Movin'On Up

Movin' On Up

Robert Gordon
Tom Burgoyne

Middle Atlantic Press
Moorestown, New Jersey

Manufactured in the United States

1 2 3 4 5 08 07 06 05 04

Cover design: Vicki Manucci

Interior design and composition: Vicki Manucci

For information write:

Middle Atlantic Press

10 Twosome Drive

Moorestown, NJ 08057

Acknowledgments

Special thanks to the Phillies organization for all their support for this book, especially Larry Shenk, Leigh Tobin, Christine Negley, Mary Ann Gettis, Tina Urban, Melissa Maani, Mike DiMuzio, Chrissy Long, and Mike Boekholder.

To Rosie Rahn and Heddy Bergsman for their beautiful photos.

To Rich Westcott for his love of the Phillies.

To Bonnie Erickson and Len Epstein for their artistic contribution.

To John Schiffert for his ideas and support

To Ernie Montella and the Philadelphia A's Society

To Jim DeLorenzo for his help

Dedication to Tug and the Pope

At 11:29 PM, EDT, October 21, 1980, Frank Edwin McGraw Jr.'s leap of joy moved all of Philly on up to its highest high. Throughout the seventies, Paul Owens wheeled, dealed, and managed the Phils through their most exciting and successful era ever. Thanks to each of them for their unbridled spirit and the joy they brought to all of us. This book is dedicated to their memory—Tug and the Pope who have moved on up to a better place.

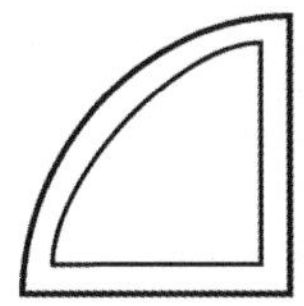
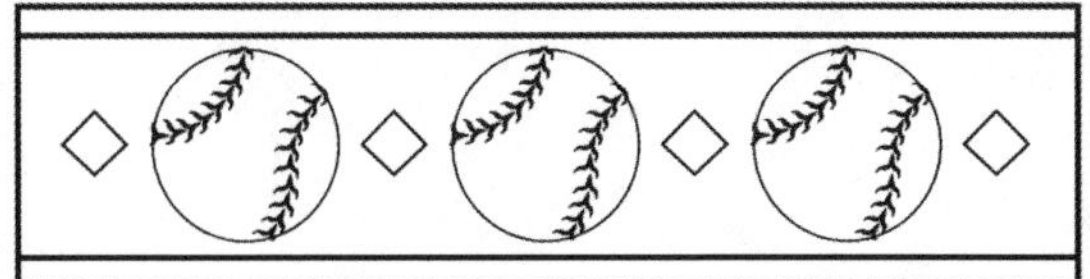
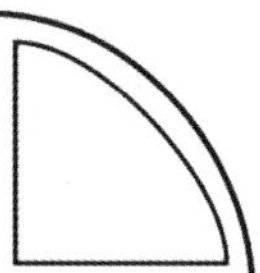

Contents

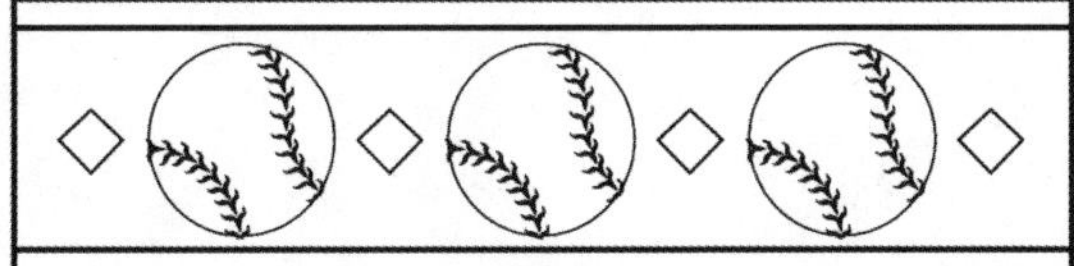
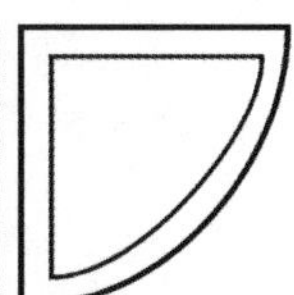

Foreword

By Jim Thome

I left a good city in order to come to Philadelphia. My family and I lived many happy years in Cleveland. Any decision to pull up stakes and leave was bound to be a tough one.

So, when it comes to movin' on up—well, believe me, I figured if there's anyone who knows what movin' on up to Philly is all about, it's me. At least that's what I figured till this book came along! I knew a little bit about Philly before. But I never realized how much more there is to know! I never knew how much pride and joy Philadelphians feel for their city, their traditions, and their teams. This book brings all those sentiments to life. It brings the present and past of my favorite team, the Philadelphia Phillies, to life. It brings this dynamic city to life. And, just as Philly's wacky Phanatic does it better than any other mascot, this book brings the spirit of our wonderful fans to life.

Best of all, in typical Philly style, this book is full of fun.

Fun—you know, I think that played a big part in why I chose to move on up to Philadelphia. Back when I was a free agent, I knew it would take something special to take me away from Cleveland. It wasn't going to be just money. I wanted to play on a team where coming to the ballpark every day was fun. I wanted a city where it would be fun for my daughter to grow up. But really, if you asked me exactly what I was looking for, I couldn't have answered you. I just hoped I would recognize it if I saw it.

Well, I saw it here in Philadelphia. Did I ever! From the moment I hit this town, I knew something special was going on. I could see it everywhere I went. Philly's a beautiful town, getting more beautiful all the time. Just look at the Broad and Pattison Avenue area and you'll see what I mean. If those two new stadiums aren't beautiful, I don't know what is. Then too, there's so much to see and do. And eat! Do we have some great food in this area!

But when you get right down to it, the really special thing about Philly is the people. I could feel the energy of Philly people as soon as I walked into the Phillies offices. The whole place was jacked up about the organization and city. Same with the team. And I could see that the people in this city were bustin' to move right on up to a new stadium and a new era. The fans are the tenth man on our club. They made a hit with me right off the bat.

There's real excitement in the air in Philly. I love to breathe that air. I was blessed to feel this same sense of excitement when I played in Jacobs Field when it was brand-new. I was a youngster back then, but I'll never forget how invigorating that atmosphere was. A ballplayer lives for that feeling. I'm so fortunate to be able to experience it again. And to think Philadelphia has *two* brand-new stadiums to showcase two exciting sports.

Besides knowing how to have fun, Philadelphians have a blue-collar, take-care-of-business ethic that fires me up. We players are having fun playing baseball, but first, last, and always, every one of us runs out on that showcase diamond every night proud to play in a place like Philadelphia.

I came to Philly so I could be part of a franchise that's movin' on up, even if 2004 didn't go the way we hoped. I'm proud to be a Phillie, and I couldn't be happier to be in Philadelphia. I think this book that Tom—our beloved Phanatic's "best friend"—and Bob have put together really hits a home run.

Preface

A WORD ABOUT PHILLY AND ITS FANS

There's a painting in the Philadelphia Art Museum. Actually, there are several. It's a big building. But this particular painting has been a family favorite for half a century. It's the Paul Rubens painting, "Prometheus Bound," which hangs in the European Paintings Collection, 19th Century European Gallery on the second floor. Years ago, it loomed over one of the landings on the staircase.

"Prometheus Bound" has been a perennial kid favorite. When I was a kid, it was one of the oh-gross! paintings where Cub Scout packs congregated to ogle the gore while the Boy Scouts scoured the galleries for nudes—nude paintings, that is. They wouldn't have known what to do if they found nudes. I never believed any of their back-of-the-bus, Girl-Scouts-Gone-Wild-at-the-Art-Museum stories anyway.

The Rubens painting is epic in scope and size. It features Prometheus on a spooky, jagged promontory. He's bound and he's buff—which is really impressive for a guy who didn't juice, except for an occasional nip of ambrosia. A huge eagle, wings spread, talons out, is ripping Prometheus' liver out.

Some people think it's a perfect painting for Philly. At least, one of my cynical friends feels it is. Here's a little background on the Prometheus legend. Then I'll give you his take on what the painting means.

Prometheus was the guy that Zeus told to create mankind. Prometheus followed Zeus' orders and perhaps earned an "attaboy." However, controversy followed. Prometheus then stole fire from the gods and gave it to his creatures. Unlike Dr. Frankenstein's creation who grunted when he saw fire like a trucker scarfing down nuclear wings, Prometheus' creatures loved fire. Eons later, it's still Donald Trump's favorite word.

But the gods didn't appreciate what Prometheus did. The gods were convinced that mortals would make a mess of things, that mortals would take something good—fire—and turn it into something bad—fire. What fools we mortals be. So Prometheus was punished for his thievery, sentenced to spend eternity getting his liver ripped out during the day, and then having it re-grow every night (and Bill Murray thought he had it bad in *Groundhog Day*).

Now back to my cynical friend. Here's how he interprets the whole Prometheus legend, especially after the 2004 season: "Ain't that Philly? I mean, ain't that the karma of Philly sport fans? Loving our hometown teams, giving our hearts and souls over to them, and then having our guts ripped out and our souls laid bare, only to grow back for the next carnage—the next season—for eternity—year by year, season by season." My friend goes so far as to suggest that Pitchin' Paul Rubens, Nostradamus-like, did his Prometheus painting as an allegory of the Philly sport fan almost four centuries ago. He's convinced that this painting is a prophecy/allegory for Philly. Why else would Rubens have chosen an iggle to rip Prometheus' liver out?

My cynical friend goes further. He says there's another clue, something that's missing from this particular painting—something that proves that bad karma is eternal for Philly fans. Rubens is renowned for painting chubby women. OK, art history and art appreciation courses describe them as cherubic or voluptuous. Trust me. They're chubby, unless you're the type that prefers watching Roseanne Barr do Coke commercials in a tutu instead of Britney Spears in whatever it is she does them in. But back to the "Prometheus Bound" painting—not one chubby woman appears in that painting. No chubby woman in a Rubens painting is like no boos in a Barry Bonds plate appearance.

So what does that mean? The cynic says that Rubens was painting messages in his brush strokes just as DaVinci was doing in *The DaVinci Code*. His message in the Prometheus painting was a message to Philadelphia: "It ain't over till the fat lady sings. And since there ain't no fat lady in the painting, it ain't ever gonna be over for you Philly fans. You'll forever have your guts ripped out by your teams. And each time you do, you'll break your TV, sleep it off, and renew your season tickets the next day." I'm hoping *DaVinci Code* author Dan Brown picks up on this theme and writes a sequel called the Paul Rubens Code. That's Paul Rubens the master painter *not* Paul Reubens, a.k.a. Pee Wee Herman. Pee Wee *is* a master something, but it's not a master painter.

To my cynical friend and his theory, I have one word to say.

NOT!

I don't believe Philly is the black hole of bad sports karma even after the last season. In my travels, I've found that every city in the country feels like their teams underachieve. Bad karma in sports is spread fairly evenly around the nation if you exclude New York. It's always a good idea to exclude New York anyway.

Philly is a great city. Philly has great people. Philly fans simply pour so much of themselves—so much of their hearts and their souls—into their Phillies and Iggles and Flyers and Sixers that they feel the agony of defeat more intensely than others. Whereas fans elsewhere can shed a tough loss by popping down a Tums, a Philly sport fan feels like his guts are getting ripped out and a Tums is useless. Philly fans are passionate about their hometown teams. And proud. OK, sometimes they're a little overly boisterous, but no one's perfect.

When ballplayers call Philly fans the toughest in the world, they quickly add that Philly fans are also the greatest. Philly fans suffer for their teams the same way parents suffer for their kids. You parents know what that means. Parents know the disorienting feeling that's always in the pit of your stomach until your kids reach the age of reason.

(Younger parents have yet to discover that the age of reason falls somewhere between 85 and some scary-looking scientific number you'd see on a whiteboard in a Drexel engineering class.)

Understanding the parent-child relationship helps in understanding the team-Philly fan relationship. A kid drives parents nuts, frustrates them, annoys them—and all in all, brings parents more joy than human beings should be allowed to have—for the most part. So does a Philly sport team. When your kid fumbles the ball in the big traditional Thanksgiving Day game and his team loses, you're still proud of him. Sure, Philadelphia parents have to throw a long-haired wig, sunglasses, and fake beard on the kid and hustle him outside to safety. But they still support him. They still love him even if he's not the big star. And they still say once more with conviction, "I'm never going to watch him play again. It makes me crazy! He makes me crazy!" And they stick to their word until his next game when they're packing hoagies to eat at halftime so they don't swallow the heart that's in their mouth as their kid almost fumbles another game away. (And also because they're allowed to eat a hoagie in a high school stadium. They almost couldn't do that in one local professional stadium.The hoagie's potential as a weapon of terror was too great.) Anyway that's the relationship of Philly sport fans with their teams. It's as though Philly fans were watching their own kids out there.

Like kids, the Phillies have alternately frustrated and delighted Philadelphia fans since 1883. But that's no different than every other baseball team in every other major-league city has done for and to its hometown fans. The difference in Philly is that family thing. Winning is a family affair here in every way. Curt Schilling once told us, "I've been in cities all over the country. Philadelphia fans—and I'll add Boston and New York to this group—are tied to their teams more than other cities. One generation is tied to the next. A father in Philadelphia raises his son to be a Phillies fan, and that son raises his son the same way, with the same passion. Most people in the Delaware Valley stay in the Philly area, but even when they move away, their love of the Phillies is so deep-rooted, they never adopt another team no matter where they move."

Sure, we've had good times and bad times aplenty over almost a century and a quarter of Phillies baseball. Baseball, like art, imitates life, although life should *not* imitate baseball. Most bosses don't like employees spitting sunflower seeds all over the office carpet. OSHA isn't crazy about it either.

As for local prophets of doom and Philly bashers, let them join my cynical friend. Let them think that the Prometheus painting is an allegory for Philly sport fans. People in that camp are missing a real high right now in the Delaware Valley. Despite the disappointing year the Phils had, Philadelphia is poised to move on up at the dawn of this new millennium. Since the new millennium, Philadelphia has advanced into the top fifteen U.S. tourist destinations, and the top ten destinations for foreign visitors. We've added two brand-new dynamite stadiums. We've got a trophy city too—with sites like the Art Museum, Fairmount Park, the Water Works, the Kimmel Center, the Constitution Center, Independence Mall, and Boat House Row. Our native sons and daughters include Princess Grace, Bill Cosby, Ben Franklin, and Will Smith. And our Fightin' Phils have added another soon-to-be Philly institution to be proud of—one of the grand old game's premier sluggers, Jim Thome.

The disappointment of 2004 is behind. The Phils didn't move on up in the standings. But they did move on up to a great new, take-me-out-to-the-ballgame park. In bad times and good, our city and a team we consider family have been linked for 121 years. And will be forever linked.

Eat your heart out, Prometheus.

A WORD ABOUT THE BOOK

We've been rooting professional baseball on for more than a century in this town. Philadelphia has come a long way since 1883, the year the Phillies first set up shop in Phillytown. The Quaker City had a population of 650,000 that year. Today the census counts 1.6 million Philadelphians.

In baseball's halcyon days in the city, Philadelphia was in the process of reinventing itself—or more accurately, continuing to reinvent itself. Once the largest, grandest city in the New World, Philadelphia watched New York overtake it as the nation's major center of commerce in the back half of the nineteenth century. By 1883, the last brush strokes of America's Gilded Age had dried, and the nation found itself in the clutches of a new era of discovery, invention, and modern marvels. The unthinkable suddenly became doable. Long-distance travel and communication revolutionized everyday life. Big cities bloated. Commerce churned and Philly was caught in the eye of that storm.

A scant six years before the birth of the Philadelphia Phillies, the City of Brotherly Love hosted the nation's Centennial celebration in Fairmount Park. One of many luminaries in Philly that Centennial summer was Alexander Graham Bell who proved conclusively that human beings can be conditioned to say "Hello" at the sound of a ringing bell. Two or three decades later, Pavlov proved that dogs can be conditioned to salivate at the sound of a ringing bell. Dogs have stayed the same. Humans have not. In this generation, humans, at the sound of annoying repetitive tunes, are conditioned to yell "'Wassup?" followed by the incessant plea, "Can you hear me now?" Evolution is not always a good thing.

Thomas Alva Edison also showed up at the Centennial, along with peculiar-looking people with even more peculiar names like Hiram, Ichabod, and Ezekial. Those names had faded away by the time the Bicentennial rolled around. Evolution is not always a bad thing.

As for baseball in the 1880's, the game had not evolved. Baseball wasn't the national pastime yet. Professional baseball was one of the dot.coms of its era. The game that would grow into "the Grand Old Game" was only a shaky new enterprise with an uncertain future.

Such was the terrain when the Philadelphia Phillies first pitched their tent here back in 1883. Philly's new hometown team drew only 55,992 fans into a rickety stadium called Recreation Park that first year, but attendance shot up to 100,475 the following year. That was the first time the Phillies moved on up. They've been doing so ever since—more or less. The lesses outnumber the mores. But Citizens Bank Park, without question is a more—and, as they say in South Philly, "*That's Amoré.*"

Granted, movin' on up hasn't been an unbroken ascent for Philly's hometown team. The Phils have done more than their share of movin' on down. The Phils suffered through years—actually entire eras—when, for every step forward, the team and franchise took two steps backward. But then, hasn't everyone?

Despite some horrific teams, people around these parts liked the idea of forking money over for a leisurely day at the ballpark. The Phillies became an organic part of a world-class city. Even if they weren't a world-class team. And as the city grew and the hometown team became more a part of it, the Phils have had to move into progressively bigger and better stadiums to accommodate bigger and better crowds.

It's been a long, uneven haul from 1883 to 2004. The path that connects Recreation Park and Citizens Bank Park has more zigs and zags than a Phillie Phanatic ramble through the stands. But the Phillies juggernaut never plunged off the road, though it certainly has rattled along the road shoulder for a good portion of the trip.

The Philadelphia Phillies have existed as the same entity longer than any other team in American professional sport. They are as much a fixture in the City of Brotherly Love as the William Penn statue atop City Hall—which stands to reason. The Phils have been in town longer than Billy Penn has been on his perch. Billy didn't start standing sentinel till 1894.

Regardless of a bad season and a legacy of more losing teams than winning teams, this book celebrates movin' on up. Phillie fans have to acknowledge and accentuate the positive from time to time too. The Phils are movin' on up to a trophy stadium, Citizens Bank Park, destined to become a temple for memories of sunny days and fun times and dates and family bonding and all those other little pleasures that baseball enables. Meanwhile down in Clearwater, the Phils are movin' on up from Jack Russell Stadium. Spiffy new Bright House Networks Field is not only the site for the Phillies' Grapefruit League games, but also the home park for the rechristened Clearwater Threshers.

Movin' on up—from Recreation Park to Citizens Bank Park. This isn't a textbook or historical analysis. It's a loosely themed, lighthearted, and hopefully entertaining look at the Phils' continuing journey. It's a celebration of Philly, Philadelphians, and our passionate sport scene. We'll revisit the places the team once called home. We'll talk about Philly's other professional baseball team that loved us and left us. And we'll talk with the Society that honors them today. We'll talk with Hall of Fame announcer Harry the K, Hall of Fame candidate Jim Thome, and some hometown guys, past and present, who moved on up to the big leagues. We'll talk with a guy who made Phillies videos before movin' on up to national acclaim as producer-director of one of the top movies of 2003. We'll talk about a transplanted Philly folk singer who moved on up in the music industry by peppering his performances with songs about Dick Allen, Eddie Waitkus, and other Phillie stars of the past. We'll look at some local folks who have moved on up inside the Phillies organization.

Throughout the book, we'll toss in "Stadium Stuff" and "Joltin' Joltin' Joe" sidebars. The "Stadium Stuff" generally makes comparisons about past and present stadiums. The "Joltin' Joltin' Joe" sidebars propose various Philly and Phillies records that appear more unbreakable than Joe DiMaggio's 56-game hitting streak, which is usually acknowledged as baseball's most unbreakable record.

And of course "Phanatic Philes," our popular, inside-out looks at the Phillies and the world through the eyes and snout of the Phillie Phanatic, will be profusely and randomly distributed throughout the book, just as they were in our first book, MT3B (*More Than Beards, Bellies, and Biceps . . .*).

Yes, the Phillies recorded lots of history in 121 years—too much for one small book. We even chose *not* to include chapters on the 1980, 1983, or 1993 teams. So much has been written about them already. We wanted to use history as a framework for human-interest stories about the people who add the color to the Philly sport scene—not only the players, but the institutions and the fans.

Yes, the 2004 Fightins didn't do it. No, all is not lost. All is not doom and gloom. Philadelphia still has a lot to celebrate, a lot to be proud of, and a lot to get excited about. We've come a long way together—the city, the fans, and the team. And in the words of another great Philadelphian, Jim Croce, *"After all, it's what we've done that makes us what we are."*

CHAPTER 1

MOVIN' ON UP TO THE VET

Don't it always seem to go
That you don't know what you've got
'Til it's gone.
They paved paradise
And put up a parking lot.
—Joni Mitchell, *Big Yellow Taxi*

Kaboom! Phillytown shook early Sunday morning on March 21, 2004. Veterans Stadium imploded. Across the way, spanking new Lincoln Financial Field glistened. Maybe it gloated. Citizens Bank Park was busy gestating, its working parts painstakingly taking shape. Looming against the Philly skyline it gave every indication of growing into a beautiful baby. Down with the old, in with the new. Rejoice.

Imploded means that everything once supported by concrete and steel rushes inward. What a fitting end for the Vet—fitting as a burial at sea for an old sea wolf. The old place harbored so much of our past. For years people couldn't wait to see it torn down. Then when the time came, the city found out there was more than concrete and steel to that structure. And the city's exterior bravado imploded into melancholy for the loss of an old friend.

After years of bellyaching, Philly fans found that their stadium was not lifeless. It was not an empty shell. In fact, it never matters how beautiful or ugly a place is—any place. A place comes to life when it's peopled—in the same way a house becomes a home. We never seem to grasp that nuance no matter how many times we live it. John Merrill, the Elephant Man, lived that tragedy. His body was a rank and ugly shell, but the soul that gave it life held beauty unsurpassed. Of course, people realized that only after the Elephant Man was gone.

Don't it always seem to go, that you don't know what you've got 'til it's gone. They paved paradise, and put up a parking lot.

Now we're not taking the stance that the Vet was paradise, or that it hadn't already seen its best days, or that CBP isn't a boon to our baseball scene. But the Vet is a parking lot at this point and the crush of eleventh-hour nostalgia for the old lady as she was downed is sadly typical. Our kids grew up in that place. Fathers took sons and daughters there to their first baseball and football games. Teens rocked at mega concerts. And when the time came to say goodbye to the Vet, and people flipped back through the pages of their lives, they found a lot of those pages were written on Veterans Stadium stationery.

Arguably the Vet and its teams hammered out a new national reputation for Philly (we hasten to throw the old Broad Street Bullies in there too). Is it a positive image? We think so. The image is at least assertive and proud, with a soft underbelly—soft as in soft-hearted. In W.C. Fields' day and for decades later, Philly was slammed as the dullest place in the country. The sidewalks, so the story went, rolled up at sunset. There were no restaurants, no clubs, no nightlife. There was no fun. Philly was the whistle-stop between New York and Washington. Stop the tour bus, rush in to gawk at the Liberty Bell and Independence Hall, grab a soft pretzel with mustard, and hop back on the bus. Then burn rubber to get to a *real* city. Philly had nothing else to offer.

Then along came the Vet, the biggest, grandest new park in all of pro sports—multipurpose, the hippest trend in design—as hip as bell-bottoms, hot pants, long hair, facial hair, and leisure suits. The Quaker City owned something new and better than other cities, something to spur civic pride.

Philly's image morphed completely during the life of the Vet. The nation's 1976 Bicentennial gave our city a new facelift. A world-class dining scene emerged. The city rehabbed beautifully. In the Yuppie era, center-city Philly transformed into a hot property. Upscaled neighborhoods like Manayunk, Fairmount, Old City, and Queen Village reinvigorated city living.

Meanwhile out at the ballpark, after decades of frustration, our teams started to show promise. And for once, the promise was fulfilled. Phillies teams came on strong by mid-decade and fans cheered the Phillies' greatest era on the diamond. By the end of the seventies, Dick Vermeil had made the Eagles contenders too.

The "Game of the Week" and "Monday Night Football" broadcasts showcased our city's stunning sights and pressed them into the national consciousness. *Rocky* did the same. Just watch the Art Museum steps any Saturday. Americans slowly started to dispel the world's hackneyed biases against the City of Brotherly Love. Philly was no longer a one-(Liberty) bell city. It was a One Liberty Place city with a newfound classy skyline courtesy of a battery of attractive modern skyscrapers. From the resort twinkle of Boat House Row to the grandeur of the Art Museum to the funk of South Street, Philly's image was movin' on up.

The success of our sport teams thrust Philly more and more into the national spotlight. Ex-jocks-turned-broadcasters spiced up the Philly rep. They hyped Philly's wild and crazy fans. OK, usually they trashed them, but the way it goes down is that *any* publicity, even negative, works. In any event, the same jocks who once winced at the prospects of playing in front of Philly's in-your-face partisan crowds now made the Philly fan—and by extension the Philadelphian—unique and intriguing instead of dull and boring.

Naturally, Philly's change of image didn't *all* happen at the Vet, but the Vet was arguably the movement's flagship—or spaceship. That alabaster, spaceship-like, glowing sphere reeling and rocking with Philly fans packed inside really looked happening from the Goodyear Blimp above. The whole nation watched those shots. And these days, the whole nation agrees Philly is better when you stay over.

So we grew up at the Vet, our generations. Actually the Vet gently stifled us from growing up. What we did there was stay young. We loved the Vet for years and then turned on her 'cause she got old. We criticized the Vet every step of the way along her inevitable, stumbling trip down Sunset Boulevard—a trip we all take sooner or later. In the swirl of anticipation for a trendy new ballpark, we forgot the glee and joy that old park brought to us and our city.

So out with the old and in with the new. That's the way life goes—and long live baseball, because that's the way baseball goes. When the Vet was rockin' and intimidating opponents, the Vet was Philly's indomitable tenth player in the summer and unyielding twelfth player in the fall and winter. Fans and foes alike conceded that the place had soul. More important, the Vet has *a* soul. Here's why we say that.

We had a cat named Scruffy, our *attitudinous* cat. Scruffy was a lovable grump. He used to follow us around from room to room, everywhere, always doing his cussed best to act independent, detached, and aloof, like he wasn't *really following* us—he just happened to be going the same place we were. The little guy played a role in every memory we spun at our house. For ten years we were blessed to have his constant companionship, at once ornery, lovable, and irreplaceable. Scruffy has a soul. You know how I know? It's not because of faith or religious convictions. It's because after Scruffy died, I swore I still saw him. I saw him in every room. My son saw him too. And for the very same reason, I know the Vet has a soul. Because my son and I swear we still see that special place. We see it as it stood so long ago on the day I took him to his first ballgame. We see it looming over a parking lot, rising mammoth and majestic, as real as a pinch, as real as Ray Kinsella's ballfield growing out of that Iowa cornfield. We two approach the corner at Broad and Pattison, and just for a moment, we see it, vibrant and alive, same as it ever was. The two of us are standing there. And just for that fleeting magic moment, he's not the handsome, strong, intelligent 24-year-old who now dwarfs his dad. He's my little boy again, my little guy—that tiny, innocent, towheaded, starstruck, marvelous wonder of a boy wearing the Juan Samuel glove on one hand, and clutching his daddy's in the other.

"God, I love this game."

—Roy Hobbs in *The Natural*

Philadelphia's newest crown-jewel, Veterans Stadium, opens on April 10, 1971. A record 1,511,233 fans poured through the turnstiles in its Innaugural Season.

(Photo: Courtesy of the Phillies)

Manager Frank Lucchesi (right) stands at attention for the Natioanl Anthem with the rest of the '71 Phils on Opening Day.

(Photo: Courtesy of the Phillies)

FIELD OF MEMORIES

All good things got to come to an end.
The thrills have to fade
Before they come 'round again.

—Jackson Browne, *All Good Things*

"Field of Memories." Larry Shenk, Phillies Vice President of Public Relations, came up with that tag line. I loved it. It was a season-long reminder that after 2003, the baseball field at Broad and Pattison would be nothing more than a memory.

Once there was a ballpark . . . .

My memories of the Vet will never die. The first game I ever saw in person was at the Vet on April 10, 1971, the day the giant stadium opened for business. That's like sharing the same birth date with a friend. That's how I feel about the Vet, like it's an old friend, one I'll never see again. One I'll think about often. One I'll never forget.

Some of my Vet memories drift back to the huge stadium itself, when it was in its infancy and it had all that stuff! Funny, funky-looking yellow and orange seats, perfectly choreographed dancing waters that sprayed up from behind the center field fence, the larger-than-life statues of Philadelphia Phil and Phillis that graced the 400-Level façade, and the cannon that puffed smoke every time a Phillie hit a home run. There were hot pants girls who dusted off your seat (the plastic one attached to the floor, not your . . .), and delivered Tastykakes and water out to the umpires after the fifth inning. There was a cool-looking bullpen golf cart shaped like a Phillies cap, and bright green carpet called Astroturf. There were two gigantic scoreboards looming above the outfield fence that flashed silly animations of the ballplayers. I particularly liked the caricature of Greg Luzinski with his arms folded across his chest and the phrase "Strong like a Bull" spelled out above him. I was fascinated by the way baseballs were used as the "font" to spell the name D-E-L whenever Del Unser slapped a clutch hit. Another animation depicted a nervous father pacing in the maternity ward waiting room. If a Phillie hit a double, the nurse opened the door and brought two babies out to the father. If he hit a triple, the nurse brought three babies.

Memories.

Some of my memories drift back to the players that performed through three decades of Philly history. A Bull blast . . . Garry Maddox tracking down a deep fly ball at the base of the fence . . . Willie Montanez flipping his bat as he walked up to the plate . . . Larry Bowa ranging deep to his right in the hole, then gunning down a runner at first . . . Downtown Ollie Brown going downtown . . . Tommy Hutton's puzzling mastery over Tom Seaver . . . Bake McBride's dramatic three-run homer in game one of the '80 World Series . . . Cincinnati's Pete Rose legging out a bunt single in the ninth inning to extend his 44-game hitting streak in 1978 . . . doubles that Juan Samuel blazed into triples . . . Tug leaping into the air or walking and pounding his glove against his leg . . .

Memories.

Some of my memories drift back to the fun promotions and crazy contests and events that colored the Vet's history. There were almost as many of them as there were Mike Schmidt home runs. That's saying something. But it seems like the Vet always had spectacles going like Karl Wallenda's death-defying skywalk or Kiteman's crashes, or maybe Cannonman's or Rocketman's or Benny the Bomb's antics. I remember cherishing the giveaways at the turnstiles like they were Christmas presents—treasures like team posters, beach blankets, or a Denny Doyle or Juan Samuel glove.

The best part of every Burgoyne family Fourth of July was a trip to the Vet. Before the game, the players and broadcasters competed in old-fashioned contests, like a three-legged race, a water balloon toss, and a sack race. Our whole clan would hang around after the game to gawk at the spectacular fireworks show. We'd run all around the field, crashing into the outfield walls, pretending to make game-saving catches.

Memories.

The goal of the Phillies organization in 2003 was to bring those memories of the stadium, the players, and the promotions back to life. What a job they did!

The Phillies decked out the Vet in finery for its final season. The Phils made sure the old park went out with dignity. I've got to admit, the grand old lady looked great. On the 400-level façade that wrapped a good portion of the park, a colorful Vet timeline banner hung. In chronological fashion, the banner recognized the Phillie greats and near-greats who performed on the Field of Memories for the past three decades.

The "Field of Memories" logo—a picture of the Vet with the years 1971-2003 posted below it—was omnipresent all season long. It was sewn on the Phillies uniforms and stitched onto the bases, which were given away each game to a lucky fan in attendance. Certain seats in the 500 and 600 Level in the outfield were marked with a yellow "Vet Blast" sticker, marking the spots where each one of the Vet's 93 upper-deck home runs landed.

LONGEST VET HOME RUNS

The longest home run ever hit at the Vet was rocketed on June 25, 1971. Willie Stargell hit a ball off Jim Bunning that landed in the exit tunnel in section 601. A yellow star was permanently fixed at the tunnel and remained there until the Vet was demolished in March 2004.

Not surprisingly, Greg Luzinski belted the most upper-deck home runs at the Vet (10) and his slugging partner, Mike Schmidt, was second on the list with six. Bull's blast off the Liberty Bell that used to hang from the façade in center field is considered one of the most spectacular in the 33-year history of the stadium.

In Jim Thome's first and only year at the Vet, he walloped three home runs into the upper deck. How many do you think he could have hit if he had played eight, ten, or twelve years there? We'll never know.

There was a spot set aside in the 600 Level where fans could take a panoramic shot of the park, and with one 180-degree turn, tack on a shot of Citizens Bank Park under construction in the adjacent parking lot.

Philadelphia Phil and Phillis were resurrected on Opening Day, 2003. They returned from time to time throughout the season to visit the Phanatic. My oldest brother Joe dressed up as Phil on Opening Day. He earned his mascotting stripes (by agreeing to a lobotomy) as the Griffin at Canisius College in Buffalo. He had never ridden an ATV before as the Griffin. That may explain why he almost took a header (and lost his mascot head—yeah, I know, I'm a fine one to talk) on Opening Day when I gave him a ride.

Something was happening every day, all season long in the Vet's final season. A giant Countdown Clock was attached to the right field wall, marking the number of games remaining to be played at the Vet. That countdown made everyone feel like a second-semester senior trying to squeeze in all the fun he could before tumbling out into the real world.

We honored the teams of the eighties one weekend and the crazy '93 team another weekend. We gave out bobbing-head dolls of Mike Schmidt and Steve Carlton, the Vet's two greatest performers. We scheduled a weekend dedicated to all the wacky promotions over the Vet's 33-year run. We even brought back the first giveaway item ever—an official Little League-sized Louisville Slugger bat.

To make that freebie more relevant to this generation, we emblazoned the name Pat Burrell on the barrel.

By the time the Final Innings Weekend crashed down on us in September, the Vet was poised for one parting tribute. The final three memories—a Carlton wind-up, a mighty Schmidt swing and trot around bases, and the Tugger's 1980 leap of joy—culminated the season-long 2003 Field of Memories campaign.

The fans filed down the ramps and out the gates one last time. As the lights around the ballpark flickered into history, Phillies employees and stadium workers milled around the playing field. Some dug up dirt at home plate, scooping spoonfuls of the reddish clay mixture into paper cups. Some took pictures standing next to the Countdown Clock, now a blank square patch. Others hugged friends and soaked in the Vet air one last time. The Season of Memories was itself now a memory. And what beautiful memories, and what great promise 2003 brought! Newcomer Jim Thome provided a season-load of memories all by himself with his mammoth home runs. We saw a no-hitter, a thirteen-run inning, and tons of late-game heroics from a gang calling itself the "Bench Dogs."

Till I die, I'll not ride by the plot of real estate at Broad and Pattison without thinking, "Once there was a ballpark . . ." There sure as hell was. And it was a Field of Memories.

CONCRETE AND STEEL

Lyrics and music by Skip Denenberg

It was so much more, than concrete and steel
This place where so many dreams were made
And now that we've come to the end of the road,
These memories we share, will never fade

We'll remember the way it used to make us feel
It was so much more, than just concrete and steel

A special place, like sacred ground,
Where so many faithful came to pray
The young and the old were one and the same
We all were a part of so much more than just a game

We'll remember the way it used to make us feel
It was so much more, than just concrete and steel

I've heard it said it had a life of its own
I swear that once I heard it cry,
Filled with magic, this place we called home
A field where heroes never die

We'll remember the way it used to make us feel
It was so much more, than just concrete and steel

So much more, than just concrete and steel

IN THE BEGINNING

Back in the sixties, a barren tract of land in the Northeast along State Road was under consideration as a site for a new sports stadium for the Phillies and Eagles. The papers named it "Torresdale Tundra." To kids like me who grew up in Philly's Great Northeast, Torresdale Tundra was "the Answer." A stadium there would be like having Disneyland in our own backyard. (There was no Disney World yet. These were the Dark Ages.) Having a ballpark in the Northeast meant no more treks to Connie Mack Stadium in North Philly—no more start-and-stop jaunts on the "66" line, the trackless PTC trolley that ran on Frankford Avenue (the PTC was taken over by SEPTA in 1968). No more switching sides on the trolley to read the marquees at the Mayfair and Merben Theaters. No more straining to see what was playing at the Devon Theater. The Devon showed "art" films. We wanted the trolley to go slow past the Devon.

It was a long haul by PTC from the Northeast to 21st and Lehigh. After the "66" ride, we had to transfer to the "el" at Bridge Street, then hop out at Somerset Station and board the "54" bus to the park.

Torresdale Tundra was going to save that long trek.

But alas, Torresdale Tundra was not to be. Philly had been jawing about building a new ballpark for years. Siting was an issue as was funding. As early as 1953, city officials in conjunction with the Phillies and Eagles staged discussions on constructing a new multi-purpose sports stadium. The parties never agreed on a site and no one knew where the money to build it was coming from. Then in November 1964, Philadelphia voters approved a $25 million bond to build a new stadium, Philadelphia Veterans Memorial Stadium. South Philadelphia was selected as the site and Torresdale Tundra was forsaken, as were numerous other proposed sites for the park, like Cheltenham, Fairmount Park, and Cherry Hill.

Three years later, on October 2, 1967, ground was broken and construction got underway. Veterans Stadium sprawled out over 74 acres of former marsh land. The stadium itself was laid out in the shape of an octorad—eight points plotted equidistant around a circumference, each point joined to its flanking neighboring points by a straight line. The final tab amounted to $52 million. Seating capacity for the baseball field, which was to be the largest in the National League at the time, was originally 56,371.

On April 10, 1971, the Phils took the field against the Montreal Expos in the Veterans Stadium debut. The largest baseball crowd in the history of Pennsylvania, 55,352, braved temperatures in the low 40s and watched the oldest pitcher in major league baseball, Jim Bunning, get Montreal's Boots Day to ground the first pitch weakly back to him. Bunning threw to first baseman Deron Johnson to record the stadium's first out. Later, Larry Bowa slapped the park's first hit, a single. The Phillies went on to win 4-1 and baseball in South

Philly was underway.

Throughout its 33-year history, the place underwent numerous physical changes. The original scoreboards in left-center and right-center were removed to free up more space for seats. Colonial-dressed Philadelphia Phil and Phillis vanished from the fourth-level façade in center field. So did the dancing waters beyond center field. An electronic scoreboard and video board were added. More Super Boxes were built and Sky Boxes were constructed at the top of the stadium for Eagle fans to nest.

Everyone loved the Vet at first. But over the ensuing decades, the hometown soured on its stadium. The Vet was showing its age. It was also getting shown up. Philadelphians watched the new wow-packed generation of ballparks lift civic pride everywhere they went up. For fans, these new parks added dimensions and possibilities that older parks couldn't match. For the Phillies, a new facility upped the prospects of upping the bottom line.

There were other factors contributing to disenchantment with the Vet. America started greening in the seventies, and the trend has gained momentum (hopefully it's not a fad, but a national imperative). Americans wanted real grass (so did the seventies' hippies, but that's a different book), not artificial stuff. People grew more nostalgic for simpler times so "old-fashioned" ballparks became the in thing. Realistically, real grass is the lone link that new, big, expensive parks have to the parks of yore. Yet somehow the new generations of ballparks manage to evoke the game's past. Rather than being bona fide replicas of old-fashioned parks, the new ballparks are time machines, albeit classy time machines. And why shouldn't they be? As the Doc told Marty McFly why he chose a DeLorean for his time machine in *Back to the Future*, "Marty, the way I figure it, if you're gonna go back, why not do it in style?"

In the last decade, the Phillies and the City of Philadelphia pumped more than $40 million into the Vet to keep it afloat. The earth-tone-colored seats were phased out and replaced by blue seats. The blue looked so good, the Phils carried the color scheme over to Citizens Bank Park. A state-of-the-art video board replaced the old center-field Phanavision.

Those improvements were not sufficient. The most virulent complaints about the Vet came from players. The turf was a killer. The playing surface was like concrete—hard and unforgiving. On October 10, 1993, the Chicago Bears' wide receiver Wendell Davis blew out both knees on one play on the Vet's Astroturf. He ran a post pattern, planted his feet to leap for the ball, and ended his career.

Many hometown athletes felt their careers were shortened because the unforgiving turf stressed and strained their knees. The stadium's two tenants—the Eagles and Phillies—didn't sit idly by. Prior to the 2001 season, a new synthetic grass surface, Nexturf, was installed. Nexturf was just not natural turf, though.

By the mid-nineties, the Vet was as out of place as a shortstop in the Thome shift. The Vet was unhip, bloated, and passé. When both the Phillies and Eagles signed new stadium deals, the old stadium was relegated to the same fate that befell all our old stadiums. But the Phillies took it upon themselves to send the old lady out in style.

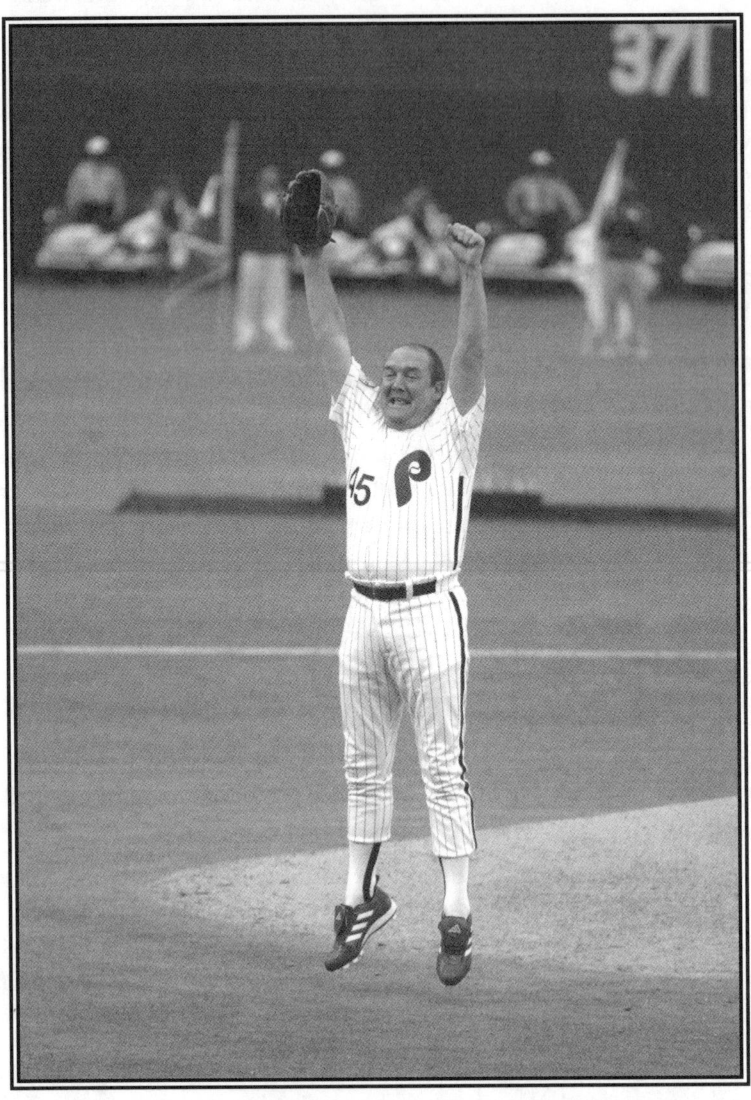

The Vet's final memory—Tugger's leap of joy.

(Photo: Rosemary Rahn)

THE COUNTDOWN CLOCK

My favorite highlight of the Vet's farewell season was the game-by-game ritual of counting down the games remaining at the Vet. Every game day, someone who played a role in the history of the Vet had the honor of removing the number hanging on the "Countdown Clock," and replacing it with the next lower number. Adding by subtraction. The "ceremony" took place at the Countdown Clock that hung prominently on the right-field fence throughout the 2003 campaign.

Before the season got rolling, the Phils' promotions team decided to add some pizzazz by letting the Phanatic escort the guest to the Countdown Clock. I was thrilled. I chauffeured a veritable "Who's Who" list of notables in my four-wheeler. Naturally, that list included a lot of great ballplayers. But it also included Phillies employees, broadcasters, sponsors and fans.

Every game, we hooked up the red sidecar to the Phanatic's ATV. It looked like the contraption Batman used to cart Robin the Boy Wonder around in. The sidecar is a bit on the small side and rides close to the ground. Getting in and out proved a challenge for a select group of dignitaries like the Bull, Greg Luzinski. When the Bull came down to the right-field truck ramp, he took one look at the sidecar and uttered three words:

"Ain't no way."

In any event, I didn't argue or correct his English. Neither would you. The Bull's forearms are approximately the size of a radial tire that's overinflated. They've gotten bigger since his playing days. Even Jim Thome is impressed.

The Bull chose to ride western style on the back of the ATV instead. My shock absorbers are still in shock.

John Kruk declined the sidecar seat as well, electing to limp—er, I mean walk—out onto the field as I led the way on the ATV. John may have fit into that sidecar if I had been able to find a 6-foot shoehorn on eBay. But getting out would have required the jaws-of-life.

On the other hand, Larry Andersen was a gamer—sort of. He wedged his gangly legs into the sidecar, then asked me a little nervously, "You're gonna take it easy going down that ramp, aren't you, Phanatic?"

"Su-u-u-u-u-u-re, LA," I lied (actually, the Phanatic lied, not me). I gunned the accelerator and caught air flying down the ramp. LA screamed louder than Zell Miller during a Chris Matthews interview. Maybe LA was having flashbacks about facing Barry Bonds.

I had some great surprises. Some guys you wouldn't expect to get excited about changing the number were downright giddy. Lenny Dykstra was all smiles, pumping his fist like he did after that clutch home run in the '93 playoffs. The normally reserved Steve Carlton did a little jig as he changed the number from three to two on the Vet's final weekend. Lefty wasn't as excited about changing the number as he was about fighting off the effects of a long plane ride. Steve enjoys his wine, even airplane-brand wine. He had made a mad dash from the airport to the stadium and took a bouncy ride in the sidecar. He didn't have time to make any *other* stops along the way, if you know what I mean. I think that's why Steve was hopping around.

Even hardened sports columnist Bill Conlin got caught up in the act, startling me with a running chest bump. Bill was either caught up in the moment or prepping for a second career in Sumo wrestling.

Philly favorites Rick Wise, Tony Taylor, and Willie Montanez had the honors each night of the opening weekend. Each got huge ovations, as did Rico Brogna, Jim Eisenreich, and Gary Matthews.

If you were sitting in the upper deck on June 18th, you needed to squint real hard into my sidecar to catch the head of Hall of Famer Joe Morgan poking up. After changing the number from 46 to 45, Joe hopped back into the sidecar without a hitch, or without his famous chicken wing. Joe was comfortable in that little sidecar even though his feet didn't reach the floor.

Connie Mack's daughter, Ruth Mack Clark, got a warm reception in the first game of the doubleheader on June 8th when the Phillies hosted the Oakland A's. Those cheers turned to boos in the second game when weatherman Tom Lamaine made his grand entrance onto the field to change the number from 48 to 47. Tom's a great guy and one of the Phillies' most loyal fans, but his timing couldn't have been worse. It was pouring rain.

TV sports anchor and ex-Eagle kick returner Vai Sikahema used the padding on the outfield wall as a punching bag after changing the number from 15 to 14. Vai was reenacting his much-imitated end zone celebration after a spectacular kick-off return against the Giants at the Meadowlands.

The August 16th countdown ritual was a sobering reminder of how quickly my job changes from the ridiculous to the sublime. At the end of the fifth inning, I zipped onto the field and danced in front of the dugout with Sponge Bob Square Pants—along with Sponge Bob's friend, a pink, colossal starfish named Patrick. Other assorted large-headed cartoon characters from Nickelodeon TV joined us. Three outs later, I was dutifully escorting the Governor of Pennsylvania, Ed Rendell, onto the field to change the number from 18 to 17. Off the record, Ed chose not to ride in the sidecar. Gee, I wonder why.

Longtime workers at the Vet got their minute and fifteen seconds of fame too. A group of nineteen people that included Vet hosts, hostesses, and security staff personnel changed the number *en masse* one night. This particular group of game-day employees had worked together *every year since the Vet opened.* Even more amazing in longevity, Wally Brando changed the number on April 8th. Old Wally has been employed by the Phillies for 67 years, dating all the way back to Baker Bowl. Tom Reiter, whose career traces back to the old Connie Mack Stadium days, has holed up in the tiny Courtesy Window for 33 years at the Vet. Tom got a ride in the sidecar too. So did many other loyal employees who have meant so much to the Phillies organization over the years.

What are my most lasting Countdown Clock memories? For starters, there were some misty eyes in the crowd when a tuxedo-clad Harry Kalas stood at the base of the fence in right field. Harry the K held the square piece of cloth with the black number 1 stitched on it in one hand, while with the other, he blew kisses skyward to his old sidekick Whitey Ashburn.

Ex-Phillies pitcher Mike Krukow honored his old roommate Tug McGraw when he ripped down number 67 from the wall and put up a sign that read "Get Well, Tug" instead. Two and a half months later, on July 3, the Tugger made his first 2003 Veterans Stadium appearance. Tug changed the number that night. It was fireworks night and the place was packed. I dressed the Phanatic in an Irish leprechaun outfit in honor of Tug, and rode my ATV from home plate to the Countdown Clock with the Tugger close behind me in a golf cart. Decked out in his blue Hawaiian Phillies shirt, Tug and his youngest son, Matthew, hopped out of the cart and changed the number from 39 to 38. Then came the best part. After I high-fived him and got him back into his golf cart, I hopped on the ATV to lead him on a victory lap around the field. I took it nice and slow, letting the Tugger feel the love.

This was one time when no one was going to fault me for taking a little extra time between innings. Some things are bigger than a baseball game.

WHEN A CLOCK IS NOT A CLOCK

OK, before you say the "Countdown Clock" was not actually a clock as we normally think of a clock, read on. A standard clock gives the time of day, like 3 o'clock, which is a contraction for 3 of the clock. The Countdown Clock was more like an Advent calendar. It was *not* like the old Longines clock at Connie Mack, or the clock in the Big Ben tower, or the Bavarian glockenspiel clock in Munich. However, the Merriam Webster dictionary—the final word on word matters (much as Greg Luzinski is the final word, and resting place, for barbecued ribs)—defines "clock" as 1: a device other than a watch for indicating or measuring time commonly by means of hands moving on a dial; 2: *broadly: any periodic system by which time is measured.* So by that broad definition, using "clock" in the context of a Countdown Clock is correct. Besides, even if the Phillies were wrong on that one, cut them some slack in wordsmithing. In their world, you don't have to actually strike a ball for a "strike" to be recorded.

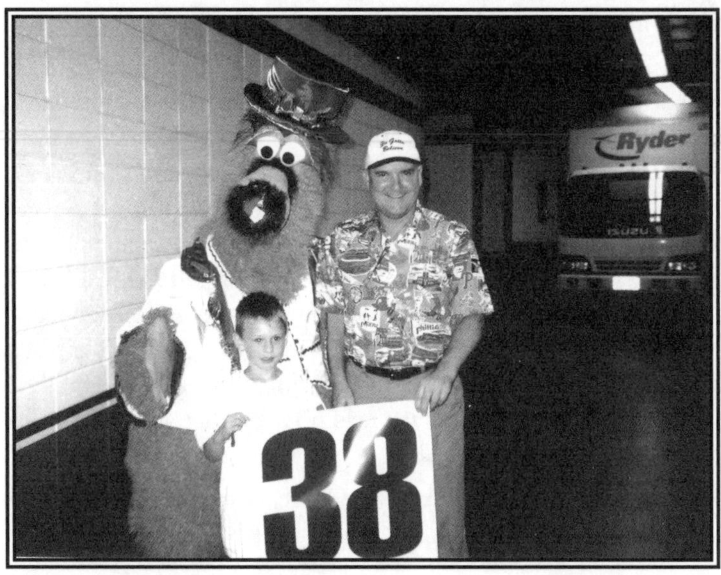

Tug McGraw and his son Matthew pose with the Phillie Phanatic after changing the Countdown Clock on July 3, 2003.

(Photo: Heddy Bergsman)

THE FINAL INNINGS

"Don't cry because it's over. Smile because it happened."

The final game wasn't memorable. The final day was.

Chase Utley grounded out to end not only a lackluster game, but also what turned into a disappointing season for the Fightins. It *turned into* a disappointing season because the Phils couldn't beat the Marlins. But it *turned out* to be not nearly as disappointing when we saw by October's end that *no one else* could beat the Marlins either.

The collective mood during the game was somewhat like the feeling guys try to hide at a wedding ceremony—that when-the-hell-is-the-marriage-ceremony-going-to-end-so-we-can-hit-the-open-bar sense of containment that overpowers guys two bars (not the kind of bars the guys are thinking of) into the Wedding March.

It was worth the wait. The Phils threw a going-away party the city won't soon forget. All season long, the Phils celebrated their Field of Memories. On the final weekend, Steve Carlton removed the #3 on the Countdown Clock and put up #2—his position on the all-time strike-out list till Roger Clemens dislodged him in his 2004 reappearance. On Saturday, which fell on his birthday, Mike Schmidt removed the #2 and strung up #1. Also on Saturday, the all-Vet team was announced. Sartorially resplendent in black collarless shirts and white-and-red pin-striped blazers, these guys looked like they could still win.

Then came the final game.

The Phils added all the right touches. Philadelphian Jerry Crawford umpired the final game. His dad Shag had umpired the Vet opener. The ground crew performed their chores in tuxedos. Harry Kalas, golden-voiced and emotional, emceed the event in a tuxedo. Harry had been the emcee the day the Vet opened.

Skip Denenberg's song (you'll be introduced to Skip in Chapter 14) "Concrete and Steel" lilted across the field where 500 Phillies ballplayers had swung or pitched, and where 25,000 innings had been played in front of 68,000,000 fans. That number doesn't include the South Philly kids who slipped in uncounted.

The Phillie Phanatic emerged onto the field from behind the plate. Sporting a rumpled tuxedo, the Phanatic spun and danced to Donna Summer's hit single, "Last Dance." He made his way onto the top of the Phillies dugout, a place he had performed for 26 years, and invited fans sitting in the first couple of rows to join him one last time for a dance at the Vet. It was like closing down an old saloon, with patrons dancing on the bar and squeezing out the last drops of good times.

THE PARADE

After the Phanatic's last dance, the Pope, Paul Owens, sitting next to VP/GM Ed Wade, was driven to home plate in a golf cart. The Pope, though seriously ill, summoned enough strength to wave to the crowd. Owens, the architect of some of the greatest Phillies teams of all time, got a chance to marshall the grand parade that highlighted the end of the Vet. Here's who walked the green turf for the last time that day.

1971—Jim Bunning, Rick Wise, and Don Money. Hall of Famer Bunning won the Vet opener. Rick Wise pitched a no-hitter and hit two homers in one of baseball's greatest-ever pitcher performances. Don Money—for whom Girard Bank launched a "Girard Bank Likes Money" campaign in an effort to land him an All-Star berth (it didn't work)—hit the Vet's first homer.

1972—Terry Harmon, Willie (the Phillie) Montanez, and Irish Mike Ryan. Willie's trade to San Francisco brought Garry Maddox to town.

1973—Mike Rogodzinski and Wayne Twitchell.

1974—Gentleman Jim Lonborg. Lonborg, then with the Bosox, battled Cardinal HOFer Bob Gibson in the '68 World Series when Lonborg won two and Gibson three. Jim is now a dentist.

1975—Tony Taylor. The Tony Taylor trade marked one time the Phils got the best of the Cubs.

1976—Gene Garber and manager Danny Ozark. There's no truth to the story that before the final game, Ozark told the 2003 Phils, who had been mathematically eliminated, that they could *still* win the pennant.

1977—Jay Johnstone.

1978—Jerry Martin.

1979—Warren Brusstar.

1980—Dallas Green, Marty Bystrom, Dickie Noles, Ruben Amaro Sr., John Vukovich, and Del Unser.

1981—Dick Ruthven. (with his shaved head)

1982—Greg Gross.

1983—Bob Dernier and Al (Mr. T) Holland. Dernier slid head-first across the plate. Holland was winner of the Rolaids Relief Man Award that year.

1984—Larry Andersen. Andersen, fittingly, didn't touch home plate because on the hill LA lived just *off* the plate, and on offense he seldom got to touch any of the bases, let alone home plate.

1985—Ozzie Virgil. Virgil got into the catcher's squat behind the plate.

1986—Kent Tekulve.

1987—Steve Bedrosian. Bedrosian won the Rolaids Relief Man Award that year. Free spirit Bedrock did angel wings out on the mound, as he had years before.

1988—Don Carman.

1989—Von Hayes. Hayes grabbed some dirt and pocketed it.

1990—Tommy Herr.

1991—Tommy Greene.

1992—Mariano Duncan. Mariano smiled same as ever.

1993—Mickey Morandini and Mitch Williams. Williams got one of the loudest ovations. Mickey and Mitch each had short hair and goatees.

1994—Randy Ready.

1995—Tyler Green.

1996—Rickey Bottalico.

1997—Ruben Amaro Jr.

1998—Rico Brogna.

1999—Paul Byrd. Byrd characteristically flapped his arms like a bird.

2000—Ramon Henderson (coach since '98), Amaury Telemaco, Tomas Perez.

2001—Tony Scott (coach), Nick Punto, Brandon Duckworth, David Coggin, and Jason Michaels.

2002—Carlos Silva, Todd Pratt (with his bleached blond hair), **Larry Bowa** (who hopped on home plate), **Dan Plesac** (who pocketed some dirt from the mound), **and Vicente Padilla**.

2003—Joe Kerrigan (coach), Chase Utley, Brett Myers, Rheal Cormier, Kelly Stinnett, Josh Hancock, Travis Chapman, Ryan Madson, and Anderson Machado.

After the parade, the Phils brought out the 2003 incumbents at each position. Each stood at his position on the diamond along with two former Vet greats who played the same position. As the ceremony wound down, Harry Kalas announced Veterans Stadium's final three memories.

First, Steve Carlton took the mound as he had 499 times as a Phil. Lefty went through his windup with Harry the K chiming, "He struck him out—3,000 strikeouts for Steve Carlton."

Next, Mike Schmidt grabbed a bat, dug in (but didn't do his famous butt wiggle), took a stroke, and headed around the bases. He reenacted the running-in-place routine he unveiled for his 500th homer. On a slight disconnect, Kalas announced, "Number 548 for Michael Jack Schmidt!"

Then, as Kalas crooned, "When it's time to get one out, who do you call up?" a limousine rumbled toward home plate. The crowd chanted in unison, "Tug!" PA announcer Dan Baker screamed, "Now pitching for the Philadelphia Phillies, #45, Tug McGraw!"

The hometown favorite—sickly but smiling—impishly stepped out of the limo, hustled to the mound, and reenacted the most-played, most-beloved moment in the history of Philadelphia sports—his strikeout pitch to Willie Wilson at 11:29 PM, October 21, 1980.

The festivities were nearing an end. Harry Kalas uttered the final words over the Veterans Stadium PA system.

"It's like a 3-1 pitch to Michael Jack or Jim Thome. It's a long drive. It's outta here. God bless you."

God bless you. With those words, the book on Veterans Stadium sports closed. Harry Kalas hearkened to the words from the last line in Charles Dickens' classic, *A Christmas Carol:* "God bless us, everyone." That's another nice call, Harry. The Dickens tale shows the combined power the spirits of the past, present, and future wield. That's pretty much what the Phillies did in 2003. They summoned the past, related it to the present, and hitched it all onto the future. Their Field of Memories year at the Vet instilled fans with a deeper appreciation of what baseball means to this town, and what a grand theater for the game the Vet was. Movin' on up to a stunning new stadium does not diminish the glory the Vet was in her times.

The Phils put on a great show in those final innings at the Vet, but Philly's sport theater is interactive. Granted, it's often theater of the absurd, but it wasn't this day. Looking around the stadium, we saw a sea of banners. The corny outnumbered the clever, but all were ingenuous and straight from the heart, intended to express emotion rather than attract attention. "Thanks for *Vet Memories*," "The Vet's Been Good *Tho-me*"—that kind of stuff. One modest, unslick sign will stay with me though. It was held aloft by a shy, demure-looking woman, seeking to see more than be seen. Handwritten in rough penmanship on a piece of cardboard, she had scrawled a few lines that corralled the day's sentiment:

- *2 tickets to a Phillies game—$50*
- *3 hot dogs and some beer—$25*
- *33 years of Vet memories—priceless.*

STADIUM STUFF

THE ALL-VET TEAM

SS	Larry Bowa	CF	Garry Maddox
1B	John Kruk	2B	Juan Samuel
RF	Bobby Abreu	C	Darren Daulton
3B	Mike Schmidt	RHP	Curt Schilling
LF	Greg Luzinski	LHP	Steve Carlton

STADIUM STUFF

AROUND THE HORN

The 2003 Incumbents and the Two All-Vet Stars Chosen at Each Position for the Final Innings Ceremony (incumbents are in bold)

1B **Jim Thome,** Dick Allen, John Kruk

2B **Tomas Perez,** Manny Trillo, Juan Samuel

3B **David Bell,** Dave Hollins, Mike Schmidt

SS **Jimmy Rollins,** Kevin Stocker, Larry Bowa

LF **Pat Burrell,** Milt Thompson, Greg Luzinski

CF **Marlon Byrd,** Lenny Dykstra, Garry Maddox

RF **Bobby Abreu,** Jim Eisenreich, Bake McBride

LHP **Randy Wolf,** Danny Jackson, Steve Carlton

RHP **Kevin Millwood,** Larry Christenson, John Denny

•Placido Polanco, the starting second baseman in 2003, could not attend.

COST OF YEARLY TUITION & FEES AT PHILLY COLLEGES

	When the Vet opened 1970	When the Vet closed 2004*
Bryn Mawr	$1880	$31,390
LaSalle	$1400	$25,000
Villanova	$1870	$27,025
University of Pennsylvania	$2250	$30,716

**These figures are approximations. Deciphering the Rosetta Stone was easy compared to getting tuition and fees figures from colleges today. Here's a challenge. Get on any college website and try to get a figure for tuition and fees. It's easier to find the name of the college president's pet dog.*

PHILLY SKYLINE MOVIN' ON UP

Tallest Philadelphia Buildings in 1971

City Hall	548′
PSFS Building	490′
5 Penn Center	490′
IVB Building, 1700 Market	482′
PNB Building, Broad & Chestnut	475′

Tallest Philadelphia Buildings in 2004

One Liberty Place	945′
Two Liberty Place	847′
Mellon Bank Building	791′
Bell Atlantic Tower	738′
Independence Blue Cross Tower	627′
Two Commerce Square	564′
One Commerce Square	564′
City Hall	548′

THE VET'S FINAL DH

Here's a quick test to find out if you're an old-time baseball fan. Answer quickly. In baseball, what does DH mean? If you answered Designated Hitter, you're a new kid. If you answered doubleheader, you're an old-timer.

We may have seen our last DH in Philly—doubleheader, that is. We hope we *never* see our first Designated Hitter, aside from interleague play.

The Phillies scheduled a doubleheader against the Pardres on August 2, 2003. That's two games for the price of one, for you youngsters out there. And, even though a rain-out resulted in a two-fer at Citizens Bank Park on September 29, 2004 versus the Pirates, the day-night doubleheader will most likely become the norm. If two games are scheduled for the same day, they'll play an early game followed by a late one. In between games they'll close down the park. The first day-night doubleheader at Citizens Bank Park was on June 17, 2004 against the Detroit Tigers.

If traditionalists are appalled, here's how to find relief. Call the Sameric or Regal Theater nearest you. Ask them when their next *double feature* is showing.

GETTIN' MOVIN'

We don't know exactly what a *Phillie* is. We hear the word occasionally in old movies. But it's not spelled "Philly." It's spelled "filly." And as Yogi says, you could even look that up.

In the movies, it's mostly big burly guys from the Deep South who say "filly." Usually those burly guys have names like Buford or Jethro, and usually they say filly when they're talking about petite women. Or what's even more amazing, when they're talking *to* petite women. Buford will say something like: "Now ain't you a perty little filly!"

The dictionary meaning of "filly" is a young female horse less than four years old. But the guys in these movies are definitely calling people, not horses, "fillies," at least on camera. Off camera, we can only guess.

Nowadays, if you say filly to a Delaware Valley woman, you can expect trouble, especially if you say it to a filly in your workplace. Telling a woman she's a perty filly will get you an uncomfortable, daylong interview with your company's Human Resources officer, especially if the Human Resources officer happens to be the one you called a filly. And especially if the HR officer happens to be a man, but that's a filly of a different color altogether.

That being said, we can't imagine that the founders of the Philadelphia Phillies intended to name their team the *Fillies* but misspelled it (although later on in the book you'll read that one of Philadelphia's and the nation's greatest symbols has an embarrassing misspelling on it). At least *Fillies,* unlike *Phillies,* is a real word. It's possible the 1883 founders didn't know the word *filly* since they didn't have old movies to watch. We do know there wasn't a single person named Buford or Jethro in the entire Phillies organization. We checked. Besides, only in the Phanatic's era have "f" words (please stay in context here) caused orthographic problems. "F" words in the Quaker City have a higher "ph" value than Schuylkill River water. The phenomenon started when the Phanatic arrived in Philly from the Galapagos Islands in 1978. Ever since then, Philadelphia spelling has become a nightmare. Fun has become "Phun," fever "phever," and fantasy camps, "phantasy camps"—although phantasy campers can't even spell their own names in the wee small hours of the morning in Clearwater (a problem that keeps Camp Commissioner Larry Andersen up nights—concerned yet never dehydrated).

So what does "Phillie" mean? Reportedly when pressed, Phillies founder Al Reach stammered, Jon Lovitz-like,"It tells who we are and where we come from." He may have added, "Yeah, that's the ticket," and mumbled something about Morgan Fairchild. We don't know. We do know that ever since he gave that answer, whenever anyone gives a far-fetched excuse, we say the guy is *Reaching*.

Al Reach did seem to be reaching. First of all, it appears that Snoop Dogg has claimed the exclusive right to invent or bedizzle words. Besides that, we don't call New York residents *Yorkies*. Animal groups would protest that term as a cruel affront to a beautiful breed of canines. Nor do we call Pittsburgh residents *Pittsies*. ZaSu would be offended, and the term might be construed as a characterization of what life is like in that gray, three-river city. Philadelphians—or, as Reach would say, Phillies—have earned a global reputation for hospitality, restraint, and graciousness. Well not quite global. They don't love Philly in the North Pole. Santa never got over that snowballing episode. The guy's got to get out more often.

SNOWBALLIN' SANTA–THE STORY

Philadelphia's reputation as a tough place to play has really snowballed. Philly gets whammed by every national broadcaster as being somewhat inhospitable. The rap started on December 15, 1968 at halftime of the Eagles-Minnesota Vikings game at Franklin Field. It was cold and snowy. Welcome to Philadelphia. Things weren't going the Eagles' way. Welcome to Philadelphia. The band couldn't go on the field at halftime because of bad field conditions. A float made by Zaberer's of Atlantic City was too heavy to move onto the field. That left Santa as the entire halftime show.

Santa sauntered onto the field as "Jingle Bells" reverberated around the stadium. When he made it to the 35 yard line, which was farther downfield than the Eagles had advanced all day, a snowball flew out of the stands. By the time Santa reached the 50, he was walking through a snowball storm.

Santa scurried off the field. At the 20 yard line, he halted, whirled, and shook his fist at the upper deck. Or so some say. Santa was wearing mittens. You would think they prevented him from making finger gestures, although some eyewitnesses (who now number approximately 25 million in a stadium with a seating capacity of 60,000) swear he did.

Did Babe Ruth really point to center field? With which finger?

WHAT IS A PHILLIE?

It's hard to believe, but there are thousands, make that millions, of Phillie fans who have never attended a Phillies game where the Phillie Phanatic was not cavorting around the field and creating havoc in the stands. An entire generation of Phillies rooters has grown up with the Phanatic playing as big a part in a Phillies game as a hot dog or a post-game traffic jam.

The Phanatic has been at *every* game, save a half dozen or so, since Carter was President. He rode the flatbed that led the 1980 World Champions down Broad Street. He stood tall, holding back the tears, when baseball resumed after the tragic events of 9/11. He has helped raise championship banners and retire numbers and he has goofed around at every All-Star Game since '96. He has parachuted into the Vet, zipped down a cable wire from the top of the stadium to the dugout. He has gone toe to toe with Rocky and Joe Carter. Fathers and mothers who once trailed the Phanatic on his rounds at the Vet as kids, now scoot down the aisle with their own kids tucked under their arms. Those parents wait in lines so their kids can get a high-five or a signature smooch from the Phanatic.

And after the city and fans have been Phanaticized for all these years, the big question, the one I hear most, remains: "What the heck *is* the Phanatic? What's he supposed to be?"

Bill Giles, the driving force behind the Phanatic's creation, said that the Phillie Phanatic was named after the passionate and, yes, *fanatical* fans of Philadelphia. Incidentally, Bill spelled fanatical correctly.

But what *is* the Phanatic? Is he an aardvark? An anteater? A green monster (not likely since the green monster already resides in Boston)? The correct answer is that the Phanatic is a rare species of bird from the Galapagos Islands. Charles Darwin developed his theories on evolution when he studied the wildlife that inhabits this remote Pacific island chain. There's no evidence that Charlie ever stumbled upon any Phanatics in his travels in the Galapagos. He may have been frightened to bring him back to England. The Phanatic has no ears. He would look terribly out of place standing next to the British royalty.

Anyway, years later, for some unknown reason, the Phanatic uprooted himself from the tropics and sailed east towards the New World. He ended up in South Philly, which he inexplicably found very tropical. He obviously didn't arrive in January. He waddled into Veterans Stadium on April 25, 1978 and witnessed his first baseball game. He was hopelessly and forever smitten with the team, its city, and its fans. That night, he decided to make Philadelphia his permanent home.

That's my story and I'm sticking to it. I don't know if our current ballplayers know this crucial piece of history. I'm more interested in whether they know something more fundamental; namely, what is a *Phillie*?

"It's a young lady, I guess," answered Jimmy Rollins. Randy Wolf had another opinion: "It's a horse." Randy pitches better than he spells. David Bell concurred, "I agree with Randy. It's a horse, but don't quote me." I think I just did. David's probably afraid our HR people will grill him now. Pitcher Kevin Millwood added his two cents, then voted for "horse." It's starting to sound like we should be playing at Philadelphia Park instead of Citizens Bank Park. Billy Wagner chimed in. "I have to be honest with you, I have *no idea* what a Phillie is but I do know that an Astro is short for astronaut." Billy himself was short for an Astro. He's also short for a Phillie (what we mean is Billy is the most vertically challenged pitcher in MLB and we hope he has a sense of humor).

In 2004, Mike Lieberthal became the pro athlete with the longest tenure in Philadelphia. I figured he would surely know the origins of the word that has been written across his chest for so many years. Of course, his chest protector hides it half the game . . . but still. "It's a girl or a cigar, I think," Lieby muttered a bit sheepishly. Don't run that combination by Bill Clinton—oh, that was girl *with* cigar. Tomas Perez and Bobby Abreu just shook their heads. "No idea," they both said. Or was it "*Ninguna idea*"? "You got me on that one," was Placido Polanco's response. Evidently "Phillie" isn't a Spanish word either.

Jim Thome's eyes got wide as he pondered the answer. "Wow, that's a good one but I think a Phillie is short for Philadelphia." Does Jim mean they shortened "Philadelphia" because the word was too long to fit across most guys' chests? You could spell "Philadelphia-City of Brotherly Love" across Thome's chest. Young Marlon Byrd wrapped up the mystery of what the word on all his paychecks actually means. "I think the name Phillie is short for the people of Philadelphia."

That's right, Marlon. The team was named after Philadelphia and its people. About 201 years after after the first Philadelphians, "oops," I mean, the Phillies settled here.

IN THE BEGINNING WERE THE RUBY LEGS

The Philadelphia Phillies debuted in the National League in 1883. The National League debuted after the demise of the National Association, the first generally recognized professional baseball league, which struggled through five years (1871-1875) of existence. The National Association's first champion was the Athletics of Philadelphia, which was *not* the same organization Connie Mack set up in the City of Brotherly Love in 1901.

In the National Association's final year (1875), three of the league's thirteen teams wore Philadelphia uniforms (the Athletics, the Centennial, and the Phillies). The Centennial, however, dropped out of the league by June, after drawing only 4,500 fans. Sports have grown. That's how many showed up at Philadelphia Park to see Smarty Jones the Saturday after the Derby.

The National League of Professional Base Ball Clubs (the current National League) was founded on Groundhog Day, 1876 in New York's Grand Central Hotel. The NL debuted in 1876, with the Athletics of Philadelphia representing the Quaker City. The A's ran short on cash. They couldn't afford to make the final western trip of the season, so the League ousted them. With the 1876 departure of the Athletics, the National League lacked a Philadelphia representative.

Enter the Philadelphia Phillies. The Worcester Ruby Legs (sometimes referred to as the Brown Stockings, perhaps when the ruby ones were in the wash) dropped out of the National League. They spent two of their three NL seasons in the basement. NL President A.G. Mills was anxious to colonize the Philadelphia market since Philly was the nation's third most populous city at that time. To make that happen, Mills asked an adopted Philadelphian named Al Reach to transplant the Worcester franchise in the City of Brotherly Love.

Move on up Chestnut Street between 18th and 19th Streets, right in front of Boyd's Men's Store. There you'll find an historical marker for Alfred J. Reach (1840-1928). The Pennsylvania Historical and Museum Commission set the marker at 1820 Chestnut Street because that address is the former site of Al Reach's sporting goods store, once a part of Reach's thriving sporting goods empire. But that came later. Back in 1883, Reach became the Phils' co-owner along with a Philly lawyer named John Rogers.

REACH AND SPALDING

The Phillies first owner, Al Reach, was a second baseman—a left-handed second baseman. He played in the National Association from 1871 to 1875, and finished with a career batting average of .247. Off the diamond, Reach was quite the entrepreneur. Born in London, England in 1840, Reach and his family emigrated to Brooklyn when he was a year old. In his twenties, Reach played with the Brooklyn Eckfords but Philadelphian Thomas Fitzgerald lured him to Philly by offering to pay him as a full-time ballplayer. Some historians credit Reach with being the first paid professional baseball player although at best, he shares that hazy distinction. A pitcher named James Creighton played for the Brooklyn Niagaras in 1859, but the Brooklyn Excelsiors allegedly handed him a wad of cash to jump to their club in 1860.

As for Al Reach, he remained in Philly where he opened a cigar store at 404 Chestnut Street. In 1874, he opened a sporting goods store at 6 South 8th Street. By 1881, he had to move on up the street to larger digs at 23 South 8th Street.

In the 1880's, Reach approached Ben Shibe, future owner of the American League Philadelphia Athletics, about partnering with him in the manufacture of baseball gloves and baseballs. Shibe owned a leather-working business and was manufacturing whips. The whips were for horses, in case your mind is too fertile. The partners set up their first plant at Palmer and Tulip Streets, in the section of Philadelphia known as Fishtown. (Legend has it that Charles Dickens gave Fishtown its name because of the stench from area fish markets. In retribution, we now say Fishtown used to smell like the Dickens.) In little more than a decade, the Reach Company opened a second plant in Canada. Meanwhile, Reach's Philly store moved on up Chestnut Street to 18th Street, where that historic marker is now set.

Reach died in Atlantic City in 1928. Earlier in the twenties, he had sold off his manufacturing plants to the company owned by Albert Goodwill Spalding, another ex-baseball player. Like Reach, Spalding made a fortune in sporting goods. Spalding himself was an early superstar on the diamond. He led the Chicago Cubs to the National League's first title in 1876, pitching *every one of the 66 games* the Cubs played. He won 47 of them (if you're wondering, that's twelve short of the all-time single-season record of 59 wins recorded in 1884 by Providence's Charley Radbourn). Spalding hung up his spikes after that 1876 season, assuming his arm had enough left in it to lift his spikes. From then on, he devoted his full time to front-office duties for the Cubs and his sporting goods store in Chicago.

Spalding made a name for himself as a front-office innovator of sorts, although some of his ideas should have drowned in the think tank. For instance, Spalding sent his team out on the field with hats that were color-coded by position. Most fans—even Cub fans—were sharp enough to figure out what position everyone was playing by casually observing where each guy stood in the field. Of course, maybe it was the Cub players who needed the hint. As for Cub fans, then as now, nothing gets by them—not even foul balls. Ask Moïses Alou.

Spalding's store and business prospered. Even today, the Spalding name is one of the most recognizable brands in the sporting goods industry. Spalding himself was a respected national figure—so much so that President McKinley appointed him U. S. Commissioner of the Olympic Games in Paris in 1900. In 1939, Albert Spalding was elected to the baseball Hall of Fame.

The Phillies' opening day loss to the Providence Grays was an ominous harbinger. The NL's new kids on the block got out of the blocks slowly. Make that glacially. They finished the season at 17-81. Their .173 winning percentage (an oxymoron) remains, and presumably will remain, the worst in franchise history. For Philly-bashers, other major-league baseball teams *have* had lower winning percentages. In 1876, Cincinnati went 9-56 for a .138 percentage, and in 1899, the Cleveland Spiders spun out a 20-134 record, for a .130 percentage. The Spiders netted 101 *road* losses alone! They played a lot more away games than home games. The hometown Cleveland fans avoided home games the way arachnophobes avoid attics in abandoned houses. To make sure there was someone in the stands, the Spiders agreed to play several scheduled home games at the opponent's field.

The Phils' first home park was an odd-shaped lot bordered by Columbia, Ridge, 24th, and 25th Streets. The site had been used for baseball for a quarter-century prior to the Phils' arrival. Al Reach purchased the plot of land, threw up a three-section grandstand, and christened it Recreation Park.

STADIUM STUFF

PHILLIES BALLPARKS . . . THEN AND NOW

RECREATION PARK

Dimensions: left field 300′, center field 331′, right center 369′, right field 247′.

CITIZENS BANK PARK

Dimensions: left field 329′, left center 369′, center field 401′, right center 398′, right field 330′.

On that first Phillies squad, Reach let two different players take a shot at being manager: second baseman Bob Ferguson and left fielder William Aloysius "Blondie" Purcell. Ferguson was more successful. His winning percentage of .235 pushed him a full .075 ahead of Purcell's pathetic .160 winning percentage. Purcell never again managed a major league team, nor did anyone else with the name Blondie. Ballplayers today would balk at playing for a guy named Blondie. Their wives would have an even tougher time. After coming home late on a game night, a ballplayer could get into a lot of trouble telling his wife, "Blondie and I went out for a few drinks."

Anyway, no one can blame Blondie for quitting. He managed to hang on for one more year in Philly before heading to Boston where he hung up his spikes and perhaps a blond wig after only one more year. As for Ferguson, he was in the latter stages of a 16-year managerial career. Ferguson took off for Pittsburgh after that season.

Slow starts are not becoming, but they're becoming a Philly thing. The Eagles started 0-2 in their new stadium. The Phils lost their opener at CBP and had an underachieving 2004 campaign. Almost a century after the Phillies debuted, Mike Schmidt kicked off his Hall of Fame career with a .196 rookie batting average. There was one notable exception. Steve Carlton had a sensational first year in Philadelphia. Remember his glittery 27-10 record in 1972? Lefty was responsible for a mind-boggling 45.8% of his team's wins. The 1883 Phillies desperately needed a Steve Carlton (so who doesn't?). At first glance their staff appeared to be saddled with the anti-Carlton—but that's only at first glance. Phillie pitcher John Coleman accounted for 48 of the Phils' 81 losses. That's a whopping 59.3%. But lest we judge Coleman too harshly, his twelve wins also accounted for 75% of his team's sixteen victories. Viewed in that light, Coleman was not the anti-Carlton. He was the Carlton precursor. Coleman pitched an arm-crippling 538-1/3 innings (for comparison, Carlton pitched 346-1/3 innings in 1972) while posting a team-best 4.26 ERA (Lefty's 1972 ERA was 1.97).

The 2004 staff had an off-year. However, the next time you sing the blues about any Phillie pitching staff, consider this. Only one other 1883 Phillie hurler besides Coleman finished with an ERA lower than 5.00, and the *rest of the staff combined* pitched only 326-1/3 innings.

How did that stack up against the rest of the League? Not good. Five of the eight NL clubs finished with staff ERA's lower than 3.00. That made the Phils' staff ERA—5.34—an embarrassing 1.35 higher than the *next* worst ERA in all of baseball.

STADIUM STUFF

PHILLIES BALLPARKS . . . THEN AND NOW

RECREATION PARK

The fabled John Coleman threw the first no-hitter at Recreation Park on April 2, 1883 in the park's first exhibition game as the Phillies beat Ashland, a club from Manayunk. Charley Ferguson threw the only regular-season no-hitter at Recreation Park when he shut down Providence 1-0.

BAKER BOWL

Red Donahue threw the Phils' first Baker Bowl (called National League Park at the time) no-no, a 5-0 win over Boston on July 8, 1898. Johnny Lush threw the third and final Phils' Baker Bowl no-hitter on September 18, 1903, besting Chicago 10-0.

CONNIE MACK STADIUM

Oops! No Phillie pitcher ever threw a no-hitter here, but eleven opponents did.

THE VET

Terry Mulholland, on August 15, 1990, threw the Phils' first no-hitter, topping the Giants 6-0, and of course, Kevin Millwood tossed the final Vet no-hitter on the Phanatic's birthday, April 27, 2003.

Ah, but how about the hitters on that first Phils team? Unfortunately, they were worse than the pitchers. The only .300 hitter was Emil Gross who batted .307. Emil retired after that .300 season, much like Ashburn and the Krukker did years later. Blondie Purcell had the team's second-best average at .267—miles behind the .397 posted by the League's top hitter, Hall of Famer Dan Brouthers. The NL boasted two 40-game winners that year: Charley Radbourn and Jim Galvin. Both are now Hall of Famers. And speaking of Hall of Famers, you guessed it. There were no Hall of Famers on the Phils' 1883 roster. Not even close.

JOLTIN' JOLTIN' JOE'S RECORD – TAKE 1 AND 2

Some call Joltin' Joe DiMaggio's 56-straight-game hitting streak baseball's most unbreakable record. With all due respect to the Yankee Clipper, we'll propose two Phillie records that should jolt Joltin' Joe's record as the game's most unbreakable. Throughout the book, we'll propose some more. Here are the first two.

We can characterize John Coleman's 48 losses in a single season as more than a dubious achievement. Coleman's loss total that season smashed a mark that had only stood for three years. Coleman's should stand forevermore. Will White set the original mark when he was tagged with 42 losses in 1880. Thanks to Coleman, Willie, we suspect, will be the eternal also-ran for single-season losses.

To put Coleman's "achievement" in perspective, consider this. The entire Cleveland Indians pitching *staff* had only one more loss in the 1954 season than did Coleman all by himself in 1883. We don't think that'll launch a "Bring back Omar Daal" movement, but it does give a platform for comparison.

No one has even *approached* Coleman's record since he set it. Pitchers don't put those kinds of numbers up any more. To find the last pitcher who was even remotely close to Coleman, we have to move on down to the thirties. Doing his part for the Depression, Paul Derringer lost 27 for the 1933 Cincinnati Reds. Derringer's 27 losses ranks third for the twentieth century. Since 1950, the most games any pitcher has ever lost in a single season is 24—a figure shared by both Roger Craig of the Amazin' '62 Mets and Jack Fisher of the '65 Mets.

OK, Phillie phans, let's not get negative here. Another Phillies record that jolts Joltin' Joe's is one to be proud of. The Phillies' 1894 outfield accomplished something no other outfield ever has. It also seems safe to say that no *other* outfield ever will. All three Phils outfielders batted over .400. Ed Delahanty hit .404, Billy Hamilton .403, and Sam Thompson .415. All three were eventually elected to the Hall of Fame. Oh, one other thing. For good measure, a fourth Phillie outfielder, Tuck Tucker, topped them all with a .416 average. They just couldn't find a regular spot to put him. Too bad that old problen doesn't come back.

In spite of that forgettable 1883 start, the Phillies were in the NL to stay. The New York Giants—now the San Francisco Giants—also joined the NL fold that year. At the time, the city of New York was establishing itself as the country's unchallenged metropolis. The Philadelphia Phillies debuted the same year the Brooklyn Bridge opened. A month after the Phils' debut, on May 24, 1883, 150,300 people strolled across the Brooklyn

Bridge and 1,800 vehicles paid five cents each to cross. The behemoth structure cost a mind-boggling $15,100,000—slightly more than Jim Thome's yearly salary (we're not suggesting here that you could sell Jim the Brooklyn Bridge). The Statue of Liberty was erected three years later as New York was assertively morphing into the Big Apple we all know and . . . know.

Meanwhile down in Philly, things were getting better and better for the baseball club. In 1884, the Phils hired future Hall of Famer Harry Wright as manager. Wright had skippered the legendary Cincinnati Red Stockings, baseball's first professional team. He's buried in Philadelphia's historic West Laurel Cemetery. Harry's tombstone reads: "Father of Professional Baseball."

Under Wright's leadership, the Phils improved their 1884 record to 39-73 and moved on up two slots in the standings. The following season, they crossed over to the good side of the .500 line, finishing third behind the Cubs and Giants.

Harry Wright managed the Phils for a decade—one of the finest decades in Phillies history. They never grabbed the pennant flag, but they were perennial first-division finishers and remained so well past the Wright era.

STADIUM STUFF

PHILLIES BALLPARKS . . . THEN AND NOW

RECREATION PARK

The outfield wall was white at Recreation Park. Of course, in those days the white contrasted with the dark, tobacco, and dirt-stained color of the baseball that was used for the entire game. The white background probably *helped* hitters.

CITIZENS BANK PARK

In May 2004, the Phils darkened the brick on their brand-new outfield walls so batters could pick the pitch up better. These days, baseballs have less dirt than a dossier on Clark Kent. The average life today of an MLB baseball is less than nine pitches, which exceeds the average attention span of a fifth-grader by five pitches.

SOUTHPAWS

Philly has a thing about southpaws—a good thing. Southpaw Rocky Balboa gave Apollo Creed fits. Rube Waddell, Lefty Grove, Eppa Rixey, Chris Short, Lefty Carlton, and now Randy Wolf gave anyone who ever waved a bat fits. All are or were southpaws. *Southpaws.* Everyone uses the term but few know why lefthanders are called southpaws. At least, we're pretty confident that the origin of the term southpaw is a mystery to most people. We heard the question on *Jeopardy* and nobody knew the answer. If *Jeopardy* contestants don't know, we figure most people don't—not that *Jeopardy* contestants aren't people.

In any event, here's where the term southpaw originated. Credit a sportswriter, Finley Peter Dunne, who came up with the term in the eighties—the 1880's, that is.

Most old stadiums were designed so that the batter faced directly east and the pitcher faced directly west *into the sun*. The reasoning for the orientation would shock Richie Ashburn and John Kruk, perhaps the two biggest Phillie pitcher-bashers of all time (in terms of verbal comments as well as batting prowess). Games were all played in the afternoon in the old days, so this setup forced the pitcher, not the batter, to squint into the afternoon sun. *Batters got the advantage*. Of course, that's not the way things actually worked out.

As it turned out, batters faced *bigger* problems with that orientation. As the afternoon wore on, the shade crept into the 60′-6″ area between the pitching rubber and home plate, stealing in like a blanketing black tide. Batters from the middle innings on had to fix their eyes on a rapidly moving sphere that left the pitcher's hand in bright sunlight and then, in mid-flight, zipped into dark shadows. And *that* phenomenon gave batters more fits than squinting into a setting sun. I'm sure Richie and the Krukster would agree that pitchers were the evil geniuses behind it—that pitchers had the shadow thing figured out from the beginning, and pushed for orienting the park that way from day one.

So back to the term southpaw. In a park oriented with the pitcher facing west, a lefty's pitching arm (or, in Mitch Williams' case, his *throwing* arm—"Mitch was a thrower not a pitcher," excerpted from the Gospel according to Kruk) points south. Hence the name southpaw. Or in Mitch's case, "Wild Thing."

PHLATLINER

17 and 81 . . . OUCH! Now that's what I call a rough start. Good thing no modern manager piloted that 1883 team. They wouldn't have made midseason before the men in the white suits took them away. If talk radio existed back in 1883, I'm sure the phone lines would have lit up with irate callers threatening to march down to Recreation Park and fork over their season tickets. I can just hear some caller named Joe (well, maybe he would have had a name like Tobias) from Old City (I guess it was Aging City or Middle Aged City in 1883) screaming at host Ezekial Eskine: "And another thing, that guy Coleman has *got* to go! They should trade that clown for a bucket of oats! Not Quaker Oats, not Johnny Oates, not Hall and Oates, but just plain old oats! And another thing, Ezekial, what the hell is a Phillie anyway?"

You can imagine what Philly fans must have thought about the collection of unknowns that were thrown together to represent their city that inaugural year in the National League. Philly fans probably felt like the good people of Cleveland—which includes many of them—in the movie *Major League*, with one major difference. The fictionalized Cleveland squad was put together for the express purpose of finishing last. Cleveland had Rick Vaughn, the bespectacled convict and "original" Wild Thing (not to say that Mitch Williams is not an original). Cleveland had Willie Mays Hayes, Roger Dorn the pretty-boy third baseman, and others. But the real-life 1883 Phillies had Sid Farrar, Jack Manning, Bill McClellan, and Bill Harbridge—names that to this day inspire diehard Phillie fans to say, "Who?"

As a sports-obsessed kid growing up just outside Philadelphia, I've lived through some tough times as a Philly fan. I suffered through the 1972-73 season when the 76ers were 9 and 73. That's a .109 percentage, which makes the 1883 Phils, to say nothing of the 2004 Phils, seem dominant. I also suffered through some bad Mike McCormick-coached Eagle teams in the early seventies. Eventually, Doctor J and Dick Vermeil rescued those franchises and helped to usher in a decade-long run of relative success for all four of Philly's major professional sports teams.

The closest thing to the Phils' 1883 season that I experienced personally was our 1997 season. If you recall (why am I doing this? I had blocked that season out up till now), our Phils were on pace to break the Mets' record for most losses in a season. That's 120 if you're counting. Fortunately we didn't break the record, but speaking for myself, it was still a rough year both for the team and the Phanatic.

I like to say (or believe) that Julius Erving and the Phanatic are the only two sports figures never to be booed in Philadelphia. But then, I also like to say, "I think I could get around on a Billy Wagner fastball." Well, in '97 when the team was sagging, the *Daily News* decided that the Phanatic was as lousy as the team. They splashed a photo of the Phanatic lying flat on his back on the front page. The headline read "Phlatliner" (again, all our "Ph" problems in Philly don't come from Schuylkill water). I remember pulling up to my neighborhood Wawa in my gaudy Phillie Phanatic van, picking up the *Daily News*, seeing that cover story, and wanting to crawl into a hole. With my head down and my hand covering my face, I slid sixty cents to the checkout girl across the counter, and then slinked back into the Phanatic van. Turns out that one of the editors of the *Daily News* was at a sparsely attended Phillies game early in the season. The weather was dreary and so was the game. He was underwhelmed by the fans' response to the Phanatic's antics and decided to target Philly's phavorite mascot.

He assigned a female reporter to the story. She had *never* been to a Phillies game. She telephoned me and asked me why the Phanatic had lost his appeal. I told her the fans still loved the Phanatic. To be honest, early in '97, the fans were even better with the Phanatic than prior years.

I invited her to come to a game. If she were actually in the crowd, she could judge the fans' reaction for herself. What a concept!

What a mistake.

She *did* come to the park. Amazingly, she picked a night when the Phillies actually played, although that might have been a coincidence. I never asked. Her column next day offered her observations and interpretation of the Phanatic's antics. She only stuck around for five innings. She may have left early because she didn't foresee either team scoring a touchdown.

As for how accurate her interpretation of the Phanatic's popularity was, I can best explain it with an old joke. A scientist sets a frog down, shouts "Jump," and the frog jumps. The scientist measures and records, "Frog jumps six feet when he hears 'Jump.'" He then binds both front legs, and shouts "Jump." He measures and records, "Frog jumps five feet when his front legs are bound and he hears 'Jump.'" He then binds both front legs and one back leg, shouts "Jump," and measures and records, "When three legs are bound, frog jumps three feet when he hears 'Jump.'" Finally, the scientist binds both front legs and both back legs, shouts "Jump," and the frog doesn't budge.

The scientist draws the following conclusion: "When all four frog's legs are bound, the frog goes deaf."

Now, back to my favorite writer and how she interpreted what she saw.

A big part of Phanatic shtick is to interact with the opposing team. The visiting team was throwing baseballs at me the night she was there, and having a lot of fun doing it. Her interpretation: "The visiting team was so uninspired by the Phanatic's shenanigans that they began throwing baseballs at the green mascot." Well, duh. That's all part of the act, Lois Lane. If I can get a player to splash water, throw a resin bag, or lock me in a full nelson, I've done my job. She wrote further that the Phanatic shamelessly stole the thunder of an inner-city dance troupe, denying them their moment in the spotlight during the pre-game entertainment. Here's another news flash, Lois. The kids and their instructors *insisted* that the Phanatic join them in their routine. The kids were thrilled to pose for a picture afterwards with the big green guy to memorialize their, not the Phanatic's, special night.

The article created quite a stir among Phillie and Phanatic faithful. WIP Sports Radio was deluged with calls defending the green guy. The *Daily News* was bombarded with letters in support of the Phanatic. One indignant fan wrote, "Let's ditch Santa Claus, too. His act has gotten old, his suit out of style." I guess I should explain what he means to my favorite reporter. He was being facetious. You see, the guy actually *likes* Santa. Sure, he might throw a snowball or two Santa's way, but that's a Philadelphia thing. Like jazz, if you have to explain it, you'll never understand it.

Two hundred six Phillies employees staunchly backed the Phanatic and sent a joint letter protesting the article (to those of you who haven't received my check yet, it's in the mail).

The story even hit the national news. *USA Today* came to the Phanatic's defense. Now that's movin' on up! They ran a cover story with the headline, "Mascot Stands Test of Time—The Phillie Phanatic Keeps 'em Laughing Even if the Team Is in Last Place." The *USA Today* article cited marketing studies that proved the Phanatic was still a fan favorite. The piece included quotes from fans, ushers, and players like Curt Schilling who said: "Are you kidding me? I love watching the guy. He's the best mascot in sports." (Thanks, Schil. The check is in . . . never mind.)

Anyway, to me, the *USA Today* piece was total vindication. As for the editor who decided that it was time for the Phanatic to take a bullet—he was transferred to Hartford, Connecticut later that same year. At his going-away party, the staffers at the *Daily News* autographed a huge sign with a drawing of the Phanatic driving him out of town—in a car, not with one of Ben Shibe's whips.

Pharewell!

CHAPTER 3

MOVIN' ON UP TO THE FIRST PENNANT

Harry Wright had just piloted Providence to a National League pennant in 1883 when he arrived in Philly in 1884. Old Harry had played sporadically and managed Boston in the old National Association from 1871 through 1875. He finished his playing career with a .274 average.

It took only three seasons for Wright to whip his hapless new Phillie charges into contenders. Today professional baseball remembers Harry Wright as one of its immortals. The Veterans Committee inducted him into the Hall of Fame in 1953 under the category of "Baseball Pioneer."

In his decade as Philadelphia's skipper, the Phils finished in the first division all but the first two seasons. They nailed a couple second-place finishes and a couple of third-place finishes but never managed to move on up to the very top. Not that they didn't have the talent.

In the late 1890's, Wright-piloted teams (that's Harry Wright, not Wilbur or Orville who were piloting other things around the same era) featured a constant parade of future Hall of Famers. For you seventies-era naysayers, the Phils of the Gay Nineties surpassed their latter-day counterparts in underachieving. From 1891 through 1902, the Phillies always seemed to have a *trio* of Hall of Famers-in-waiting on their roster. You could say they had "many a trio" long before Manny Trillo.

The first Hall of Fame trio played in 1891. Sam Thompson arrived from Detroit in 1889. Billy Hamilton came to town in 1890, followed by the enigmatic Ed Delahanty in 1891. The threesome stayed intact for five consecutive seasons before Hamilton was shipped to the Boston Braves. The following year, in 1897, Thompson retraced his path to the Motor City (though it wasn't called that yet) where he closed out his career. The void left by Thompson and Hamilton was filled quickly when Nap Lajoie, acclaimed as one of the sport's early superstars, became a Phil. Nap was the Phillies' best ballplayer of French ancestry till Rheal Cormier arrived.

One year after Lajoie joined the fold, Elmer Flick came onboard, as the Phillie roster of future Hall of Famers swelled once more to three. The Lajoie-Delahanty-Flick trio played together through 1900.

The big names weren't the only Phils doing big things. On April 21, 1898, pitcher Bill "Frosty" Duggleby became the first major leaguer to sock a homer in his first big-league at-bat. Others have since duplicated his feat, but Duggleby remains the only guy named Frosty who ever did it. We're betting he always will be.

HITTING A HOME RUN

Frosty Duggleby's first major-league at-bat was not only a home run, it was a grand slam. Frosty is the only Phillie pitcher ever to hit a grand slam in his first at-bat. Two other Phillies position players—Jim Command in 1954 and Chase Utley in 2003—have blasted first-hit grand slams.

In 1901, Lajoie jumped crosstown and signed with the Athletics in the brand-new American League. That same year, future Hall of Famer Hughie Jennings became a Phil. Jennings' terrific career was sputtering to an end when he started his stint with the Phils. However, the year 1901 marked the last time the Phils would field three future Hall of Famers simultaneously until 1983.

The 1983 "Wheeze Kids" had Mike Schmidt at third, Joe Morgan at second, and Pete Rose at first. Tony Perez was also a first baseman on the squad. Steve Carlton was the ace of the staff. With the exception of Rose, all are Hall of Famers.

In 1902, Flick was dealt to Cleveland where he played till his 1910 retirement. Delahanty departed for Washington. Two years later, he died under mysterious circumstances in the midst of a "sub-par" .333 season (his lifetime average was .350).

In 1902, the Phillies began a nine-year run *sans* a future Hall of Famer. Sherry Magee was the marquee Phillie player of the era. Magee batted a healthy .291 for his career and holds the dubious distinction of being the only player in major league history who ever led his league in RBI's four times and did *not* make the Hall of Fame. Magee enjoys some measure of posthumous vindication. The Society for American Baseball Research (SABR) ranks Sherry baby as the *second*-greatest ballplayer of the Dead Ball Era who is *not* in the Hall of Fame. For *Field of Dreams* junkies, Shoeless Joe Jackson is number one.

From 1902-1910, absent immortals and superstars, the Phils managed to remain competitive. After down seasons in 1902 and 1903, they cranked out first-division finishes every year but two during the leadoff decade of the twentieth century.

SHERRY MAGEE

Sherwood Robert (Sherry) Magee grew up in the oil fields of Pennsylvania. Yes, Pennsylvania *oil fields*. Pennsylvania isn't *only* pizzerias, 7-11's, hair parlors with names that are puns on anything having to do with hair, and Blockbusters. Think back to your American history. Where was oil discovered? Not in some backwater Louisiana town, not on Jed Clampett's South Forty. No, oil was discovered back on August 27, 1859 in Titusville, Pennsylvania. Sherry (Won't You Come Out Tonight) Magee was born in Clarendon, in Warren County, on August 6, 1884.

Sherry Magee was the Phils' top gun from 1904 to 1914. He holds the Phillies twentieth-century team record for stolen bases (387) and he's in the top ten in virtually every other offensive category. Magee turned in superstar years in 1910 and 1914. In 1910, his .331 average dethroned all-time great Honus Wagner as batting champ after Wagner had won four NL batting titles in a row. Magee also led the National League with 110 runs, 123 RBI's, a .507 slugging average, and a .445 on-base percentage. In fact, *Baseball Magazine* at the time called him "a greater slugger than Cobb, Lajoie or any of a score of stars whose names are a synonym for Hit."

Magee was a muscular guy for the era. At 5′ 11″, he was physically imposing and a gifted athlete. Besides being a decent basketball player and bowler, Magee was a dynamite football player who often worked out with the Lafayette College football team in Easton, Pennsylvania.

Magee was a raging competitor. He reputedly suffered from epilepsy, like teammate Grover Cleveland Alexander and later, Tony Lazzeri, the Yankee Hall of Fame shortstop. Like Lazzeri, Magee tried to hide his affliction.

He played in an era that was, let's say, edgy. Fistfights among teammates were not uncommon. In fact, the upstart American League was trumpeting a less truculent, more genteel atmosphere to snatch players from the senior circuit.

Ballplayers were a different breed back then. Take the case of Phils captain, Kid Gleason. Gleason kept a leather belt in his locker. It wasn't just for show. He used it. Whether he screamed, "Who's your daddy?" as he was belting his teammates, we'll never know. But Magee was belted more than a few times—according to some accounts. The game has changed a lot, hasn't it? Nowadays when a player says he belted one out at the ballpark, you ask how far, not *who* did you belt?

Magee himself was a guy who wasn't shy about chewing out teammates—a trait that did not make him a fan favorite. Fans hung the departure of popular center-fielder Johnny Bates on Magee. Bates was the Phils' second-best hitter. Magee of course was first. But Magee was always on Bates' case, which made coming to work a drag for Bates. So he asked out of Philly.

In 1914, Magee got into a tiff with the Phils' shortstop Mike Reed. Magee had asked for a try-out at shortstop. The regular shortstop was hurt, and the Phils were coming up short finding replacements. Replacement SS Reed took exception to Magee's comment that Sherry himself couldn't do any worse than the replacements, so the two duked it out at the pool table in the clubhouse.

Magee's most memorable gaffe occurred on July 10, 1911 in St. Louis. The Phils were in the thick of a five-team pennant race. The day before, July 9, Magee had been tossed from the game because he got in the umpire's face after being called out on a first-inning steal attempt. This particular day, Magee came to bat with his team ahead 2-1, and two runners on board. Umpire Bill Finneran called Magee out on a high pitch. Magee turned away and flung his bat. Finneran ejected Magee a little too emphatically for the taste of Sherry, so the Phillie star abruptly stopped, turned, and assaulted the ump. Sherry threw a right hand that sent Finneran buckling down to the ground. St. Louie catcher Roger Bresnahan and others subdued Magee. Meanwhile, the fallen umpire got up and rushed Magee. Finneran was stopped short by a host of Phillies and Philly cops. Then he was taken to the hospital.

Magee later claimed Finneran had called him a name. Magee didn't say what name. "Psycho" hadn't entered popular usage yet, even though a guy named Bates was on the team.

Phils manager Red Dooin countercharged that Finneran, a rookie umpire, was itching for a fight. Dooin alleged that Finneran was basically talking turn-of-the-century trash about his boxing skills—whatever trash talk sounded like back then ("Listen up you mugs, keep up the crabbin' and I'll thrash you good."). Dooin was probably not coming to Magee's defense so much as grinding a personal axe. Finneran had "offered Dooin out" (as Philly high schoolers used to say) only a few weeks earlier, Dooin claimed. Umpire Finneran told Dooin to meet him under the stands after the game, and Magee, ironically, served as the peacemaker, instead of dooin nothin'.

Magee was fined $200 and suspended for the rest of the season by NL President Thomas Lynch. The Phils appealed. The club, absent their star, played at a dismal 13-16 clip, and sank to fourth place, 6-1/2 games off the pace. President Lynch, at that juncture, relented and reinstated Magee who rejoined his club on August 16.

The following year, Magee was injured colliding with Dode Paskert, the Phils' centerfielder. One afternoon following the collision, Paskert hit a homer into the left field bleachers. Rounding third, Paskert heard Magee's sons booing him loudly (shocking that a guy who hit a homer could be booed in Philadelphia). When Paskert got back to the dugout, he and Magee duked it out, which makes the whole

Kobe-Shaq thing seem overblown.

After carrying the Phillies for a decade, Magee was traded. On the eve of the Phils' finest hour, 1915, when the Phils won a pennant, Magee was shuttled off to the Braves. The fact that the Phils won in 1915 without Magee confirmed his reputation as a jinx and/or troublemaker with many Phillie fans.

As for Magee, 1915 brought nothing but bad luck. He injured his shoulder the day spring training began and didn't regain his hitting stroke till 1918 with the Cincinnati Reds. The following year, bad luck again blindsided him. Magee finally made it to the World Series. Unfortunately, he did it in 1919, the year of the Black Sox Scandal. Our boy Sherry got one hit in two Series plate appearances but found himself jobless the next year, bringing his sixteen-year career to a close.

Sherry Magee died of pneumonia in Philly on March 13, 1929. He was living at 1152 N. 65th Street at the time of his death and overseeing a group of restaurants.

The Phils added an interesting note to the record book during that era. In 1904, 18-year-old Johnny Lush moved on up to the Big Show and batted .276—a pretty impressive mark, considering the league average was .249. Lush became the youngest position player to play in the majors in the twentieth century. Cincy's Joe Nuxhall was the youngest player ever, but Joe came up as a wild 15-year-old pitcher, not a position player. Nuxhall's 1944 debut, where he issued five walks, surrendered two hits, and left the mound with a 67.50 ERA in 2/3 of an inning, was far less impressive than Lush's mature debut.

As for the Phils, their fortunes took a turn for the better in 1911. A 24-year-old rookie named Grover Cleveland Alexander arrived from Nebraska—the home state of another Phillie great, Richie Ashburn. Pete, as Grover preferred to be called (with due respect to Philadelphia comedian Grover Silcox, who would want to be called Grover?), fashioned a 28-13, 2.57 ERA rookie season. A star was born, and the Phils were about to hitch to that star and move on up to where they had never been.

The following season, another budding immortal, rookie Eppa Rixey, the Phillies' alpha "lefty," made his debut. For the first and only time in history (unless Kitty Kaat gets his due), the Phils could trot two Hall of Famers out to the mound in the same season.

After back-to-back 10-win and 9-win seasons, Rixey plummeted to 2-11 in 1914. So did the Phils who dropped from second to sixth place.

The year 1915 was a different story. Alexander won 31—his first of three consecutive 30-win seasons as a Phil. Rixey bad-lucked his way to an 11-12 record, belying a sparkling 2.39 ERA. But Erskine Mayer picked up the slack, recording his second straight 21-win season. The Phils dominated the competition on arm strength. They outdistanced the defending pennant-winning "Miracle Braves" by seven games. The Phils' miserly 2.17 staff ERA compensated for an unimpressive team batting average of .247. Actually, that BA is misleading; 1915 was a pitcher's year. The NL's highest team batting average was only .254 that year.

The Phils packed remarkable pop for the era. They led the majors in homers with 58—a disappointing season nowadays for Sammy Sosa, but an astonishing team total for its day. Gavvy Cravath was the team's Jim Thome. Cravath belted 24 round-trippers. How good was that? Cravath's total topped or equaled the output of all but one NL *team!* Not surprisingly, Cravath doubled the individual output of *every* National League player except Phillie-great-in-waiting Cy Williams.

THE WILLIAMS SHIFT

When Fred "Cy" Williams retired in 1930, he was second on the all-time NL home run list behind Roger Hornsby. Baseball might have forgotten that factoid, but the game shouldn't forget for whom the Williams Shift was devised. The answer is the Phils' Cy, *not* the Red Sox' Ted.

Credit for devising the Williams Shift usually goes to Cleveland Indians manager Lou Boudreau. Actually, the original Williams Shift was a device to thwart the power of the Phils' Cy Williams. The Chicago Cubs dreamed it up in the late twenties.

The two Williams boys—Cy and Ted—had more in common than a last name and a shift. Both guys were left-handed power hitters, both led their leagues in homers four times and home-run percentage five times. Both were dead pull hitters who resisted hitting the ball to left, and both steadfastly refused to bunt the ball toward the third base area invitingly vacated via the shift. Both Williamses approached the Williams Shift the same way. Both tried to pummel the ball to the right side—and both had great success doing so.

SHIFT THIS

Jim Thome's first year with the Phillies was one for the books. Forty-seven home runs. One hundred thirty-one RBI's. One hundred eleven runs scored.

But beyond the numbers alone was the way he did it. Home run balls explored regions of the Vet where baseballs had never gone. Every Thome hit, every mammoth moon shot and every run produced seemed to come in the clutch in 2003. After he homered in his first official at-bat as a Phillie in spring training, the entire Philadelphia sports world fixed its eyes on Jim Thome. It seemed fitting that, once again, a player wearing red and white pinstripes could replicate the feats of long ball specialists Mike Schmidt and Greg Luzinski in the Vet's farewell season. There was a noticeable jingle of electricity running through the crowd every time Thome strode to the plate.

Now to be honest, when I'm running around in a furry, green costume, jumping over chairs, stealing food and flirting with ladies, I sometimes lose track of what is going on in the game. You'd have a tough time concentrating on the game too if you were busy smooching the blonde in the twelfth row one minute and goosing the fat guy carrying three cheesesteaks and two beers down the aisle the next.

But when Thome is digging into the batter's box, no matter how cute that blonde is or how funny the fat guy looks dribbling beer after the goose, the Phanatic's eyes join all the other eyes in the stadium. They're fixed on big number twenty-five—until I notice that the shortstop is standing next to the second baseman on the right side of second base. Maybe we shouldn't have cut up Al Spalding's color-coded-by-hat scheme after all.

Roaring on up from the twenties to the new millennium, the Williams Shift has morphed into the Thome shift.

JIM THOME: "It all started when I was playing for the Indians. Art Howe was managing the A's and he was the first one to do it to me. From then on, a bunch of teams started to do it. I guess you can look at it two ways. In one way, it's flattering that they would go to such lengths to stop me. But in another way, it might be like saying they think they have the book on me. Either way, I really don't pay much attention to it. I don't make any adjustments at all."

He could have said, "It makes no difference *Tho-me.*" But he's not as silly as me.

The Phils faced Boston in the 1915 World Series. Alexander spun his magic in the opener, winning 3-1 in front of a home crowd of 19,343. The next three games all ended 2-1. Unfortunately, when they all ended, Boston had the two. Games three and four in Boston each drew 41,000-plus spectators. Limited by the stadium's capacity, crowds in Philadelphia were only half that number.

After Boston took two at Fenway, the Series returned to Philly for game five. The Phils were down three games to one. Twice in the game the Phils took a two-run lead. Twice they lost it. Twice, Harry Hooper hit home runs that gave Boston the lead back. His top-of-the-ninth homer was all she wrote.

STADIUM STUFF

THE PHILLIES' FIRST WORLD SERIES

• Babe Ruth made his first World Series appearance at Baker Bowl at the age of twenty. The Babe grounded out in the ninth as a pinch-hitter. It was Ruth's only appearance in the Series.

• The Babe did not pitch in the Series, despite his staff-leading .750 winning percentage and 18-6 regular-season record. The next two seasons, Ruth was the ace of the Bosox staff with records of 23-12 and 24-13. Over the course of the 1916 and 1918 World Series, Ruth pitched 29-2/3 consecutive scoreless Series innings—a World Series mark that stood till Whitey Ford broke it in 1961.

• The first U.S. President to attend a World Series game did it right here in Philadelphia. Woodrow Wilson attended game two at Baker Bowl.

• Size matters, or at least it mattered in 1915. Baker Bowl seated some 20,000, in contrast with 40,000 in Boston's Fenway Park. When the Series moved back to Philly after game four, temporary bleachers were erected in left field in Baker Bowl. The Phils lost the game and the Series on two HR's off the bat of Boston's Harry Hooper. Ironically, Hooper circled the bases because his drives bounced into the temporary seats.

Despite the disappointment of a World Series loss, the Phils had moved on up to their first pennant. Unfortunately, they didn't keep movin' on up. In fact, they faded quickly. The Alexander-Rixey duo was dismantled by 1918. Alexander was shuffled to the Cubs (their greatest gift till Ferguson Jenkins unpacked his bags). Alexander missed most of the 1918 season because of World War I but went on to epic success as a Cub. Rixey, though still a Phil, missed the entire 1918 season. Not surprisingly, without him the Phils plummeted from 1917 NL runner-up down to sixth in 1918. They wallowed in the second division for more than a decade.

It would be another thirty-five years before our hometowners moved on up to another pennant.

JOLTIN' JOLTIN' JOE'S RECORD – TAKE 3

In 1916, Pete Alexander threw sixteen shutouts in one season. Let's frame that a little better.

In 2003, Kevin Millwood, along with Matt Morris and Jason Schmidt, led the majors with *three* shutouts. But forget shutouts. In the past fifteen years, no major leaguer has thrown sixteen *complete games*. Roger Clemens racked up eighteen CG's back in 1987. But nine CG's was tops for all major league hurlers in 2003.

To find the last time a pitcher reached double figures in shutouts, you have to go back to 1985 when John Tudor recorded ten—the same number Jim Palmer attained ten years earlier.

In this era of low pitch counts, early yanks (we're not referring to Willie Keeler), and automatic save situations, it seems unlikely that any pitcher will ever *approach* what Grover Cleveland Alexander did in 1916. Ol' Pete holds second place on the career all-time list for most whitewashes. He tossed ninety of them. Let's compare that to the current crop of surefire Hall of Famers.

Roger Clemens has 46 shutouts. His best single-year total was eight in 1988. Career totals for Greg Maddux, Pedro Martinez, Randy Johnson and Tom Glavine are 34, 15, 35, and 22 respectively. Of that group, the Big Unit's six in 1998 is the highest seasonal total.

PHANATIC PHILE

THE BEST BIRTHDAY PRESENT – EVER

Phillies fans waited 15 years to see a Phillies player throw the first nohitter at the National League Park. The year was 1898, and on July 8, Red Donahue earned the distinction. I'm sure Red was really dealin' that day. But all old Red had to deal with was the Boston Braves. OK, he might have been preoccupied, planning an off-season steamboat trip to Hawaii, which the U.S. acquired that very day. (Hey, the Phanatic might have been chillin' in the Galapagos, but he always kept up with world events.) We'll never know what was on Red's mind that day. But one thing is certain: Red was *not* harassed or distracted by a giant clam devouring an umpire whole. Nor was he harassed by other costumed creatures running around in the outfield between innings.

Kevin Millwood had to endure all those distractions on April 27, 2003—the day he tossed his no-no at the Vet. Just as Donahue had tossed his no-hitter on a momentous day—the day the U.S. acquired Hawaii—so too did Millwood. The momentous occasion for Millwood's gem was the day all of Philadelphia celebrates—the Phillie Phanatic's birthday.

The Phillies have been celebrating the Phanatic's birthday yearly ever since his arrival in Philadelphia in 1978. How old is the Phanatic? Nobody really knows and the Phanatic isn't telling. He may be as old as some of those giant tortoises on the Galapagos Islands but like ex-Philadelphian Dick Clark, he never ages. In any event, on a spectacular spring day when 40,000 fans packed the Vet, Kevin Millwood gave the Phanatic his best gift ever.

The Phanatic's annual birthday party rocks. Some think it rocks too much. One baseball purist once complained that he went to watch a ballgame on the day of the Phanatic's birthday, and a Muppet Show broke out instead.

The beat went on in 2003.

Before the game, hundreds of kids wearing party hats and holding balloons were invited onto the field along with their parents. Clowns, face painters and guys on stilts mingled in the crowd. Mascots from various colleges and pro teams were on the field too, creating havoc. A group of ten-foot inflatable characters called the Zooperstars were making their third straight appearance at the Phanatic's birthday. The name of each Zooperstar is a pun on baseball players. There's a giant inflatable great white shark called "Shark" McGwire, and a creepy crawler called "IchiRoach." There's a long-necked Ken "Giraffy Jr." and a non-baseball star called "Stallion" Iverson. Philadelphia TV legend Captain Noah and his wife, Mrs. Noah, joined the 2003 party too—same as they did on the first Phanatic birthday in 1979. We thought it was a nice touch to bring them back for the last party at the Vet.

Since it was the last Phanatic birthday at the Vet, I came up with a good idea. (Or a really stupid idea. That's the beauty of my job. The really good ideas are really stupid! Don't try my method where you work though. I'm a paid professional.) My idea? Zip down a cable wire from the last row of the stadium to the top of the Phillies dugout. The Phanatic had done it twice before—once when I was dressed as Batman for a birthday celebration and once to kick off the 1998 season. Since I had clean underwear waiting in my office, and since the third time's the charm (not a popular saying in Philly since the Carolina Panthers visited the Linc in January 2004), I decided: "Why not go for the glory since this is the last Phanatic birthday at the Vet." Later in the 2003 season, we were planning to honor all the great thrill acts the Vet had hosted over its 33-year history. My death-defying leap from the 700 Level would *have* to be included in the highlights film. Besides, if Kiteman could jump one final (bad choice of words) time to honor the Vet, as he had to open the 2003 season, so could the Phanatic.

So just before Kevin Millwood took the mound, I whipped down from the upper reaches in the right field 700 Level, clocking 35 miles per hour. I had a baseball in one hand and a strap attached to the other. If anyone wanted that strap they would have to pry it from my cold, dead hands.

The last thing that passed in front of my eyes (other than my life) when I jumped was the vision of opening ESPN's *Sportscenter* that night—every mascot's dream.

After a clumsy landing, I unstrapped myself, dropped to my knees, repeatedly kissed the dugout, and delivered the first ball. Mission accomplished (not delivering the ball but surviving the slide).

The game was officially under way, although I would never have known. After a quick break (to put those underpants on), I was back out into the stands with the Phanatic's mom Phoebe, greeting all the kids at the birthday bash. Every year, the Phanatic sends an invitation and a free ticket to the 15,000 kids enrolled in the Phillie Phanatic birthday club. If they come to the game with their family, the Phanatic or his mom will visit their section. The youngsters wear Phanatic caps and Phanatic T-shirts. They clutch Phanatic dolls until they're green in the face (the kids—the dolls are already green). Many kids bring birthday cards or craft projects to give to the Phanatic. One kid put a dollar bill in his card. I get so rich on perks. Actually, the extra buck helped pay the additional life insurance I—actually my wife Jen—bought for my leap out of the 700 Level.

At the end of the fifth inning, all hell started to break loose. I streaked across the field on the Phanatic's trusty red Honda ATV and began to dance with the third base umpire. But instead of the real ump, a guy dressed as an umpire came out and played the part. After I gave an unexpected goose to his backside, public address announcer Dan Baker barked out, "Ladies and gentlemen, I can't believe it! The Phillie Phanatic has just been ejected from his own birthday party!"

I protested. While I was pleading my case, I thought I heard Michael Jackson's "Beat It" blast out. But it wasn't "Beat It," it was the Weird Al Yankovitch's version/perversion, "Eat It." At that moment, a giant inflatable clam waddled out from behind the plate. Thanks to the vigorous (and let's face it, warped) imaginations of the Zooperstars, "Clammy" Sosa (I guess Roger "Clamens" must have been busy that day) was coming to rescue the Phanatic from the evil umpire impersonator. While the umpire's back was turned, Clammy opened his mouth wide and chomped down on the ump's head. Clammy started chowing down—or *chowdering down*. The exposed legs and torso of the umpire twitched and convulsed like Quint's final meeting with Jaws. Quint had it coming. So did the ump. Any Philly fan will agree with that. Anyway, in one smooth, clean-and-jerk motion, Clammy hoisted the morsel in his mouth as the wriggling legs of the ump pointed straight up, then slowly disappeared into the clam's belly.

I'm not sure if Clammy had a bit too much scrapple for breakfast or was still feeling a little motion sickness from his flight into town, but *something* he ate just wasn't agreeing with him. As Clammy staggered in front of the visiting dugout, he spit out one of the poor umpire's shoes. A couple of woozy steps later, the ump's pants came spewing out, followed by a pair of red-and-white polka-dotted boxer shorts.

The crowd was into the whole scene. So were the players and coaches in both dugouts. As Clammy was nearing the tunnel to exit, I checked out the field. Uh-oh. The game! I forgot about the game! There was Kevin Millwood standing off to the side of the mound, expressionless, staring—no, glaring—my way. The home plate umpire was gracious enough to cut me a little extra time. But now he was striking a menacing hands-on-hips pose. The batter, Giants third baseman Pedro Feliz, was clearly itching to stand in the box. I hurried back to my four-wheeler, took the shortcut across the field to the right field exit ramp and prayed that I hadn't delayed the game too much. At the top of the exit ramp, I was greeted by about fifteen mascots all dressed and anxious to start the next routine. "Great job, Tom! That was hilarious," called out Socceroo, the mascot for Philly's pro soccer team, the Kixx.

"That was beautiful," Swoop, the feather-brained mascot of the Eagles, kicked in.

It's hard to take a man seriously when he's dressed like a farm animal, unless your name's Buford or Jethro. But from all accounts, all the mascots thought Clammy Sosa had knocked 'em dead. Kurt Funk, the talented, serious-minded Phillies Director of Promotions, popped in and said he loved the routine. It's one thing to have a giant inflatable fowl, Pee Wee "Geese," say you were funny. It's another for Kurt to say it.

"Awesome job, Tom," Kurt chipped in. "Just one thing to keep in mind, though. It's the sixth inning and Millwood's throwing a no-hitter. You and your friends better do your thing at the Countdown Clock fast and hustle off the field."

The Countdown Clock . . . For his birthday, the Phanatic had the honor of changing the Vet Countdown Clock.

No-hitter? Are you kidding me? With all the birthday-party hoopla, I had lost track of the game. I already made Kevin wait too long once. I wasn't about to do it again. I stood up on top of the four-wheeler, Phanatic head still on (something I couldn't do when December came—but more on that later), and barked out commands to the motley mascot group. General Patton, eat your heart out.

"Yo! Listen up," I yelled. "Millwood's got a no-hitter going. We've got to get out there fast, change the number and get the hell off the field!"

"Cow" Ripken looked stunned, as did the rest of the group. They had never heard the Phanatic speak so sternly. Of course, trying to tell a bunch of loonies they have to follow a few rules is pretty daunting.

After the last out of the inning, the Phanatic paraded his merry band of misfits towards the Countdown Clock. I ripped the number 66 down (or was it 666?), put the number 65 up, and started screaming, "Let's go! Move it! Move it! Go! Go!" It was tougher than hustling Rush Limbaugh out of a Mexican pharmacy. Mascots tend to milk every drop out of their moment in the spotlight. Not this time. A couple of them jumped on my bike while the others ran close behind. Our exit was really quick—about the same time it takes Britney Spears to get married and divorced.

I spent the rest of the game—my birthday—trying not to break Kevin's karma or concentration. We were supposed to stage a Zooperstar encore performance along the first base side. We switched it to the top of the Phillies dugout. The last thing we wanted was to delay the game again. This nightmare passed through my mind where we had to forklift a deflated Harry "Canary" off the field as he was milking his final bow.

But all went well, and when centerfielder Ricky Ledee had safely cradled the Cooperstown-bound ball in his mitt for the final out, was I ever relieved! The second Phillie no-hitter in Vet history was over and I hadn't screwed it up. After Kevin's curtain call, he sat down in front of the Phils' dugout with Phillies broadcaster and ex-reliever Larry Andersen. Larry, an admitted wannabe mascot, hit Kevin with *the* tough question:

"Kevin," LA started, "Don't you feel a little bad that you stole the Phillie Phanatic's thunder on his big day?"

"Not really," Kevin countered with a laugh, "the Phanatic gets to have a birthday once a year. These [the no-hitters] don't come around that often."

Whatever, Kevin. That night, I didn't even appear on ESPN, not even for an instant, because of your damn no-hitter.

As the Phanatic watches "Clammy" Sosa chow down on the third base umpire. Despite the distractions, Kevin Millwood hurls the second no-hitter in Vet history.

(Photo: Rosemary Rahn)

STADIUM STUFF

PHILLIES BALLPARKS . . . THEN AND NOW

BAKER BOWL

Al Reach introduced one of the Phillies' first promotions. Every fan who bought a 50-cent ticket received two free horse-trolley tickets that were worth 12 cents. The Phils were in competition with the Athletics of Philadelphia who played in the American Association. They charged only 25 cents per ticket.

CITIZENS BANK PARK

Promotions have come a long way since the days of Al Reach. The Phillies set aside a series of special dates when kids can run the bases. Dollar Dog Days—a buck a hot dog—bring back the past and bring in the chowhounds. CD's, books, bobble-head dolls, baseball gloves, bats, batting gloves—all kinds of things have been given away as promotions.

CHAPTER 4

THE PHILLIES PHAMILY

MOVIN' ON UP

"When the one Great Scorer comes to write against your name, he marks—not whether you won or lost—but how you played the game."

—Grantland Rice

"Behind every great man, there's a great woman." That's an *old* saying. We've gotten more real over the years. "Behind every great man, there's a woman rolling her eyes"—now that's more like it, closer to the real deal. Deep down, every guy knows it.

Too many big companies suffer from eye-rolling—too much eye-rolling and too few great men. Great men are hard to come by no matter where you go. But eye-rollers are everywhere nowadays.

As a consultant and executive coach, I get to work with some "good' companies—"good" as long as "good" means having a profitable bottom line.

But the bottom line by itself doesn't tell the whole story, any more than batting average by itself tells the whole story in baseball. A company is supposed to be much more than a soulless place where business is conducted. After all, people devote more than 50% of their waking hours to their company's cause. *Devote* . . . For many, it's a devotion of time, not of heart and soul. The hours spent are not rewarding, not fulfilling, not satisfying. The sad truth is: if it's drudgery just to be at work every day, "things" are not good. Things are not good for the employee. Things are not good for the company. And the company is *not* a good company, regardless of what the bottom line seems to indicate. The company might be generating profits in the short term, just like an April phenom in baseball might generate a lot of hits early in the season. But a company that breeds malaise and operates under such conditions has deep-seated weaknesses. That company will tumble. It's a matter of time—just like it's a matter of time before the weaknesses of an April phenom land him a spot in a trivia book rather than on a lineup card.

People won't perform in the long run in an atmosphere they despise. Nor will they stay, nor will they be loyal, nor will they go the extra mile. Employees are supposed to be enthused about their company and their workplace. Check out the work scene these days. Employees are not a happy lot. Groucho Marx once said, "Eighty percent of life is just showing up." That's what a lot of employees do. They show up. Period. They force themselves to show up, like they force themselves to go to the dentist. Showing up is 80% and job fulfillment (and the effort they give) is 20%. It's strange math, but it holds true. I almost wrote, "It's strange math *but it works.*" That's the point. It doesn't work.

Besides being profitable, businesses are supposed to jack up the quality of life for employees. Businesses are supposed to enhance and embrace the community.

This isn't a harangue at employers. Actually, in team-building and leadership workshops the Phillie Phanatic, his "best friend" Tom Burgoyne, and I conduct with business groups, we focus on *employee* responsibility. The workplace belongs to everyone. Simple concept—tough to grasp. Tougher yet to embrace. If "This place sucks" (which we hear all the time) is on everyone's lips, listen. They're right. They make themselves right with every interaction they grind through.

The attitude, enthusiasm, and behaviors that the lowest-paid individual brings into a workplace shape that workplace atmosphere just as much as the president of the company. People *are* the company just like a dancer is the dance. No dancer, no dance. No people, no company.

Again a simple concept. But how often in the workplace do we hear the expression "They just don't get it"? Both sides scream "They just don't get it" while pointing futilely at the other side across the management/labor line. *They* don't get it. Futile is a bad choice of words. Futile sounds neutral. "They don't get it" is far from neutral. It's active and harmful. It makes both sides dig in and stray further from a sense of fairness and honesty.

I spend a lot of time working those issues with business groups. When I look at the Phils, however, I'm struck by their teamwork. Calling a business organization a family sounds hokey. Every organization has its prodigal sons. But there can be an abiding sense of togetherness. The Phillies seem to value that sense and strive for it.

Phillies employees share a sense of responsibility to each other. They practice some old-fashioned values that enhance quality of workplace life—even though those practices may arguably *negatively* impact their bottom line or the quality of their product in the short run. The Phillies organization is often fiercely loyal to past employees. Fans would shudder at the icy reception I've seen many other professional sports organizations give their former stars.

The organization tends to promote from within. They tend to partner with employees to develop career paths for them. The employee issues and complaints I hear at client companies center on such issues. The way an organization views and handles such matters is a matter of commitment and trust, as well as dollars and cents.

Is this organization perfect? No, far from it—same as every other organization on earth. My first boss years ago pretty much hit the mark. He told me our company never had a single personnel problem till we hired a second employee. That's the way it works. But the Phils organization seems to have fostered more harmony than the typical modern workplace. That in itself is an achievement.

Phillies President David Montgomery, stands with the Phanatic moments after the Vet crumbled to the ground.
(Photo: Rosemary Rahn)

OUR PHAMILY

There is nothing in the world like a close-knit family. Family members love to be together. They care about one another. And they have fun. Let me hit that one again. They have fun. You love to visit their house. As soon as you walk through the door, you sense warmth, hominess, coziness, and togetherness. Everywhere people are talking—loud and long. Conversations go on forever. Children play and run through the kitchen while mom and/or dad desperately try to get dinner out on the table or bring a pinch of sanity to the scene. And that never seems to happen. The TV is usually cranked too loud. The phone rings incessantly, and the soundtrack for the entire scene is laughter.

Always laughter.

I'm blessed to say that I just described a Burgoyne-family Christmas or holiday or get-together any time. When our family gets together, I never want the day to end.

It's impossible to get that feeling in a place of employment. I guess that's why I'm so happy at the Phillies. The organization *feels* as much like a family as a big business can.

I'll always be amazed at how many Phillies employees have spent most of their lives working for the Fightins. Remember those old-fangled notions like fostering dedication and loyalty? I watch it happen here. My co-author and I do team-building workshops with other companies. I see what happens when employees feel nothing toward their employer. Those sessions make me appreciate my work environment even more.

We've got a number of people in significant positions who worked their way up from entry-level jobs. Hot Pants girls from the early days of the Vet, like Chrissy Long and Debbie Nocito, now hold key jobs in the marketing department. You'll find Rosie Rahn, the poster girl of the Hot Pants Patrol, on the other side of the camera these days. She's the club's main photographer. And some of our higher-ups like Vice President of Public Relations Larry Shenk and ticket guru Ray Krise are now reporting daily to their third different ballpark.

Most of our employees are not only Phillies fans. They're Philadelphia fans. They grew up in the Philadelphia area and grew up with the Phillies.

Here is a look at just a few of the Philadelphia people who have moved on up in the organization. I would like to include more—and you know who you are, so get over it.

DAVID MONTGOMERY

"The first job that I ever had was in baseball," Phils President David Montgomery told me, sitting behind his desk in his new third-floor corner office at Citizens Bank Park. "When I was 12 years old, I got $2.00 a day for taking care of the new baseball field off Henry Avenue in Roxborough. I cut the grass, lined the field, and kept score. They gave me a key to the shed where all of the bases and equipment were stored and put me in charge."

David Montgomery is a grassroots guy. Sure, he has an Ivy League degree but he scaled those ivy walls from the modest streets of Roxborough. He was born in 1946. His father was a coal-company credit manager who grew up in East Falls. His mother was an elementary school teacher, a native of Roxborough. David himself only ever managed to migrate as far away as Wyndmoor—not very far from his childhood 'hood.

David was a good student in elementary school. After grade school, he moved on up to Penn Charter because his grandfather had willed him $5000 expressly to go there. Good grades at Penn Charter nabbed him admission to the University of Pennsylvania where he majored in history. After getting his BA, he was off to Penn's Wharton School of Business. While at Penn, he befriended Ed Rendell. They have retained the friendship.

Dave Montgomery is a dedicated employee and a dyed-in-the-wool fan of the team he's loved all his life.

DAVID MONTGOMERY: "I went to Connie Mack Stadium a lot. I lived and died with the Phils. I remember seeing the lights of the ballpark above the neighborhood as you approached Hunting Park Avenue. You'd have to park five or six blocks away and walk past all the row homes. I remember the feeling I got when I'd see that grass. It always looked so lush. We'd sit in the General Admission section in the upper deck on the third base side and always try to get there early so we wouldn't get stuck in the obstructed-view seats."

Ever since he became a Phillies employee thirty-four years ago, Montgomery has put in notoriously long hours. He says you can count the number of Phillies home games he's missed on one hand in all those years.

So how did the Roxborough kid move on up to President of the Phillies? He was driving a delivery truck for Dydee Diaper Service. His friend Ed Rendell had helped him get an interview for a job with the 76ers. Dave had started coaching Germantown Academy's offensive and defensive lines on the football team while he was at Penn. He also helped out coaching the baseball team. Two kids on his baseball team were named Roberts and Simmons—the sons of Phillies greats Robin Roberts and Curt Simmons.

Right before his interview with the 76ers, David met Bill Giles courtesy of an introduction from Roberts. Timing is everything (the Phanatic knows that better than anyone). Giles told David to stop by the Vet, which was then under construction. The two hit it off, and David sucked up the $20 less per month he would earn as a Phillies sales apprentice than as a Dydee Diaper deliverer. I guess David just figured it was high time to get out of diapers (sorry, I couldn't resist). It turned out to be a great choice. In 1980, he moved on up to Director of Sales and Marketing. They tell me he was the first baseball exec who ever had the term "marketing" on his business card (I tell myself I'm the first one who ever had "mascot-author" on mine). When Ruly Carpenter sold the club in 1981, Montgomery moved on up to executive VP. Then in 1997, David moved on up to club President, the chair Bill Giles vacated.

Needless to say, when Citizens Bank Park opened its doors for business on April 3, 2004 with an exhibition game against the Cleveland Indians, the Roxborough kid with the deep Philadelphia roots was a happy man.

DAVID MONTGOMERY: "I had the opportunity at Penn to attend college basketball games at the Palestra. You get such a sense of history there when you walk through the doors and walk around the concourse. All the pictures and trophies from past years are hanging on the wall. It's such a great place to watch a basketball game, with great sight lines and the fans so close to the action.

"In baseball it's the same thing. A baseball venue is very important and it adds to the overall experience. Connie Mack Stadium did that in its day. It added to the overall experience and made for special days. I was there once for a doubleheader and saw Sandy Koufax pitch a no-hitter. He beat Chris Short. I was at another game when Frank Howard hit one over the huge sign in left field. They are great memories, and I associate them with the stadium itself. Those signs on the roof at Connie Mack—well, I can see them yet. In Citizens Bank Park, we wanted to build a ballpark that, all by itself, would create a memory for each fan attending. I'm thrilled with the way the fans have reacted to the place."

LARRY SHENK

Larry Shenk, or the Baron as he is known, is a walking Phillies baseball encyclopedia. He has worked in the Phillies public relations department since 1963. Back then, he actually *was* the public relations department. He probably knows more about every player, coach, scout, or employee who ever walked through the Phillies' front door than anyone else.

He was born in Myerstown, Pennsylvania, a sleepy town located two hours outside of Philadelphia in the heart of Pennsylvania Dutch country. Larry's is a classic small-town-boy-comes-to-the-big-city story.

LARRY SHENK, PHILLIES VICE PRESIDENT, PUBLIC RELATIONS: "As a kid, I loved baseball. At some point in my life, I realized that I couldn't run or jump or hit or catch a baseball. But I still wanted to be associated with baseball somehow when I grew up. They didn't have big league ball where I lived, but there were a lot of other smaller leagues like American Legion and semipro leagues. I'd hang around the ball fields all the time and help out as a bat boy. Those hometown leagues gave me a real love of the game. The teams used to organize trips to Connie Mack Stadium and they always invited me to tag along. Seeing those light towers at Connie Mack Stadium from Henry Avenue and then seeing that beautiful, green patch of grass in the middle of the big city always gave me a thrill. Living in a small town, I was in awe of the big city."

Larry got an even bigger taste of the big leagues and the big city when he was a senior in high school. Still dreaming of a career somehow connected to baseball, he entered the Atlantic Junior Sportswriters Contest. He had to write an essay on why he wanted to be a sports broadcaster.

LARRY: "I was one of eight finalists selected to go to Connie Mack Stadium to compete. Before going to the ballpark, we met and had dinner with [Phillies broadcasters] By Saam and Claude Haring at the Drake Hotel in Center City. When we got to the park, we each got a chance to announce an inning on tape. The winner got to spend time in the broadcast booth with the announcers during the game. I lost but I still have that old tape lying around the house somewhere."

Actually, that particular contest turned out to be a springboard. The contest winner the year before was none other than long-time Phillies broadcaster Andy Musser.

When Larry moved on up to Millersville University, he began to develop a passion for journalism and started writing for the school paper. Eventually he landed a job with the *Lebanon Daily News* working as a general news reporter and covering sports one night a week. In 1963, he moved further east and wrote sports for the *Wilmington News Journal.*

LARRY SHENK: "The Phillies were looking for a PR guy back in 1961. I applied for the job and didn't get it. The following year, the position opened up again. I applied again and didn't get it. One year later, the Phillies tried to fill the position again. After getting turned down two years in a row, I was going to forget about it. But [longtime sportswriter] Hal Bodley was the night sports editor at the Wilmington paper and he, along with another colleague named Al Cartwright, encouraged me to throw my hat in the ring again. I typed a letter on a beat-up typewriter on some brownish paper lying around the newsroom and sent it in. And the third time was the charm!"

The job duties of a PR man back in the mid-sixties weren't much different from a PR man's duties today. But the technology certainly was. There were no computers, e-mails, fax machines and cell phones, which means you couldn't reach people as easily as nowadays. On the other hand, there were no answering machines, so on occasion you might actually speak to a live person rather than leaving ten unanswered voice messages.

LARRY: "My first day on the job, they opened a door to an office. It had a desk and a phone with buttons that occasionally lit up. At that point, I had no idea what the buttons were for. The Phils basically showed me to the office and said, 'Good luck.' (With their track record in retaining PR guys, they probably went back to their offices to write the next help wanted ad.)

"My office was small. Pillars and pipes ran through it that I was forever bonking my head against. I had lots of duties. I had to keep track and type all of the players' statistics. Sometimes the visiting team didn't supply statistics so we had to crank them out ourselves. I started a 'Newsy Notes' feature in the press notes that highlighted quirky stats from the day's game.

"Back in '64, every team in baseball put out a media guide but the Phillies. I took it upon myself to make one. I typed it up and my wife Julie and I did all the graphics. We mimeographed about three hundred media guides and bound the pages together. The Phillies put one out officially the next year."

Larry has other reasons to remember 1964. There was a pennant chase that year that would stick in his craw and the craw of every Phillies fan forever.

LARRY: "I was on top of the world for most of that 1964 season. Here I was, working for my favorite team, we were in first place and we were planning for the World Series. I was still new to the organization and didn't have a clue what I was doing but it was an exciting time.

"We had the World Series tickets printed and the World Series program all ready to go. Frank Powell, who was director of sales at the time, was in charge of finding a place to host the World Series party. He wanted to have it at the Warwick Hotel downtown but they had a wedding already booked. The owner of the hotel was vacationing in Paris. Frank called the guy in Paris and told him that we wanted the main ballroom. They wound up scrapping the wedding reception for our World Series party, which, I don't have to remind you, never happened.

"Those days at Connie Mack Stadium were great days. And the way we went out—the last game there—was unforgettable. Bill Giles had just come over from Houston to help with PR and promotions. Bill had the idea to hand out the replacement wooden seat slats that would never be used again. Every fan would get a little piece of the old ballpark. Unfortunately the fans used those wooden slats to hammer out the seats, signs and fixtures. You could hear that hammering sound all game long. They ripped the seats out. They even ripped out the toilet seats. Then they tore down signs and parts of the outfield fence. We had intended to have a helicopter fly in and lift home plate out of Connie Mack and fly it to the Vet. But we called that off because fans were storming the field and ripping up the turf. I swear, the press box shook that night. It was scary."

Larry left his memories of Connie Mack behind and went ahead to spend the next thirty-three years of his life at the new ballpark, Veterans Stadium.

LARRY: "The city was swept away with pride the day the Vet opened. At the time, the Vet was the crown jewel of baseball, architecturally the best of all the multi-purpose stadiums. Multi-purpose was the buzz term at the time. The Pope [GM Paul Owens] did a tremendous job developing Phillies talent as we entered the Veterans Stadium era. Players from around the league saw that Philadelphia had a good thing going on and they wanted to be part of it. I see so many similarities in what we're doing now with our move [on up] to Citizens Bank Park. I'm hoping we can build the kind of teams we had in the seventies."

After five decades fighting the baseball wars, Larry Shenk has many memories to share.

LARRY: "I remember when Howard Cosell came to town. There was always hoopla surrounding Howard. I had never met him before so I walked up to him before a game and introduced myself, 'Mr. Cosell? My name is Larry Shenk, I'm the PR director with the Phillies. It's a pleasure meeting you and I'm here for you if you need anything.' He looked up at me and snapped back, 'Can you get me a bottle of vodka?' I went to Bill Giles and we got him a bottle of vodka!

"Then there was Pete Rose, an amazing guy. He knew so much about the game. He could tell you about the pitcher we were facing that day or about a kid that the opposing team had just brought up from Triple-A. He was great with the fans, too. He'd sign every autograph and tell them stories. One time during our winter caravan, I was in the men's room at a banquet hall with Pete and some guy came in and passed a pen and piece of paper under the stall for Pete to sign it. And he did! (I never had that happen. But a guy did slip a ten under the stall once and asked for ten ones. He was out of toilet paper.)

"Garry Maddox, the Bull [Luzinski] and Pete were all at a high school assembly in Freehold, New Jersey on one occasion. There was a long Q-and-A session with the kids. At one point, a kid raised his hand and asked Pete if he had ever attended college. Pete replied, 'Do you mean to tell me that you have been listening to us all this time and you ain't figured out yet that I ain't never been to no college?'

"The day Pete broke Stan Musial's record for most hits in the NL, we were going to surprise him with a congratulatory phone call from President Reagan. When we were walking over to the pressroom, Pete said, 'You got President Reagan calling me, don't you?' He always knew what was going on and you could never get anything by him.

"Actually there's a lot of funny stories about that night. Stan Musial was in town so he could congratulate Pete when he broke the record. Stan had been sighted in Bookbinder's [a Philly restaurant] a couple of nights in a row eating lobster and having a good time. I got a call from a restaurant owner in South Jersey who said he wanted to present Pete with an eighteen-pound lobster for breaking the record. He said that the eighteen pounds represented the eighteen years Pete had been in the league.

"I took the guy down to the clubhouse after the game. He went over to Pete's locker and handed him this big box with this giant lobster crawling around. Pete looked into the box and said, 'That thing's not going to crap in my Rolls Royce, is it?' It was classic Pete."

The Baron certainly outlasted his two one-year-term predecessors. The Phils haven't had to post for his position in 41 years. Now that the Phils have moved on up to Citizens Bank Park, Larry Shenk no longer has to duck to avoid low-hanging pipes in his office. His is the office with the computer and the funny-looking phone with all the buttons. Larry has moved on up in the organization, but some things don't change. I'm not convinced he knows yet what the buttons on *this* phone do either.

MIKE DIMUZIO

To kids growing up in South Philadelphia in the spring of 1971, every day must have seemed like Christmas. *Their* Phillies were moving on down from 21st and Lehigh in North Philly to Broad Street and Pattison Avenue in South Philly.

For many baseball-crazed neighborhood kids, things were about to change. Instead of heading to the playground for a game of half-ball or hoops every day, they bicycled over to the new stadium, searching for autographs from heroes who had once seemed miles removed from their world. They also learned how to haggle with security guards to get into the game for free (never haggle prices with someone from South Philly). And if haggling didn't work . . . well, a generation of South Philly Phillie fans (to all the nuns who *tried* to teach these guys, close your ears, sisters) perfected the fine art of sneaking into the Vet.

To Mike DiMuzio, a Bishop Neumann High School senior at the time and a die-hard Phillies fan, the new stadium meant a chance to make an extra buck or two.

MIKE DIMUZIO, BALLPARK OPERATIONS DIRECTOR: "The Phillies were looking for a new crop of grounds crew guys for the new stadium. I applied and was chosen with about fifteen other guys. The Phils brought us all in just before Opening Day to show us what we'd be doing. I was in awe of how big the place was.

"On Opening Day [April 10, 1971], when it came time for the grounds crew to change the bases, nobody wanted to run all the way out to second base because they were intimidated, afraid they might trip and fall in front of all those people. I said, 'Give it to me, I'll do it.'"

That's how the long career of Mike D (as he is called) began with the Phillies. Since Mike made it to second base on Opening Night (which Mike didn't do on a single date in high school), he has moved on up from a junior grounds crew member to a job in merchandising and ticket sales to Director of Stadium Operations. He held that title for a few years at Veterans Stadium and now holds it at Citizens Bank Park.

For thirty-three years, Mike D was as solid a part of the Vet as its concrete and steel.

MIKE DIMUZIO: "My favorite memories of the Vet are of Ruly Carpenter [Phillies owner before Bill Giles] when he hung out with the grounds crew guys behind home plate. During the game, Ruly would come down and watch the game through the Plexiglas window behind home plate. That's where the crew hung out. Ruly was a down-to-earth guy and could bust chops with the best of them.

"One time, Froggy [Mark Carfagno, another grounds crew member since Opening Day at the Vet] and I approached Ruly and asked why the ball girls were getting $10 a game and the ground crew was only getting $6. Ruly didn't blink. He said, 'Because the fans come out to see the ball girls—not you guys!' Later that week, he came down and said that he had thought about it and he bumped us up to $8 a game.

"On the night we won the World Series in 1980, Ruly had the hot pants girls deliver champagne on silver platters to the grounds crew after the game. How great is that?"

The Vet's final year was a nostalgic one for Mike. In the ninth inning of the final game, Mike ran out to second base and changed the base one last time, just like he had done on the Vet's very first day in 1971. That act represented another nostalgic closure for the Phillies people, even though it might have gone unnoticed by most of the throng. Tradition and sentiment mean a lot in this organization. After the game, Mike carried the 1971 flag and led the long procession of former Phillies players onto the field.

MIKE DIMUZIO: "What gratifies me the most is that the whole perception of the Vet changed in that final season. So much of the criticism of the stadium was dropped. People started realizing how many of their own memories were made there, and they were losing a little part of themselves. The Vet was our home for three decades. Citizens Bank Park is great but it's just a house right now. It's not home yet. But it will be soon."

CHRIS WHEELER

Chris Wheeler is baseball's equivalent of a basketball gym rat.

The gym rat is always dribbling a basketball. When he's outside at the playground, he's constantly bugging everyone to get another pick-up game going. He's the guy pestering the custodian at the high school to unlock the doors to the gym in the morning. And once he's inside, he's the guy the custodian has to shoo off the courts so he can shut off the lights and go home.

After Wheels' family moved from Yeadon, Pennsylvania, he practically grew up on the green baseball fields in Newtown Square—if baseball people ever really grow up. Wheels could be found at the fields all summer long, baseball glove tucked under his arm, waiting to play the next pick-up game.

CHRIS WHEELER, PHILLIES BROADCASTER: "I lived and breathed baseball as a kid. If I wasn't playing, I was going to as many Phillies games as I could. It was a trek from my house in Delaware County to Connie Mack Stadium. My dad took me there a lot. Other times, I'd make the trip myself. I'd take the bus to 69th Street, then hop on the Phillies Express that would take me to the subway, which took me to Lehigh Avenue. I used to love the doubleheaders—a whole day at the ballpark. That was like a slice of heaven."

When he realized his destiny was not to be a major leaguer himself, Wheels decided to give it a go as a broadcaster. He majored in broadcasting at Penn State where he hosted a radio show with Joe Paterno in 1966. After he graduated, he flooded the Philly sport scene with résumés. Eventually he landed a job with radio behemoth WCAU. The Phillies were looking for someone to help out in the public relations office in 1971. They asked Andy Musser, a WCAU sportscaster at the time, for a recommendation. He recommended Wheels.

CHRIS WHEELER: "Andy told [PR Director] Larry Shenk, 'Wheels is your guy.' My first day with the Phillies was July 5, 1971. I thought I had died and gone to heaven. I reported to the PR office that morning. My first assignment was to drive some of the Phillies hot pants girls to a promotion at Dilworth Plaza in Center City [then he really thought he'd died and went to heaven]. When I got back to the Vet that afternoon, Phillies manager Frank Lucchesi brought me into the clubhouse and showed me around. He sat me down and we talked baseball for over an hour. I kept thinking to myself, 'This is all I ever wanted. I better not screw it up!'"

But Wheels' lifelong dream of working for his hometown team was destined to move on up—much higher.

WHEELS: "The Phils clinched the division in 1976 in Montreal in the first game of a doubleheader. Harry and Whitey had to leave the broadcasting booth to go down to the clubhouse and do the post-game interviews with the champagne flying and everything. They were short people in the booth and needed somebody to fill in. I wound up filling in. That was my first game as a broadcaster. I was on cloud nine."

Wheels has been broadcasting ever since, living out the dreams he had as a kid in Newtown Square. He shakes his head at his own story of movin' on up.

WHEELS: "My buddy, Ed Pappas, lived right across the street from [legendary Philadelphia broadcaster] Bill Campbell. We used to play baseball and football in his front yard and do Bill Campbell impersonations while we were playing. We hoped Bill would hear us and someday give us a job!"

RUBEN AMARO JR.

Here's the ultimate movin' on up story. It's the story . . . of a lovely lady—oops, wrong story. No, this is the story of the son of a popular Phillie player. It's the story of a guy who hung around the Vet as a kid, became batboy on a pennant-winning club, played on the diamond for the Phils, and then the day after his playing days ended, slid into a Phillie front office job that reported to the GM.

Ruben Amaro Jr. is the prince charming in the Phairy Tale (just thought I'd give Ruben another nickname that his friends can bust his chops for—actually Ruben might like this nickname better than some others).

RUBEN AMARO JR., ASSISTANT GENERAL MANAGER: "I've always been around the game of baseball. It's been my life. My dad [Phillies shortstop Ruben Sr.] was finishing his playing career when I was growing up. He spent a lot of time on the road as a scout and a coach. I spent a lot of time around that '80 Championship team. Boonie's [catcher Bob Boone] and Pete's [Rose] kids were always hanging around too. We had fun together.

"The main batboy back then was Mark Andersen. [Mark's another movin' on up story. Mark is now the Phillies assistant trainer.] He showed me the ropes and I wound up being the batboy from '81 to '83.

"Some of the guys on those teams were real characters. The pitchers, especially Mike Krukow, Dick Ruthven and LC [Larry Christenson], all razzed me pretty good. They were constantly spitting big wads of chewing tobacco on my shoes. Gary Matthews was a great guy. He would get all fired up before the game. I can still hear him yelling, 'It's *showtime*, kid. You'd better be ready to go.' Then he would purposely knock off his own helmet when he ran the bases so I'd have to run out onto the field and retrieve it."

After graduating from Penn Charter High School, Ruben headed west and enrolled in Stanford University, playing the two sports he loved most—baseball and soccer. Eventually baseball won out and he was drafted by the California Angels. He wound up traded to the Phillies in 1991.

RUBEN AMARO: "Playing in Philly was both a blessing and a curse. On one hand it paved the way to where I am now. But as a player, playing in my hometown where my father played, I think I put too much pressure on myself."

PHANATIC PHILE

After making stops in Cleveland and Toronto, Ruben landed back in Philadelphia in 1996, finishing his playing career in 1998.

RUBEN AMARO: "Ed [Wade] had just taken over as general manager in December of '97. We talked throughout the '98 season about my life after baseball. I don't know if it's ever happened before that a player has retired and immediately taken a job where he reports directly to the GM. I still can't believe how great it all turned out."

CHARITY STARTS FROM HOME

The Phillies have been a contributing member of the Delaware Valley community for a century and a quarter.

• The Phillies have raised over $8 million for ALS research since adopting it as the club's official charity in 1984.

• Overall, in 2003, the Phillies and Phillies Charities Inc. combined to donate over $1 million in cash, autographed items, merchandise and tickets to hundreds of worthy causes and organizations in the Delaware Valley.

GRANNY

Granny (Granville) Hamner played longer for the Phils than any other player except Mike Schmidt. In fact, in the history of Philadelphia professional sports, no *Philadelphia athlete* has ever played more years continuously with one franchise than has Mike Schmidt. Schmidt played 18 consecutive seasons with the Phils. Hamner places second on that same list with 16 (Jimmy Dykes with the A's, Steve Carlton with the Phils, and Bobby Clarke with the Flyers tie for third with 15 consecutive seasons each).

Granville was quite a character. He played hard and lived hard. And he could be cantankerous. After he retired, the popular ex-Phillies captain worked for the Phils for practically the rest of his life. However, before coming on board with the Phils after his playing career ended, Granny hit some hard times. He was looking for work and asked his teammate and friend Robin Roberts to intercede with the Phils on his behalf. Robbie made a pitch for Granny to Ruly Carpenter. The Phils owner said hesitantly, "We'll find something, but Granny has to straighten out and behave." Robbie called Hamner back and told him the news Hamner was hoping to hear—that the Phils would find something for him and put him back on the payroll. But before Roberts could give Hamner the rest of the message, i.e., Carpenter's conditions, Hamner interrupted and said, "Look, tell him I'll come back as long *as it's on my terms.*"

ANDY

How long does a fan club last? To Anne Zeiser, it lasts forever.

Anne started a fan club 56 years ago, and her club keeps on keeping on.

ANNE ZEISER: "Bill Campbell, the radio/TV announcer, held a "Name Your Favorite Phillie Past or Present" contest in 1946. The winner got a season pass. My favorite ballplayer was Andy Seminick. I won the contest but the game was rained out and I didn't get my prize till the end of the season. The Phillies gave me a season's pass for the next year, 1947—*and* they kept giving me a season's pass every year the Phils played in Connie Mack Stadium. They even gave me a season's pass the first two years at the Vet."

That's a lot of mileage for one contest. But the Sisters Zeiser have given the Phillies a lot of miles over the years too. They've become legends in the Phillies organization. They know everyone.

ANNE ZEISER: "Our fan club sponsored three tribute nights for Andy each and every year. We worked with Babe Alexander and Frank Powell in the Phillies organization. We'd get local merchants to donate gifts. We'd bring string bands out to the park. We had 550 members at our peak. We collected dues, sent out a regular fan letter, and we donated money to charities. We didn't have much money, but we'd give it all to Little Leagues in Philly on Andy's behalf."

Anne and Betty vie with the Phanatic as the ultimate Phillie fans. They grew up in the Wissinoming section of northeast Philly and graduated from St. Bartholomeo's Grade School and St. Hubert's High. Anne worked at Phoenix Mutual for 36 years. When she makes a commitment, she sticks to it. After all, it's been 53 years since Andy Seminick first left the Phillies.

ANNE ZEISER: "But Andy did come back in '55 and played out the rest of his career as a Phillie. Then he coached for them for a number of years in the minors at places like Reading, Elmira, Lynchburg, and Williamsport. We went to every one of those cities to watch him."

The Zeisers became personal friends of the Seminicks. They used to stay with Andy's wife Bessie when the Phils were out of town. Andy taught the girls how to drive a car. He also went hunting with the Zeisers' dad, who called the Phils catcher the "son he never had."

When Andy Seminick was shuttled to Cincinnati and Chicago, the hometown fans in each of those cities approached him about starting Seminick fan clubs. Andy politely declined. He told a Cincinnati fan to join the Zeisers' club in Philly. She did."

According to the Zeisers, fan clubs were all the rage back in the fifties.

ANNE ZEISER: "Practically all the Phillies had fan clubs back then: Robin Roberts, Curt Simmons, Bubba Church, Del Ennis, Dick Sisler, Richie Ashburn, Russ Meyer, Steve Ridzik, and others. Eventually the fan clubs faded away."

The Zeisers' favorite memory is still the pennant-winning game in Brooklyn in 1950. They were stars on the small screen themselves that game.

ANNE ZEISER: "We sat behind home plate with the Lauderbachs, who were in the moving business and good friends of Benny Bengough, a Phillie coach. The Lauderbachs kept telling me: 'I don't know if you'll have us cried out or prayed out by the time this game's over!' There was a priest sitting in front of us rooting loudly for the Dodgers. We were chattering back and forth the whole game long, and at one point, I was hitting this priest with my scorecard as a joke. Bill Campbell saw it as he was broadcasting the game. Bill said, 'You want to see real fans in action?' The camera panned down and caught me! It made the news.

"We rode back on the train with the Phils. What a great time! Some drunk on the train kept telling Dick Sisler, 'I remember your father from way back when.' He repeated it over and over and over. [Dick Sisler's father is in the Hall of Fame. When you're at Citizens Bank Park, take a look at the huge 1939 photo that shows George Sisler, Connie Mack, the Babe, Walter Johnson, Grover Cleveland Alexander, and other early HOF inductees at Cooperstown.]

"We've had so many wonderful memories because of Andy and the Phillies. We've had season passes ever since 1947. After the Phillies stopped giving them to us, we got our own. We hardly miss a game. We've also been going down to Clearwater for a couple of months every winter since 1954 to watch spring training. We were invited to the '50 Phils reunion a few years ago. When we walked into the room, every one of those guys called us by name. They all remember us. I feel sorry for the young fans now. They'll never get to know the players like we did—like real people. That's such a shame. The players don't live in the same world as the fans anymore."

The Zeisers will still be cheering at every game in Citizens Bank Park. Despite the death of Andy Seminick in February 2004, his fan club lives on. Baseball, more than rock 'n roll, never forgets.

ANNE ZEISER: "We were honored when the Phillies called us and asked us to change the number on the Countdown Clock at the Vet in 2003. Betty and I didn't ride with that crazy Phanatic! We went out in the golf cart, tore down #60 and replaced it with #59. You know what John Kruk's comment was? He said, 'You can tell those ladies are intelligent. They're not riding with the Phanatic.'"

See, the Phanatic doesn't always get the girls. These girls belong to Andy forever.

STADIUM STUFF

PHAMILY TREE

The Phillies "phamily tree" has grown to great heights over the years. According to baseball historian Rich Westcott, when the Phillies played at Baker Bowl, there were only four or five people in the club's front office. When Larry Shenk started with the Phillies, there was a whopping total of 11 front office employees working at Connie Mack Stadium. That number grew to 18 in 1970, representing an increase of over 60% by the time the Phils left the ballpark in North Philly for good. The Phillies now employ 180 full-timers at Citizens Bank Park plus another 90 people working as scouts, coaches, and other baseball people around the country. Add about 800 part-time game day employees and you have a family that you might want to think twice about inviting over for holiday dinner.

CHAPTER 5

THE PHILADELPHIA A'S SOCIETY

Motorists movin' on up Route 263, Old York Road, rocket out of Willow Grove only to fizzle out in the two-lane decompression zone that is Hatboro. Hatboro is a quiet, blue-collar borough that offers sanctuary from the nonstop neon and commercial confetti strewn along Old York Road as it traces its way across Montgomery County. Hatboro isn't unique. To the south, Jenkintown still clings to its small-town, out-of-the-past roots. But Jenkintown is more toney and high-end. Tidy, blue-collar enclaves like Hatboro are rare around Philly. I value them more and more. They're buffers from complete homogenization and reminders that progress is not interchangeable with change. Progress proceeds with as many steps backward as forward.

Sure, you'll find a 7-11 at the town's fringes. There's a Wendy's too. But the chain of national/regional franchises that links the little towns along Old York Road unlinks in Hatboro. The town center remains a citadel for small, independently owned shops. Remember them? You can actually patronize them in Hatboro.

The town coffeehouse is the Daily Grind. It's not Starbucks. At least not till progress gives in to its gluttonous appetite. The Daily Grind is an independent, old-timey, sit-and-unwind coffeehouse that serves tasty homemade sandwiches and hearty java and features live local music on the weekends. Gamburg's Furniture is the only Gamburg's Furniture in existence. It's the same Gamburg's that has anchored the town center for decades. Hatboro's a small town. Somebody's got to furnish it. Burdick News Agency is one of those lazy, endangered small-town magazine and newspaper depots. Café La Fontana, Ming's Chinese, the Old Mill Inn, On a Roll, and the *Happy Days*-like Daddypops Diner animate a fun little dining scene. Towey's Tavern and P J Keene's Tavern are the local watering stops. There's even a reliable, old-fashioned hardware store. They carry two of practically everything you can't find anywhere else.

Hatboro doesn't seem small-time. It doesn't seem fake. It's a good spot for an unpretentious, un-glitzy baseball museum. The museum is also the headquarters for a low-key, low-profile organization called the Philadelphia Athletics Society.

Love of the national pastime alone fuels this group. After all, the Philadelphia Athletics, the Society's *raison d'être*, disappeared a half-century ago.

Ernie Montella and Ted Taylor co-founded the Society. You probably remember Ted Taylor as a sportswriter for the *Philadelphia Daily News*. Ernie Montella is just a lifelong baseball lover and native Philadelphian. We asked Ernie how the A's Society came to be.

ERNIE MONTELLA: "A guy named Bob Schmerier runs the Eastern Pennsylvania Sports Collectors Convention twice a year. He used to do it at Willow Grove, in the George Washington Convention Center, which is now gone.

"I was raised as an A's fan. My dad loved the A's more than the Phillies. He took me out to Connie Mack Stadium to watch Bobby Shantz, Gus Zernial, Eddie Joost, and all those forties-fifties-era A's play. Well, I used to go to the convention in Willow Grove [named after Lefty's brother Willow] and found out that the *Philadelphia* A's still had plenty of fans. After the conventions, a bunch of Philly A's fans would always gather and share all the Athletics' memorabilia they rounded up. It was kind of an A's 'show and tell.'

"Then in March 1990, Eddie Joost was invited to the convention for a card signing. I was amazed. The autograph line must have stretched a half-mile. That night, we took Hank Majeski [another former Philadelphia A] and Eddie to dinner at the Country Squire [the restaurant's name has changed; it's now Julie's] in Hatboro. I was thrilled. That was the first time I ever met any of the old A's personally, and it was great to get to know them all these years later.

"A couple of years after that night, Lou Spadia was trying to help Joost get inducted into the Bay Area Sports Hall of Fame [BASHOF]. Eddie himself really wanted in. I volunteered to write a document pleading his case. I wrote twenty-five pages! People out there in San Francisco didn't really know much about Eddie Joost. He played here on the East Coast when there wasn't any major league baseball on the West Coast. Well, long story short, Joost made the Hall of Fame in 1996, and it was a great experience for me."

Ernie spearheaded a couple of Eddie Joost for Hall of Fame campaigns. They helped to reawaken Philly love for the prodigal Philadelphia A's.

ERNIE MONTELLA: "Eddie was going to be inducted into the Wall of Fame at the Vet in 1996. They used to elect a Phillie and an Athletic each year. There was a dinner at the Four Seasons for the induction. I had bugged Larry Shenk of the Phillies [Larry is the VP of Public Relations in the Phils organization] for a couple of years to induct Eddie. Larry was great. The Phils did a terrific job and handled everything great. Anyway, since a lot of the old A's were in town for the banquet, we all got together for breakfast. That was back in March 1996. Elmer Valo, Wayne Ambler, Al Brancato, and others were there. I guess you could say that was really the first Philadelphia A's reunion breakfast. We talked about starting an official Philadelphia A's Society at the breakfast. Nothing would have happened, but a couple of days afterwards, a guy named David Stephan—a sportswriter from the West Coast—really got behind it. He telephoned me practically every day, bugging me: 'You've got to start a Philadelphia Athletics Society!'

"So we did. Ted Taylor and I pooled our Philly A's memorabilia. We each kicked in $25. That was the seed money for the A's Society—big-time operation, huh? We organized a reunion breakfast that coming September [1996], and I guess you'd call that our official birth. About seventy people attended.

"Next thing we had to do was find a place for all our Athletics memorabilia. My main reason for starting the Society was to preserve A's memorabilia and keep it in one safe place. I had been keeping everything in my garage and my wife was about to kill me! Then we found this storefront in Hatboro which turned out to be perfect, and we turned it into a museum."

Since its serendipitous start, the group has become a force on the sport scene. Membership has swelled to almost a thousand, and the Society boasts members on every continent but Antarctica (perhaps Ron Cey could convince some of his relatives there to join).

ERNIE MONTELLA: "By the end of 1996, we had already grown to two hundred members, totally by word of mouth. We had no website. We did no advertising. But people somehow heard about us—people from all over—and joined.

"We've had some special things happen. Like with Carl Scheib. Carl pitched for the A's in the forties and fifties. His wife passed away a while ago. Carl came to a reunion, and, don't you know, one of his big fans *from forty years ago*—a female fan named Sandy—read that he was going to be here. Sandy came to the reunion breakfast to meet him and they ended up getting married!

"That's not our only 'special' story. We brought the Mack clan together. They had been estranged for years when Connie Mack's sons, Earl and Roy, had a falling out years ago. As a result, the two branches of the Mack family grew apart. Mr. Mack himself was married twice. Roy and Earl were the children from the first marriage. Connie Junior, Dorothy, Ruth, and Mary were children of the second marriage. Over the years, the family lost touch. There were generations of Mack descendants that never met. They wound up reuniting because they got wind of our Philadelphia Athletics Society reunions. They decided to have one huge Mack family reunion at the same time. Dozens and dozens of descendants, or spouses of the descendants, of Connie Mack showed up. They all came to our reunion breakfast. We're proud that we helped bring them all together."

The A's Society is not unique. You'll find a few other groups that honor defunct baseball teams like the Washington Senators, the St. Louis Browns, the Brooklyn Dodgers, and the New York Giants.

ERNIE MONTELLA: "The Milwaukee Braves formed a society recently too. Remember Johnny Logan, the Braves' shortstop who played on those great teams with Hank Aaron, Warren Spahn, and Eddie Matthews? Logan founded a Milwaukee Braves Society, but they're a for-profit outfit. We're not."

The A's Society is anything but for-profit. Ten volunteers donate countless hours manning the museum and store, updating an excellent website, tracking down former Philly A's and Phillies, and preparing for the annual breakfasts and special events that the Society sponsors. And *none* of those other groups honoring defunct teams has a museum.

And this is no dinky, ham-and-eggs museum. It's a must-see for every baseball aficionado. Hang around this place awhile and you'll discover what a destination it is, not only for locals, but for baseball fans from all over the country. Where else can you see the baseball from Lefty Grove's 299th win, or Connie Mack's 1929 Edwin Bok Award, or a 1910 World Series program?

ERNIE MONTELLA: "We've collected some pretty impressive stuff. A guy named Chism moonlighted as a security guard for the visiting team's locker room at Connie Mack Stadium. Connie Mack took a liking to the guy. He even invited him down to spring training. Mr. Mack used to let Chism come into the A's locker room too. Well Mr. Chism wound up getting sixteen baseballs signed from 1947 through '49, one ball autographed by every team in both leagues. Chism went to games that Mack used to arrange against local prison teams. The inmates at Graterford Prison took a liking to Chism. They built a display case that you can't break into. He donated the case to our museum! We've picked up all kinds of memorabilia like that from lots of great people."

The A's Society has also been responsible for the erection of at least eight historical monuments. Working in concert with the Pennsylvania Historical Museum Commission, the A's Society has initiated and helped fund the installation of numerous historical markers. Among them are Mickey Vernon's home in Marcus Hook, Nellie Fox's house, Eddie Plank's home in Gettysburg, Rube Waddell's home, and Chief Bender's home in Carlisle.

All fine and dandy you say, *but* why such a fuss about a team that jilted Philly fifty years ago, and drew a puny 1,715 spectators to its farewell game at Connie Mack Stadium? Here's one good reason. Many would argue that the A's of 1929, '30, and '31 were the greatest team of all time. Current-day fans are unaccustomed to a Philly team getting that adulation. Everyone just assumes a Yankee team must be the greatest. But the Yankees were not always the uncontested Zeus on the national pastime's Olympus.

Let's move on back to the beginning of the last century, or what Philly and Boston fans should call the good old days. From 1903 (when Boston beat the Pittsburgh Pirates five games to three in the first World Series) to 1918, Boston and/or Philadelphia appeared in *ten of those first fifteen* World Series. In fact, the World Series in 1914 and 1915 pitted two different Boston teams against two different Philadelphia teams. In 1914, Boston's Miracle Braves, as they were called, swept the Philly A's in four. Then, in 1915, the AL Boston Red Sox beat the NL Philadelphia Phillies four games out of five.

The 1911 Athletics featured one of early baseball's most famous taglines. The Athletics' "$100,000 infield" of Stuffy McInis, Eddie Collins, Jack Barry, and Frank "Home Run" Baker referred to the foursome's *outrageously* high value. To young fans, $100,000 sounds like the price of an at-bat for A-Rod, or a funny Dr. Evil ransom routine.

Before 1920, only *two* other American League teams, the White Sox and Tigers (with a guy named Ty Cobb on their roster), managed to ace the A's or Red Sox out of the World Series. Notably absent from the list of early AL pennant winners is the Yankees (or Highlanders as they were called in the early part of the century). The Yankees didn't appear in *any* World Series till 1921. What losers, huh?

Enter baseball's most momentous moment—when the Red Sox bounced the Babe in 1920 and unleashed the Curse of the Bambino. The Ruth-less Yankees prior to the twenties were humdrum. That all changed when the Ruth-led Yankees of the twenties escalated up to the ruthless Murderer's Row.

Meanwhile back in Philly . . .

The A's fortunes plummeted after their 1914 pennant. They sank to last place in 1915, dubiously achieving the first first-to-worst tumble in AL history. They languished in last place for *seven straight seasons*. In three of those seasons (1919 to 1921), both Philly franchises were bottom dwellers in their respective leagues. In case you're wondering, Boston was the first city to claim that distinction.

Starting in 1922, however, the Mackmen notched up one slot per year in the eight-team AL. From 1925 to 1928, they finished second three out of four seasons. Then came 1929. That's the year the powerhouse Athletics outdistanced the runner-up Yanks by *eighteen games* in winning their first of three consecutive AL pennants. They won the next two pennants handily too. In 1930 and '31, they bettered the Yanks by eight games and thirteen-and-a-half games respectively.

The A's fielded Hall of Famers Mickey Cochrane, Jimmie Foxx, and Al Simmons. Hall of Famer Lefty Grove headed their pitching staff. Near-Hall of Famers George Earnshaw, Eddie Rommel, and Jack Quinn were also on the staff. At 46 years, 3 months, Quinn became the oldest player ever to appear in a World Series.

Everyone loved a winner. The A's of that era were the darlings of the Quaker City. They drew 839,176 spectators in 1929. In October that year the Depression struck. Attendance dipped to 721,663 in 1930 and 627,424 in 1931. Mack had trouble meeting his high-priced payroll. So he dealt off his superstars. Attendance sank to 297,138 by

1933, and the once-mighty A's devolved into hapless also-rans for the remainder of their stay in Philly.

The '29, '30, '31 A's are considered one of the greatest teams of all time. Their glory has been shadowed by the Babe Ruth-Lou Gehrig mystique. However, head to head, the A's *buried* the great Yankee teams of Ruth's era and won two consecutive World Series before the Gas House Gang burned down their barn for good in '31.

Still, the momentum of the glory days—the first three decades of American League play—fueled the team's popularity for two more decades. When it came to baseball, Philadelphia was a city divided. Philadelphians were either Phillies fans or A's fans. The A's outdrew their city rival *every* year in the twenties and thirties on the inertia of their *nine* AL pennants. When the Carpenters acquired the Phillies, attendance between the Phils and A's flip-flopped. The Phils became the city's darlings when the GIs came home from the War. The Phils topped the million-spectator mark in 1946, a threshold the A's never managed to scale. And once the 1950 Whiz Kids whizzed to an exciting pennant, it was over for the A's. In 1950 the Phils outdrew the A's by the largest margin in city history: 1,217,035 to 309,805. The A's never recovered.

The A's needed to take drastic measures so they did the unthinkable. They left. Even men didn't leave in those days when loyalty was part of the culture and not just an inert word in a Missions, Visions, and Values statement. The machines of progress were grinding. In 1953, the Boston Braves, a stalwart in the Senior Circuit *for sixty years*, split Beantown for Brewtown. Other weaker-sister franchises in two-team cities followed suit. After the St. Louis Browns set up shop in Baltimore, the Philadelphia A's announced they were goin' to Kansas City. Movin' on down.

As it turns out, 1954 was not the Philadelphia Athletics' swan song. Four decades after the A's went to Kansas City, Ernie Montella and Ted Taylor resuscitated this beloved piece of Philly heritage. Thanks to them, the Philadelphia A's are alive and well and living in Hatboro.

If you'd like to find out more about the Society, call 215-323-9901, or check out www.PhiladelphiaAthletics.org. Membership dues are $30 a year.

WHAT'S IN THE PHILADELPHIA ATHLETICS MUSEUM?

• The 25 original Philadelphia Athletics "Wall of Fame" plaques that were displayed on the 200 Level concourse at Veterans Stadium.

• The "Philadelphia Award," better known as the Edwin C. Bok Award, given to Cornelius McGillicuddy in 1929 for his contributions to the people of Philadelphia. The first Bok award was presented in 1921. Mack was the first recipient from the world of sport.

• One of the four Connie Mack busts formerly on display at Shibe Park.

• A turnstile from Shibe Park.

• Three seats from Shibe Park.

• Former A Irv Hall's 1945 home uniform.

• Former A and one-time All-American football player Sam Chapman's 1948 A's road uniform and his 1940 A's hat.

• A program from the 1910 World Series.

• A collection of 16 (8 American League, 8 National League) autographed team baseballs on loan from the Chism family.

• The "Millennium Ball." This ball was actually used in a 1954 A's vs. Cleveland game. In 2000, the Oakland A's dispatched a video crew and and their mascot Stomper to the Hatboro Museum to bring back some talisman of the Philly A's, hoping it would bring them luck in 2000. They carried this ball to the Hall of Fame and rubbed it on the busts of Mack and all the Philly A's players in the Hall for good luck. They then took the ball back to Oakland where Eddie Joost, the last manager of the Philly A's and a Bay area resident, threw out the first pitch of the 2000 season. This ball is considered the only one in existence that was used in a major league game in both the twentieth and twenty-first century.

• A's yearbooks from 1949-1954.

• A photo archive of more than 4000 photographs.

• The portrait of Connie Mack that once hung over the fireplace of his Mt. Airy home.

• More than 1500 sports-related books and five 1940's/1950's newspaper albums.

JOLTIN' JOLTIN' JOE'S RECORD – TAKE 4, 5, AND 6

In fifty years as a major-league manager, Cornelius Alexander McGillicuddy, a.k.a. Connie Mack, fashioned a winning percentage of .486. Hardly Hall of Fame stuff, we know. But how about this: Mack managed more seasons (53), won more games (3,731), and lost more games (3,948) than any other manager in history. Closest to Mack on each list is John McGraw, who managed one team, the New York Giants, for thirty-one years (1902-1932). McGraw's numbers *aren't even close to Mack's.* Mack managed twenty-one more seasons than McGraw, won 936 more games than McGraw. OK, he lost 2,041 more games than McGraw too. Don't forget, both guys put up those numbers in 154-game seasons. Given the itchy trigger fingers that most owners possess nowadays, these Mack records will stay as untouched as a pork chop in a vegan's refrigerator.

One other thing—Connie Mack is most likely the last manager to stroll the dugout in coat, tie, and straw hat.

MOVIN' ON UP . . . TO FIVE-FEET TALL

The Gordon family grew up listening to stories about Bobby Shantz. My great uncle, (Otto) Paul Williamson, was Bobby's baseball coach when young Shantzy played for a team in northeast Philly, the Holmesburg Ramblers. Bobby Shantz was their 5′-6″ quarterback. Eat your heart out, Eddie LeBaron and Doug Flutie. Brud Williamson, Paul's son, now lives in South Carolina. He reminisces about young Bobby Shantz.

BRUD WILLIAMSON: "Bobby was a 'big' star on the neighborhood football team—a great quarterback who could throw, kick, and run. Without question, he was the most modest guy I ever met. My father loved him. In fact, my dad had a heart attack and died in Bobby's arms in 1948 when they were both bowling at the Mayfair Bowling Alley.

"Bobby was the star for the Holmesburg Ramblers. No one could believe a guy his size could throw like he did. What an athlete! The guy could do anything and everything in sports. Boulevard Pools on Roosevelt Boulevard in northeast Philly used to put on diving exhibitions. My buddies and I would go and we'd all end up hollering to let Bobby get up on the board. He was a better diver than anyone in the show. We wangled them into giving Bobby a shot and he stole the show! He was a great gymnast too, and he could beat anyone in Ping-Pong or bowling—any sport he tried. And I'll warn you, don't ever play him in pool [billiards]. You'll lose your house!"

Bobby Shantz grew up in Pottstown, Pennsylvania. He just didn't grow very high. He was 4′-11″ when he patrolled the outfield for Pottstown High School, where he graduated in 1943. Bobby's dad loved baseball. He used to take him and his brother Wilmer (who also played major league ball) into Philly to watch the A's. The family left four hours before game time just so Mr. Shantz could hit ground balls to his kids in Fairmount Park.

BOBBY SHANTZ: "My dad loved baseball. He wanted us to be good ballplayers. But I don't think he ever dreamed we'd play in the majors."

When the war hit, Bobby went to enlist. He was rejected because he didn't meet the 5′-0″ height requirement. So Shantzy went home, grew another inch, came back in 1945 and was inducted into the Army.

BOBBY SHANTZ: "I spent eighteen months in the Philippines. They started me out in the tank corps, but I couldn't reach the pedals with my feet. I'm being serious! So they made me an infantryman instead. While I was in the South Pacific, I played baseball. Hard to believe but I grew six inches and gained thirty pounds while I was in the Army."

When he returned stateside, Bobby played sandlot baseball. While playing for the Souderton His Nibs (that's not a misprint—and, no, Bobby has no idea what that name meant—but if an astute reader knows, let us know and we'll explain it in the second printing and give you an acknowledgment), he was discovered by an A's scout, Harry O'Donnell. Jocko Collins, the Phils' head scout, told Bobby he had a great arm but felt Bobby was too small ("So did I," Bobby quips). Bobby signed a modest pro contract and headed off to Lincoln, Nebraska to play minor-league ball. There he met Shirley. When Bobby was promoted to the big club in 1949, Shirley came back with him. They married in 1950, and have been together, living around Philly, ever since.

Shantzy's rookie year (6-8, 3.40 in 127 IP) was promising. He followed up with an 8-14 record before coming of age in 1951. His 18-10 record and 3.94 ERA that year hinted at the monster season coming up. In '52, his 24-7 record and 2.48 ERA for the 4th-place Athletics earned him the American League MVP. He was hampered by arm problems from 1953 through 1956. Then in 1957, the former MVP was traded to the Yankees.

In those days, Kansas City was a veritable farm club for the Yanks. Consider this: the 1960 Yankee roster included *ten* ex-A's: Roger Maris, Art Ditmar, Bobby Shantz, Wilmer Shantz, Elmer Valo, Ralph Terry, Joe Demaestri, Jim Pisoni, Ryne Duren, and Duke Maas.

In Shantz's first season in New York, he was cruising at 9-1—all as a starter—at the All-Star break. He earned an All-Star berth. After the All-Star Game, he reported to the bullpen. The next three seasons, he worked exclusively out of the bullpen and compiled ERA's of 3.36, 2.38, and 2.79 before being traded to the World Champion Pittsburgh Pirates in 1961.

Shantz pitched out the remainder of his career in the NL, ultimately calling it quits in 1964 as a Phillie. When he retired, the great athlete that Brud Williamson touted had won eight consecutive Gold Gloves—four in the AL and four in the NL.

Postscript: I wasn't around to savor Shantz's MVP year in 1952, but I was a young baseball fanatic in 1960. One day my father surprised me and said, "Your cousin Brud's taking you to Yankee Stadium for a game as Bobby Shantz's guest. You're all going to eat dinner with the Yankees after the game." I was flying higher than Ralphie Parker in *A Christmas Story* when Santa brought him his "genuine Daisy Red Ryder Carbine Action 200-Shot Lightning Loader Range Model Air Rifle with a compass and a stock and the thing that tells time."

The Yankees played Baltimore that September day when I made my first trip to Yankee Stadium. Shantzy relieved late in the game. Unfortunately, he served up a gopher ball to Jim Gentile and the Yankees lost. Didn't matter. I was in the House That Ruth Built. Afterwards, I ate dinner with Bobby Shantz, his brother Wilmer, Joe DeMaestri, and Tony Kubek. I was surrounded by Mickey Mantle, Whitey Ford, Roger Maris, Elston Howard, Yogi Berra, and the rest of the guys who, up till then, had only been photos on Topps baseball cards.

And Bobby Shantz—well, he was every bit the humble, likable guy I had heard so much about. That's a commodity that's wanting these days in the profession he once graced.

As a writer, I've had the privilege of talking with Bobby on numerous occasions. Each time, I walk away with the same impression. In an era when too many sport figures abdicate, if not obliterate, their obligation to set a positive example for impressionable kids, Bobby Shantz remains a role model. He didn't seek the responsibility. He wanted to play baseball. But he realized he was blessed and privileged to play. He realized further that with that blessing came the responsibility to wield his power to influence positively. He did and does embrace that responsibility. It comes with the territory. The sport scene would be a healthier place if every athlete moved on up to the standard that Bobby Shantz sets.

CASEY AND YOGI STORIES

Bobby Shantz spent four years with the Yankees at the height of the team's fifties-early sixties grandeur. Bobby can spin some *plausible* Casey Stengel and Yogi Berra yarns.

Ninety percent of what Bobby remembers is possibly true. The other half is exaggerated.

BOBBY SHANTZ: "I was supposed to be a reliever. But, when I got to New York, Whitey Ford was hurt. Casey Stengel [manager] asked me if I thought I could start. I said I could, so I replaced Whitey and I was 9-1 at the All-Star break. Then Whitey came back and Casey sent me back to the bullpen. I never started again. Casey never bothered to tell me why though—he never mentioned a word about it.

"Casey used to fall asleep in the dugout. One day we needed a pinch-hitter. Frank Crosetti, our third-base coach, was yelling to Casey to send up a pinch-hitter. Casey was sound asleep on the bench. Frank ran over to the dugout, woke Casey up, and asked him who he wanted to pinch hit. Casey leaned forward and yelled down to Elston Howard to grab a bat. Trouble was, Elston had been playing the whole game.

"But my favorite story is about Casey and Yogi. I was starting a game against the Red Sox in '57 when I was on that 9-1 roll. The first three batters were right-handed hitters. They had some good ones on that team: Frank Malzone, Jackie Jenson, and Jimmy Piersall to go along with lefties Ted Williams and Mickey Vernon. [*Note to Phillie fans:* not included among the *good* right-handed hitters was a .270-hitting infielder named Gene Mauch in his final season as a player.] They'd load the lineup up with righties when I pitched. I remember 'cause you had to pitch different up there. Those guys would all open their stances on me and try to drill that left-field wall. From the pitcher's mound, that green monster looked like it was at shortstop. Anyway, the leadoff guy hits the first pitch I throw for a single. Next guy up hits the first pitch for a double. The third guy hits the first pitch for a double. Boom, boom, boom, three pitches, three hits. Casey comes moseying out and Yogi intercepts him about ten feet from the mound. I have my back to home plate because I'm upset. I hear Casey ask Yogi, 'Doesn't Shantzy have his good stuff today?' Yogi grumbles, 'How would I know? I haven't caught one yet!'"

The old and the New

Philadelphia is widely known for its role in the birth of our nation. Think Philly and you naturally think Liberty Bell, Independence Hall, Betsy Ross House, Carpenter's Hall, and soft pretzel (get hungry enough and that grouping starts to seem logical). But Philly deserves recognition for many other things that aren't as widely publicized—like hosting the nation's oldest and largest sports banquet. The Philadelphia Sports Writers Association held its 100th banquet on January 26, 2004. That's a century-long trail of rubber chickens that pecks all the way back to Connie Mack, the guy who started it all.

BOB KENNEY of the *Courier Post* and past President of the Philadelphia Sports Writers Association (PSWA): "Back at the turn of the century, baseball was just a blip on the screen [even though the only screens they had in those days were on doors and windows]. People didn't know a whole lot about the game. Connie Mack was a born promoter. He was open to new ways to popularize his business and of course, the sportswriters came up with one that happened to be self-serving, but hey, they were sportswriters. They convinced Mack to finance a banquet to help promote baseball. Basically Mack was paying for a night the writers could eat and drink and have a good time, free of charge."

The first banquet was held on February 13, 1905 at the Bellevue Stratford Hotel. And that first menu—hey, did I make a stupid comment about rubber chickens?—was awesome. There was caviar, strained gumbo soup and planked sirloin steak with béarnaise sauce. Writers from each of the area's ten newspapers served on the first committee that honored Athletics pitcher Rube Waddell and world boxing champion Jack O'Brien. All night the buzz centered around how Connie Mack and Phillies former manager and owner Bill Shettsline would get along. The two were archrivals from the moment the A's moved into the Phils' turf. According to accounts of the time, they acted civilly toward one another.

The long history of the banquet reads like a "Who's Who" in American sports. Baseball greats Babe Ruth, Walter Johnson, Grover Cleveland Alexander, Joe DiMaggio and Bobby Shantz are just a few who were honored in the first fifty years of the banquet. In 1927, Ty Cobb shocked the world when he announced towards the end of the evening that he had signed a contract to play for the Athletics. He played two seasons under Mack before retiring, posting averages of .357 and .323 in his two years in Philadelphia. When his average dropped way down to .323, I guess Ty knew he was done.

BOB KENNEY: "One year, Tug McGraw was being honored. He showed up an hour late. When he finally walked into the banquet hall, he was leading Victor the Wrestling Bear on a leash. Victor was in town for a halftime promotion at the Sixers game and Tug had 'borrowed' him for the night. You should have seen the look on [MC] Harry Kalas's face when he saw the Tugger with that bear walking towards him on the dais . . . priceless."

Since 1936, the highlight of each year's banquet has been the presentation of the Most Courageous Athlete Award. The lights fade in the ballroom and the athlete, whose name is kept secret, enters the room and steps to the podium. Legends like Pete Gray, Jimmy Piersall, Dizzy Dean, Mickey Mantle, Roy Campanella and Jim Eisenreich have all been recipients. In 2002, the award went to the New York firefighters and EMS workers who willingly risked their lives on September 11.

BOB KENNEY: "I hope the Banquet lasts another hundred years. Some people have been attending for the past 30-35 years, with no misses. They come from all over. The Sportswriter's Banquet has earned a national reputation."

While the Philadelphia Sports Writers Association has celebrated a hundred birthdays, the Philadelphia Sports Hall of Fame Foundation is in its infancy. Just two weeks after the PSWA's big 100-year bash, the charter class of The Philadelphia Sports Hall of Fame was being inducted.

On May 17, 2002, sports writer Frank Fitzpatrick put the wheels in motion for a Philly Hall of Fame when he asked the question in his weekly *Philadelphia Inquirer* column: "Why doesn't this city have a Philadelphia Sports Hall of Fame?" Ken Avalon, an information technology consultant from Abington, Pennsylvania and certifiable Philly sports nut, read the column that morning while sipping his coffee. He asked himself the same question.

KEN AVALON: "I really had no affiliation with any sports team in Philadelphia other than the fact that I've loved all the teams since I was a kid. I talked to my family and friends and everybody thought that Philadelphia *should* have its own sports Hall of Fame. I researched other Halls of Fame around the country and found out how they got started and how they operate. We spent a year behind the scenes creating the foundation and establishing by-laws and a constitution. We joined the Philadelphia Chamber of Commerce and other like-minded organizations and by May of 2003 we went public with the organization and selected an advisory panel. That helped us select our first class of inductees."

The Foundation instituted community and scholarship programs, created collegiate internships and programs, and started sports camps for Philadelphia-area children ages 6 to 18.

All was in place on February 9, 2004, at the Sheraton in Society Hill, when the first class in the Philly Hall of Fame was enshrined. Governor Rendell and Mayor Street took turns at the mic. They rhapsodized about their mutual vision of a Philadelphia Sports Hall of Fame Museum located in the South Philadelphia sports complex—another way for Philly to move on up as a tourist destination (and another reason why Philly's better when you sleep over).

KEN AVALON: "Our ultimate goal is to create a sports museum in Philadelphia and the actual Hall of Fame would be the focus. We are identifying an executive steering committee that would help us get to where we want to be. It would be wonderful to have a place where fans from around the country could see what great athletes have played in our city. The Phillies have donated some great items already. We have two turnstiles from the Vet as well as some of the aluminum railings from around the stadium. We have signage and five ticket windows and about sixty seats. Maybe we could build a theater in the museum, using the Vet's seats.

"We want the fans to be involved in the selection process. Each year we will accept nominees on our website (www.PhillyHOF.org) and will submit a ballot of the top ten nominees to our advisory panel."

On that chilly night in February, the first class was introduced. Harry Kalas and basketball guru Sonny Hill received lifetime commitment awards. Phillies greats Mike Schmidt, Steve Carlton, Richie Ashburn and Robin Roberts were honored. Ruth Mack Clark, the daughter of Connie Mack, spoke on behalf of her father. Jimmie Foxx's daughter accepted the honor on his behalf.

After the inductions, emcee Pat Williams, former general manager of the Sixers, summed up: "So there you have it—the first class of the Philadelphia Sports Hall of Fame! Selections will be debated on TV and radio, in newspapers and magazines until next year when the next class is inducted. Start the debate now and we'll see you here next year!"

And for the 98 years that follow.

PHILADELPHIA SPORTS HALL OF FAME CHARTER CLASS

Paul Arizin
Harry Kalas
Steve Van Buren
Chuck Bednaric
Wilt Chamberlain
Billy Cunningham
Tom Gola
Bobby Clarke
Bernie Parent
Sonny Hill
Joe Frazier

John B. Kelly
Connie Mack
Bert Bell
Bill Tilden
Julius Erving
Steve Carlton
Mike Schmidt
Jimmie Foxx
Robin Roberts
Richie Ashburn

(Photo: Courtesy of the *Philadelphia Sports Hall of Fame*)

CHAPTER 6

BASEBALLTOWN

For the Phillies, playing shortstop: Mike Schmidt. Playing third base: Bob Boone.

Who's on third? No, who's on first. OK, forget the Abbott and Costello routine. *Why* is Schmidt not at third and Boone not behind the plate? Every Phillie fan has to be wondering.

Not *every* Phillie fan actually. Some of the most rabid Phillie fans in existence remember watching that very lineup—before Schmidt won ten Gold Gloves at third and Boone caught 1,095 games for the Fightins (second on the Phillies all-time list for games caught). Boone, the Phillies' starting catcher for nine years, trails all-time leader Red Dooin by only 29 games. Had Steve Carlton not been on the staff, Boone would easily rank first. For young readers, Carlton had his own designated catcher, Tim McCarver, who has said, "Carlton and I will be buried 60′-6″ apart."

But let's return to those rabid Phillie fans we alluded to. They're *Reading* Phillie fans. For readers who are not from the Philly area, Reading is *not* pronounced reading, as in the activity you're engaged in right now. Reading is pronounced Reading as in *sledding*, an activity you're most likely not engaged in right now. Only inebriated college students combine the two activities.

All things considered, it's a good thing the city of Reading is *not* pronounced like reading, as in reading a book. The *Fightin'* Phils is a fitting baseball nickname. Generally, major leaguers would rather fight than read. The Readin' (as in readin' a book) Phils would be way too literary a nickname. Reading contracts once a year is enough reading for a lot of ballplayers. You'll never hear a ballplayer yell to his teammates: "Hey, you guys go out tonight without me. I'm gonna stay in my room and finish the rest of *War and Peace*." That's as unlikely as a manager telling a pitcher: "Whatever you do, *give Bonds something to hit!* "

Anyway, no matter how they pronounce or mispronounce their city's name, Reading fans are serious about baseball. So serious in fact that the city of Reading and Berks County officially claimed the title and trademarked the name "Baseballtown USA" in March 2002.

SCOTT HUNSICKER, ASSISTANT GENERAL MANAGER: "Some of the front office staff went to a seminar in Pittsburgh back in October '01. The Detroit Red Wings were represented and they made a presentation on how Detroit is known as Hockeytown. On the way home we all thought that if Detroit was Hockeytown, why shouldn't Reading be Baseballtown? We laughed about it at first but then we thought, 'Hey, why not?' Baseball in Reading has such a long and rich history, we have such a wonderful stadium and the fans are as loyal as any in the country."

Over the years, lots of lustrous baseball names have been penciled onto Reading line-up cards—names like Greg Luzinski, Jimmy Rollins, Jeff Stone, Rocky Colavito, Marlon Byrd, Andre Thornton, Bill Jurges, Lon Warneke, Roger Maris, Ryne Sandberg, and Randy Wolf, to mention a few. All-time Dodger great Carl Furillo, who lived and eventually died in nearby Stony Creek Mills, was a native son, nicknamed the Reading Rifle.

Reading has been a baseball town almost as long as Philadelphia. Back in 1883, the same year the Philadelphia Phillies debuted in the National League, the Reading Actives played a 68-game schedule in the Interstate Association, one of baseball's two original minor leagues. Brooklyn, Harrisburg, Trenton, Wilmington, Pottsville, and Camden rounded out the rest of the competition. The Actives finished in third, but the league disbanded after one season.

Baseball returned to Reading in 1897, when the Coal Heavers represented the city in the Atlantic League. Obviously better suited to heaving coal, the Coal Heavers lost a hundred games, finishing a woeful 52.5 games behind the leaders. The next year, however, the Coal Heavers bounced back like a chunk of anthracite off a Molly Maguire. They turned in a winning season that year and every year thereafter till the league folded in 1900.

But it's harder keeping minor-league baseball out of Reading than keeping Greg Luzinski away from the dessert table. The last-place York White Roses of the Class-B Tri-State League relocated to Reading and changed their name to the Pretzels for some twisted reason (sorry). White Roses doesn't sound macho. It might be OK for a British croquet team but not for tobacco-spittin' American baseballers. In 1911, the Pretzels proved worthy of their salt, winning the Tri-State League crown, but by 1917 they were gone.

From 1919 through 1932, Reading fielded a double-A team in the International League. At various times, the franchise was a farm club for the Cubs, Red Sox, and Dodgers. The team had several different names including the Coal Barons, Marines, Aces, and Keystones.

The era was far from the golden age of Reading baseball. The 1926 squad lost 129 games and finished 75 games out. That's bleak, even for Detroit. The 1927 team lost 31 games in a row. There were a few brighter notes. Reading's George Quellich rapped out 15 hits in 15 consecutive at-bats over a four-game span, setting a record for organized baseball that stands to this day. It was the apex of George's career. Those fifteen straight hits amounted to three more than his lifetime total as a major leaguer.

Minor league ball returned to Reading in 1940. The Reading Chicks played only one year and won the Class B Interstate League crown. The Chicks were unaffiliated—the same status we suspect their players claimed when talking to Reading chicks in local bars. In any event, one year later, the Chicks left Reading (but not for good—they were back in droves when Pat Burrell came to town fifty-some years later). Next the Brooklyn Brooks played one season and left.

Minor league ball in Reading then ceased till 1952, when the Cleveland Indians moved their Eastern League franchise here from Wilkes-Barre. The Indians fielded consistently good teams in Reading's brand-new Municipal Memorial Stadium for the next decade, winning two pennants and one postseason championship. Rocky Colavito led the 1953 team to a 101-47 mark, still the Eastern League record for winning percentage.

The Reading Indians slowly faded after winning a '57 title. They departed Reading four seasons later as a last-place club.

From '63 to '66, farm clubs of the Red Sox and Indians took turns playing in Reading. Then came the climactic event for Reading baseball. In 1967, Reading became the Philadelphia Phillies' Class-AA affiliate. Reading and the Phillies have been together ever since—a remarkably enduring bond. Of 118 minor league teams affiliated with major league parent clubs in 1967, only four have maintained that association with the same organization through the 2004 season. Reading is one of the four.

On the field, the Reading Phils have been fairly successful. They started like gangbusters back in '67, rattling off nine straight winning seasons. By 1973, four Reading Phillies teams had won regular-season flags. Two others had won postseason titles. The '73 squad, which *Baseball America* voted the 62nd best minor-league team of all time, did both. The roster included Juan Samuel, Darren Daulton, and Jeff Stone, and Reading went 96-44 for the Eastern League crown. They fell short in the championships because the Phillies from Philadelphia called their young guns up to the big show in September.

The Reading Phils hit the doldrums during the next decade, only once finishing higher than fourth. Then came a banner year in 1995. After disposing of Trenton in the playoffs, they beat New Haven 3-2 for the championship. Reading hit .299 as a team in eight playoff games in '95, and walloped 21 home runs.

MOVIN' ON UP TO FIRSTENERGY STADIUM

Europeans tell this joke about Americans:

"After lunch, an American tourist visits Runnymeade in Great Britain. The tour guide informs him: 'It was 1215 when King John signed the Magna Carta right here on this spot.' The American says, 'Gosh, I wish I had known about the show. I was still eating lunch at 12:15. I would have skipped lunch just to see it.'

Though it's always a good idea to skip British food, that's not the point. The punch line is supposed to parody us Americans for viewing the entire civilized world through Disney glasses. Everything has to be staged.

We need to see a King John spectacular. King John would be signing the Magna Carta. All around him would be wenches pouring and spilling ale while frolicking and flirting with noblemen. Their wives would watch their medieval moronic mates with the same look of disgust that modern wives glare when the *Sports Illustrated* swimsuit edition pops up on the family room coffee table—or other less desirable places around the house. Frustrated cats would be poking their heads in and out of mouse holes. One wily, elusive mouse would smile that Sugar Ray Leonard smile—the one he flashed when an opponent had just swung and missed 25 consecutive times. And of course, after the show, everyone would be ushered out of the room through a shop spelled "shoppe" which automatically authorizes a 50% markup on merchandise the buyer will sell for $.50 at a garage sale three years after buying it for $25.

We crave those same Disney touches in baseball nowadays. At the same time, we crave the old-fashioned, traditional vibe that only baseball, of all the professional sports, offers. We want to feel connected to the past in our ballbarks. Yet we want the cornerstones on our ballparks to be chiseled with numbers from recent years.

The dichotomy is a good thing. Citizens Bank Park is awesome. New stadiums are like blood transfusions. Look how long they've kept Keith Richards alive—transfusions not stadiums. The new parks sustain and nourish the life of baseball with younger Disney-fied generations.

A wave of modern stadiums rolled from Baltimore's Camden Yards right across the nation. They all tap into nostalgia. They're all beautiful, and they're all great for the game of baseball. But none can recreate or capture or match some indefinable element that's embedded only in the real-deal temples of the game like Wrigley Field, Yankee Stadium, and Fenway Park. They're the only parks left that can still boast that "Babe Ruth slept here," usually after a bender the night before, and usually in right field during a mound conference. They're the places that still remind us of a simpler era. They're the places that bridge back to a time when life was lighthearted, except for occasional World Wars, polio epidemics, Dust Bowls, and Depressions.

Baseball fans are conflicted between traditional and modern, but it's a nourishing conflict. Today's throwback parks feature all the things—PR people call them amenities—that the parks they're designed to throw us back to never actually had—stadium bling like swimming pools, food courts, malls, etc. Purists view these modern contraptions as impurities. Purists think we should freeze the old parks in place and preserve them the way Europeans preserve castles. They point out that no one ever skimmed a Babe Ruth home run from a stadium swimming pool. But they're wrong because European castles have been modernized too. Louis XIV never ran a "Welcome to Versailles" video on continuous loop in an air-conditioned Hall of Mirrors.

New parks built to look like old parks are fantastic. But there's something special, an added dimension to an old ballpark that gets a rehab to preserve the past *plus* an upgrade to tap the goodies of the present. That's what they've done in Reading. Doting on their stadium the way they do in Baseballtown is a bona fide phenomenon for minor league ball.

Reading's stadium isn't as old as Wrigley, Fenway, or Yankee Stadium. But the ballpark in Reading has seen more than a half-century of service. In minor league annals, that's a long, *long* time. In the Eastern League, Reading's park is *36 years* senior to any other competitor's.

The Reading Municipal Memorial Stadium was christened on April 15, 1951. It had a price tag of $656,674 and was named to honor the servicemen and women who gave their lives for the country.

The ballpark stayed pretty much the same till Craig Stein purchased it in 1987. Since then, the ballpark has done nothing but improve. In late 1988, individual seats replaced benches in the main grandstand and a roof was installed. A third-base picnic area was added in 1990, followed by an awesome right field food court in '92.

The exterior got a facelift in '93. Then in '97 a $675,000 video scoreboard went up so the fans could be treated to color video during games—including some funny old movie gags that tie into the baseball situation. In 1999, the park was renamed GPU (General Public Utility) Stadium. A statue of giant identification tags (dog tags) outside the main entrance was installed the following year in a special rededication ceremony to honor the country's veterans.

The splashiest amenity came in September 2000—a $1.4 million pool pavilion beyond the right field fence that houses a 1,000-square-foot heated pool. The Power Alley Pub went in for the 2001 season.

In 2002, the park was rechristened FirstEnergy Stadium. The next year, more good eating spots like the Harley-Davidson Classic Café under the first base bleachers found niches in the park.

Over the years, Reading has moved on up as one of the top minor-league cities and franchises in all of professional baseball. Every year, Reading is at or near the top in minor-league attendance. In fact, ever since Stein took charge, attendance has jumped from 100,000 fans per year to well over 400,000 per year. In 2002, the club set the all-time franchise attendance mark of 485,570 fans.

In 2003, the club was awarded the prestigious John H. Johnson President's Trophy, the top honor given by minor league baseball and General Manager Chuck Domino was named Minor League Executive of the Year by *Baseball America*.

SCOTT HUNSICKER: "Winning the President's Trophy really meant a lot to the organization because I think we have the reputation around the league as being these wild and crazy promotions guys. That award means that we're considered much more seriously than that. We have a healthy respect for the history of baseball in Reading and our relationship with the Phillies."

THE 1955 READING SQUAD

In all those years of minor-league ball, there has only been one 20-game winner in Baseballtown. A guy named Don Minnick turned the trick in 1955. Minnick was one of Reading's fifteen—yes, fifteen—starters that year. Three of them, Bobby Locke, Dan Osinski, and Jake Striker (not the pilot in *Airplane* who will never get over Macho Grande), as well as Minnick, all eventually made it to the bigs. They didn't fare too badly up there either. Together they compiled a 46-44 major-league record. Osinski did the best. He played from 1962 to 1970, going 29-28 with a 3.34 ERA.

There were several other notables on the roster that year—most notably Roger Maris who asterisked his way into the record book when he eclipsed Babe Ruth's single-year home run record in 1961. Carroll Hardy was another baseball notable. Barbetters might recognize the name. Carroll Hardy is the answer to an age-old trivia question: "Who is the only man who ever pinch-hit for Ted Williams?" Answer: Reading alumnus Carroll Hardy. Then there was Larry Raines, another favorite name among trivia buffs. Reputedly, Raines is the only guy ever to play in the majors, minors, Negro League, and Japanese League.

But Don Minnick was the story in 1955. Minnick's great season came out of nowhere. In 1954, pitching mostly in relief, he was an unimpressive 7-9. In '55, as the third starter in the rotation, he won 16 straight before finally losing on July 27. Minnick cooled off to 4-3 the rest of the way, and ended up at 20-4.

Minnick's magic was fleeting. He was brought up to the majors in 1957. His entire ML career lasted from September 23 to September 28, 1957. But he made his mark forever in Reading. Through all its years of minor-league competition, he's the only 20-game winner the city ever had—a veritable legend. Ask anyone in Reading about Don Minnick and they'll all say the same thing. Who?

STADIUM STUFF

FIRST 20-GAME WINNERS IN EACH PARK

Recreation Park: 1884, Charlie Ferguson, 21-25

Baker Bowl: 1887, Dan Casey, 28-13

Connie Mack Stadium: 1950, Robin Roberts, 20-11

Veterans Stadium: 1972, Steve Carlton, 27-10

Reading Baseball—Fun at the old Ballgame

The Phillie Phanatic and the Reading Phillies are a match made in heaven. Both are all about baseball and both sometimes go to extremes to make the national pastime more fun. That's why the Phanatic enjoys making the hour-long drive out to Reading Municipal Stadium (now named FirstEnergy Stadium) often. The Phanatic loves to entertain rabid baseball fans and there's no end of them in Reading.

Not that Reading baseball fans need the Phanatic to be entertained.

It's no wonder they call Reading Baseballtown USA. By 4:00 in the afternoon, more than a hundred fans are lined up outside the beautiful brick ballpark that's aging so gracefully. Everyone hangs out there, swapping stories, buying souvenirs and waiting for the gates to open at 6:00 for the 7:00 start of the old ball game.

The whole scene is a baseball junkie's paradise.

I visit minor league cities across the nation. Believe me, there are no other cities like Reading. I credit the Reading Phillies for creating that atmosphere. They're fanatic about making their ballpark fun central.

A baseball game in Reading is much more than just a baseball game. Sounds trite, but these guys work at making it true. The stadium offers a load of fun features for watching—or not watching—the game.

CHUCK DOMINO, GENERAL MANAGER: "We've used a lot of slogans over the years to describe a Reading Phillies game. The one that sums it up best has got to be—'Reading baseball—It's like a nine-inning carnival.' Basically, as soon as you walk through the turnstiles, the atmosphere is all about fun. In fact, if it sounds like fun, looks like fun, and smells like fun, then it *must* be fun. Ooh, you know what? That one sounds pretty good. We might have to use that one for next year's slogan!"

Reading baseball has some cool things you're not likely to see at other parks. Before the game, the tots can hop aboard a makeshift locomotive that runs on the dirt track surrounding the field. Practically every night, they stage wacky contests between innings and other promotions for the game. The ground crew gets into the act. They get together with the front-office guys and do the ever-popular "Drag in Drag" routine. The guys put on wigs and women's clothing and drag the field between innings—not for bodies, but to smooth the field out. Given Reading's spicy past (you can read the city's history yourself for that dirt), dragging for bodies might be a little too entertaining.

After a win, they find the most "gravity *un*challenged" intern (the guy that an Oklahoma twister couldn't lift), dress him up like an oversized female opera singer (did I mention that they like to cross-dress in Reading?), hoist him up in a Viking ship on a huge lift behind third base and let him lip-sync an opera ballad. It's the fat lady singing . . . get it?

Who thinks up this stuff, you may ask. Chuck Domino says it's not the "who" so much as the "when" and "where."

CHUCK DOMINO: "Our RBI Room turns out to be the think tank. The RBI room is the post-game employee lounge. After games, we all head there and talk. It's a place to have a post-game beverage and unwind a little bit. We've had some pretty late nights in there and a lot of times they turned out to be really productive.

"There's a local dentist in town who wanted to advertise with us. One night in the RBI Room, we came up with the idea to get the heaviest and hairiest intern we have, dress him up in a pink tutu and turn him into the tooth fairy. He goes out onto the field with a six-foot toothbrush and brushes off the bases, including home plate. Of course, he is pirouetting and prancing all around the bases as he's doing it. The crowd eats it up."

My favorite nights are the theme nights. One year, Reading invited the Phanatic to Sixties Night. The Phillies players all wore cool tie-dyed uniforms that made them look like a group of protesters from Haight-Ashbury. The club made an oversized tie-dyed jersey for the Phanatic and I got into the act by dancing to Grateful Dead songs all night. It wasn't pretty. Think Jerry Garcia with a green beard and twenty pounds heavier if you can think that big. In the first inning, first baseman Steve Carver stepped to the plate. Steve must have been a beatnik in a past life because he really got into Sixties Night. Not only was he happy wearing his bright-colored hippie uniform, but he added a flowing blond wig under his baseball cap, going for that whole "Greg Allman-turned-jock look." He proceeded to launch a pitch over the left field fence and onto the deck for a home run. That moment seemed as psychedelic as a Jim Morrison poetry reading. As he rounded third base, he was greeted by third base coach Milt Thompson, who had also gotten the sixties vibe himself. Milt greeted Carver with his jersey unbuttoned and a huge gold medallion glistening around his neck (a Mr. T starter set). He wore a huge, black afro that was so big the third base picnic area was discounted as obstructed-view seating.

SCOTT HUNSICKER: "That was one of my favorite moments since I've been with the Reading Phillies. There's always something happening on the field or in the stands. Take this year's Opening Night for instance. Elton John happened to be in town and was scheduled to perform in Reading the following night. We thought that since he was in town, maybe he'd want to sing the National Anthem for us the night before. We knew it was a long shot. He never answered any of our phone calls. I went to one of our local radio stations that morning to be part of one of their promotions. I found an Elton John impersonator there. He was six feet tall and had a wedding ring on. But other than that, he looked just like Elton. I invited him to Opening Night and told him to bring his friends. I didn't tell anyone with the club, not even Chuck or [owner] Craig [Stein]. I teased our security staff before the game that a special guest may be arriving in a limo and that they should do their best to control the crowd.

"In the middle of the anthem, a big black limo pulls up outside the stadium, right next to the picnic area. Three friends of this guy pop out of the car, all dressed in black with earplugs in their ears, like they're a some special security squad. When the fake Elton stepped out of the car and entered the stadium, he was mobbed. They even had a guy with a fancy video camera telling people that he was shooting a documentary about Elton for VH1 and was recording his every move. We never made any announcements, but between innings, we played the song, 'Philadelphia Freedom' and showed the guy on our video board sitting in the picnic area. He got mobbed even more. The mayor of Reading and Craig each came to me to get a couple of balls signed by the fake Elton. The guy was actually forced to leave in the fourth inning because of the hysteria. Craig came over to Chuck later in the game and said, 'Wow, I can't believe Scott got Elton John here.' Hopefully, they let Craig in on it. Otherwise, Craig, if you're reading this for the first time, sorry to break the news."

PHANATIC PHILE

Hey, it's hard to draw the big names to Reading, Pennsylvania. That's why those "creative" sessions in the RBI Room help. Take the night when every fan in attendance received either a construction hat, an Indian headdress, a policeman's hat, or a cowboy hat. The theme? Yes, the Village People's night. Between innings, members of the front office staff dressed like the Village People and entertained the crowd by performing classic hits like "YMCA" and "Macho Man." My advice to the impersonators that night later in the RBI Room was to leave the dancing to trained professional idiots like me.

Another thing that sets Reading apart from other teams and makes Reading a favorite stop of the Phanatic is the fact that (WARNING TO BASEBALL PURISTS: THE FOLLOWING CONTAINS GRAPHIC MATERIAL THAT MIGHT MAKE YOUR HEAD EXPLODE) there is not just one mascot running around . . . but five.

That's right, not only does Reading have Screwball, the longtime mascot with a baseball for a head, they also have his four pals: Change-Up the Turtle, Bucky the Beaver, Blooper the Dog, and Quack the Duck. Quack is no fool. You'll see him wading in the outfield pool on warm nights.

Sharing time with another mascot is one thing but having to share the spotlight with five other loonies is downright scary.

One night in Reading, on Seventies Theme Night no less, I decided to turn the clocks back to a time when the word streaking meant more than doing a bad job Windexing windows. For young fans who weren't around during the craze, streaking was a way to stretch your clothing dollar while showing your shortcomings to the world.

Anyway, I pulled out—bad choice of words—an old routine that I did several years before at the Vet. I still get a lot of requests for the routine from players and front-office mates, especially when the team needs a little pick-me-up.

Here's the shtick. I have PA man Dan Baker announce: "Fans, this reminder, any fan entering the playing field during tonight's game will be ejected from the stadium. And anyone *foolish* enough to *streak* on the field will be prosecuted to the fullest extent of the law!"

With that, Ray Stevens' infamous little ditty, "The Streak," blares over the PA system.

"Look at that, look at that. Look at him go! And he ain't wearing no clothes . . . that's why they call him the streak!"

That's when the Phanatic, *sans* uniform top, head up and arms pumping, dashes onto the field from the right field corner, running as fast as he can. By the time he reaches center field, he's covering his private parts (I'm not sure exactly *where* the private parts on the Phanatic are located—he *is* a strange bird as they say—at least the people who know me say so). He's also trying to find the nearest umpire to hide behind. Bobby Abreu is usually out there when the Phanatic decides to get naked (or as the song says, *nekked as a Jaybird*—was Ray Stevens talking about the Jaybird Jay Johnstone? I wonder). Bobby loves to play along, shielding his eyes and trying not to peek at the Phanatic in all his green furry glory.

At that point I sputter back to the truck ramp at the old Vet (wow, still sounds weird to say the "old Vet") where the mad dash began. I'm gasping for air through the fuzzy mesh screen that covers my face. I'm convinced at that moment the costume was not designed for an all-out sprint across a baseball field on a hot summer night. But listening to the crowd hoot and holler at the Phanatic in his birthday suit makes the loss of oxygen to my brain all worth it. Then again, how much oxygen does a bird brain need? Besides, the brain damage was already done long ago, probably when nuns in Jenkintown had me in a headlock.

Getting back to streaking at the Seventies Night at Reading, we decided that all the mascots should join the Phillie Phanatic in this ritual of self-expression, liberation, and not getting enough attention as a child. When the inning ended and the announcement was made about streaking, out ran the Phanatic followed by Quack, Blooper, Screwball, and Bucky, all butt-naked. Last but not least, charging out onto the field was Change-Up the Turtle, who shed his shell for the occasion. The Phanatic might be one card short of a full deck, but Change-Up was one shell short of a full turtle.

The Reading mascots do more than just get naked, but then, don't we all? (OK, some of us don't and you know who you are.) They started their own band and have been playing gigs from Berks County all the way to Philadelphia.

SCOTT HUNSICKER: "A couple of years ago, Chuck and I were thinking about buying one of those coin-operated Bear Jamboree machines that you see in places like Chuck E. Cheese. Those things cost over $30,000 so we started thinking that maybe we could put together a real band using our own mascots.

"The guy who plays Screwball is a drummer and my brother was in a band at the time. One night he got home from a gig and I asked him to try playing his guitar in the Quack the Duck costume. We went down to our basement at home and he put on the costume and started doing Hootie and the Blowfish tunes. It was 2 o'clock in the morning and he was jumping around in this goofy-looking duck costume jamming on his guitar. It was hilarious. I knew right then that we had something."

Scott and his brother are birds of a feather.

SCOTT HUNSICKER: "Believe it or not, my dad is Change-Up the Turtle. He works at Stroehman's Bread in Norristown just outside of Philly and he drives all the way out to Reading for every game to be Change-Up. At Christmas, my brother and I bought him a set of bongos and said, 'You're the bongo player' [nothing says, "Dad, we love you" at Christmas like bongos]. We recruited a bass guitar player to wear the Bucky the Beaver costume. The guys would practice in front of the office staff after the games in the RBI Room. Watching them do hard rock tunes from AC/DC and Neil Young cracked everyone up."

Before they knew it, the Mascot Band was performing regularly at Reading Phillies games. A local music store provided the boys in the band (if that's what you can call them) with sound equipment and a local bank stepped up and sponsored their van or mascotmobile. In 2003, the Harley-Davidson Classic Café was built, providing the band with their own venue. They're crying their eyes out at Verizon Hall in the Kimmel Center in Philadelphia. They couldn't contract the Reading Mascot Band. They had to settle for the Philadelphia Orchestra.

SCOTT HUNSICKER: "These guys sweat like crazy. They really go all out in a 45 minute set. We have to make sure there's an area close by where they can get out of their costumes and take a break. It's so cool to see the expressions on people's faces when they watch the band for the first time. People think these guys are lip-syncing (should that be beak-syncing?) and they start looking around to see where the real music is coming from."

The Reading Mascot Band is a traveling band. They've played the Vet and even Citizens Bank Park at the Phanatic's birthday bash. And yes, the Phanatic has sat in with the band to jam on occasion. One night at the Vet, I caught the end of Quack's guitar. More accurately, it caught me, smack in the face as he was attempting Pete Townsend's (guitarist from the Who) signature windmill strum. I got a tiny cut under my eye and I now have a little scar as a keepsake.

I know it's only rock 'n roll, but I like it.

The Reading Mascot Band rocks Citizens Bank Park at the Phillie Phanatic's birthday party. (Photo: Heddy Bergsman)

MOVIN' ON UP TO THE BAKER BOWL

Before we get into the Baker Bowl (which is impossible except as a figure of speech), let's move on back to the first Philadelphia ballpark ever to host a National League game: the Jefferson Street Grounds or Jefferson Park. For trivia buffs, the game that was played there on April 22, 1876 was the first National League game ever played. Though it didn't go well for the Philly nine that day as the Boston Red Caps scored twice in the ninth to top the hometowners, 6-5, the game officially set the NL juggernaut in motion. It's been moving ever since.

But the Fightin' Phils weren't in the contest. Philadelphia hosted Boston that day, and it was the Athletics, not the Phillies, who represented the Quaker City. And no, these Athletics weren't the same ones they honor in Hatboro. These Philadelphia Athletics were coming off a 5-year stint (1871 to 1875) in the National Association. The National Association was the professional baseball league that preceded the National League. The Athletics had won that league's first championship in 1871. When the NA folded after 1875, the Athletics immediately signed into the fledgling National League.

Unfortunately for that iteration of the Philadelphia Athletics, the 1876 season was all she wrote. They had been playing ball in the Quaker City since at least 1860, but, after one NL season, they disappeared from the scene for good.

Jefferson Park, otherwise known as the Jefferson Street Grounds, located at 25th Street and Jefferson Avenue in Philly, was the Athletics' home. The club played its National Association and National League games there.

When the Phillies moved on up to the Quaker City in 1883, they didn't move on over to the Jefferson Park facility. They bought an existing ballfield at 24th and Columbia. Owner Al Reach named it Recreation Park. The site was used since about 1860 to play baseball, or town ball as the game was then called. Union soldiers camped on the same grounds during the Civil War.

To say the least, baseball parks in the 1860's and 1870's were unsophisticated. Not till 1864 was a major-league ballpark enclosed—a modern marvel attributed to Brooklyn.

The enclosed stadium in Flatbush was plotted at the Union and Capitoline Grounds. The seating capacity was 1,500. Yes, 1,500.

The major difference between sinking capital into stadiums (*stadia* for Classical Studies majors) then and now is that baseball's prospects for survival and longevity were shaky back in the sport's halcyon days. Baseball was risky business. But sometimes you just have to say . . . .

Early owners, for the most part, were cautious and penurious (we want you to look that one up) in ballpark design and funding. Owners wanted to erect something simple and quick. In fact, players often helped in the construction, like medieval theatrical groups that built their own stages, or neighborhood kids who hammer their own lemonade stand together. Philadelphia's professional teams in the early days of the game—and well into the twentieth century—competed with numerous neighborhood semi-professional teams that had excellent talent. The major league team often shared the same park with the semi-pros.

Of course as we know, the Phils did catch on in the Quaker City—and they caught on quickly judging by the standards of the time. Reach's Philly squad quintupled the 11,000 spectators that their predecessors in Worcester had drawn the season before. The 1883 Phillies brought 55,992 fans through the turnstiles. Second-year attendance practically doubled. Attendance continued to shoot up, hitting 150,698 and 175,623 in years three and four.

Under Harry Wright, the Phillies were movin' on up as a baseball power. They soon outgrew Recreation Park and owner Al Reach had to seek out bigger digs for his growing enterprise. In 1887, Reach built a double-decker ballpark that was absolutely huge for its era. The new stadium was dubbed the Huntingdon Grounds and carried a hefty price tag of $101,000. Seating capacity was 12,500.

Al Reach went all out with his new stadium. Perhaps he was egged on by what his sporting-goods competitor, Albert Spalding, had done in Chicago. Spalding had dumped megabucks into the White Sox's Lakefront Stadium, perhaps the flagship of the NL's early fleet of stadiums. To moderns who believe private boxes are a recent innovation, they are not. Spalding's nineteenth-century Lakefront Stadium housed eighteen private boxes, each appointed with armchairs and curtains to block the sun. Spalding's personal box was equipped with a new-fangled phone—the utmost in luxury. Meanwhile, perched on a pagoda located just off the field, a house band played between innings.

PHANATIC PHILE

DELAY OF THE GAME

I wonder if the house band at Baker Bowl ever had to worry about playing a little bit too long between innings? Was there someone in the video control room (back then it might have been a huge nickelodeon) with his eyes fixed on a stopwatch, making sure they ended their song on time?

Keeping the fans entertained between innings is a big part of my job. Sure, we've moved on up when it comes to entertaining fans in the new millennium with fancy scoreboards, surround-sound technology and games to play in the concourse. But just as it was with that house band, the goal is the same: make sure that the fans are having fun.

Keep that in mind. I'm going to talk about supply-side entertainment—a Phanatic's eye view. There are two rules mascots live by:

Rule #1: *Don't delay the game.*

Rule #2: *Don't delay the game.*

If there were a Rule # 3 it would probably be "Don't repeat yourself," a problem otherwise associated with greasy tacos.

It sounds easy enough. You slip into a costume then run around the field before the game or between innings trolling for laughs. You dance with a willing player or two, goose an unsuspecting ump or coach and then scurry off the field before the batter digs into the box.

Simple enough, right?

The problem boils down to time: one minute, forty-five seconds of time to be exact. That's the time in between every half-inning. Let's do the math. Even with the Phanatic's four-wheeler rumbling flat out, it takes me at least fifteen seconds to get on the field and fifteen seconds to get off the field. That leaves me a whopping one minute, fifteen seconds to perform.

Larry Andersen has had belches last longer. Much longer.

That means I have one minute, fifteen seconds to launch hot dogs to a hungry crowd of Phillies fans. I have one minute, fifteen seconds to usher a chorus line of twenty pre-teen girls onto the field, set them up, and perform a choreographed dance routine with them that they rehearsed for months. I have one minute, fifteen seconds to get a fake umpire into position to be eaten, digested and regurgitated onto the field as we did in 2003. (Actually, that prank took a bit longer. Just ask Kevin Millwood. No, don't. I don't want to remind him. I'm hoping he forgot. And forgave.)

With MLB's recent efforts to speed up the game, the clock ticks louder these days. The pressure is *really* on for me to exit. That can pose challenges when unexpected problems arise.

Some problems might surprise you. How about this one? The red ATV I scoot around the field on is *not* equipped with a gas gauge (don't ask). Sometimes as I'm blasting out to the field, I think, "How many gallons are left in that tank?" You know, in the heat of battle, I lost track myself. So I've got to ask myself, "Do I feel lucky? Well, do I . . . punk?"

Sometimes, the problems come from . . . pigs.

In 2003, I decided to spruce up our Dollar Dog Days by inviting Smiley the Pig from Hatfield Quality Meats to help launch hot dogs into the stands during the fifth-inning routine. Smiley is Hatfield's Meats' porky mascot. Hatfield supplies the Phillie Phranks at the ballpark.

Smiley sports a perpetual smile on his pinkish face. He wears blue denim overalls that make him look like a *Hee Haw* regular (I don't mean Misty Rowe either—Smiley is definitely lower on the food chain than Misty). Since Smiley has his own hot dog launcher, I figured: "Why not launch twice as many free hot dogs?"

On the 2003 season's first Dollar Dog Day, I came blazing across the field with my hot dog launcher. Smiley followed on his launcher-totin' ATV. I hopped off at third base. Smiley barreled past and set up behind first base. I was beaming with pride. Never in the history of baseball, or of hot dogs, would so many hot dogs fly through the air as tonight. This night was destined to be the Vet's number-one aerial event of all time. Move over Kiteman and Wallenda.

I glanced over at Smiley. Something was wrong. Smiley was in a panic. He was firing his cannon but nothing was coming out—a bad case of hot dog launcher dysfunction (HDLD). Boos were raining down as he scuttled to the back of his ATV to check gauges. Scratching his oversized head with one hand and flicking at the gauge to try to get the red needle to move with the other, Smiley eventually threw up his hands and shrugged as if to say, "What can I do? I'm just a guy in a pig suit." Poor Smiley wound up grabbing hot dogs with his right *hoof* and *throwing* them into the first few rows of seats (giving new meaning to the term "hoofing it"). The ravenous fans were voicing almost as much displeasure as the old days when Mitch came in (although Smiley was throwing more accurately).

Driving up to Smiley, I thought of Rule #3 for mascots. Oh, I forgot to mention there really is a Rule #3. It's: *If another mascot is being booed, stay as far away from him as possible*. I noticed the batter was standing in the batter's box with his bat resting comfortably on his shoulder, like he'd been waiting there awhile, enjoying the spectacle of a pig making a fool of himself. It was easier than trying to hit Millwood. I yelled to Smiley, "We gotta get out." Smiley beat a hasty retreat off the field and squealed: "The psi numbers were way too low, and I think the main valve that connects to the CO_2 tanks was sticking." I listened but it's hard to take a guy seriously who's explaining the scientific principles behind a machine designed to shoot hot dogs—when all the while he's dressed in a pig costume.

Smiley *ham*-pered my act on his next visit too. The plan was to join the pig at first base and orbit three hot dogs per launcher simultaneously. Sort of like a six-hot dog salute. It was going to be another spectacular (in the annals of hot dog launching) as well as another Vet Stadium first. This time, when I got over to Smiley, *my* launcher had run out of CO_2. Our six-shooter fizzled down to a three-shooter. Philly doesn't have the Curse of the Bambino or the Curse of Steve Bartman. Apparently, we have the Curse of Smiley the Pig.

The third time is not the charm either. Smiley's third visit started off fine. Smiley was tossing hot dogs around as casually as J-Lo tosses husbands and other things around. The pig was playing to the crowd and really getting into it. In his squeal—er, zeal—he forgot Rule #1 and Rule #2. The home plate umpire did not. With the tact and compassion of a Philly airport cop writing a ticket, he asked me to suggest that Smiley vacate the premises, whenever it was convenient for Smiley. Oh, no, that's not exactly what he said. It was something about sticking an apple in Smiley's mouth and firing up the grill.

"Smiley, Smiley, get off the field!! Move, move, move!!" I screamed as I zoomed for the ramp.

Frantically, Smiley hopped on his four-wheeler and hit the accelerator. With a nod to Vin Diesel's *The Fast and the Furious*, I present to you Rule #4: *A mascot has got to know his limitations—for speed that is*. Blistering up the right field foul line, Smiley was barreling too fast to avoid the section of stands that jut out towards the field. Jennifer, our pretty ball girl, now had a manic, furry pig bearing down on her. The lovable swine swerved to his left to avoid Jennifer and the 100-Level deluxe box seats. That made the trailer hitch hauling his hot dog launcher tilt to the left and then to the right before flipping over onto its side.

Bobby Abreu should pay us for the entertainment. Bobby could hardly contain himself watching Smiley's wipeout. Smiley jumped off his ATV, scraped the remains of his damaged hot dog cannon off the turf and dragged the trailer-hitch off the field.

Surveying the carnage at the top of the truck ramp, Smiley buried his head in his hooves. In the course of just over one minute and fifteen seconds, the pig had managed to hold up the game, almost run over a ball girl, and crash his hot dog launcher.

Granted, Smiley the Pig gave us some real Dog Days, but a real dog caused the Phanatic's all-time longest delay. (Note to Phillies brass: It is *never* the Phanatic's fault if he overstays his welcome on the field. The fault always lies with his "phuzzy" phriends. Note to the readers: Sorry for the delay. I just wanted to make that point clear to the Phils brass because of Rule #5: *Never get my bosses ticked off at the mascot wearing green.*)

It was a beautiful, summer Sunday afternoon in 2002 and Disney's Air Bud was paying a visit to the Phanatic. Air Bud is the Big Dog of the silver screen. He's a beautiful golden retriever who can do it all: soccer, basketball, volleyball, and of course—baseball. He was in town promoting his latest film, *Seventh Inning Fetch* and was slated to join the Phanatic for the fifth-inning routine.

The idea was to have Air Bud and his co-star, Caitlin Wachs, play catch on the field between innings. To prepare Bud, he had to meet the Phanatic before the game, and get used to the Phanatic's scent, which has been compared to the irresistible fragrance, *eau de wet dog*. The Phanatic and Air Bud practiced throwing the ball back and forth. As Air Bud's trainers barked out commands, Bud and I became buds, practicing for close to forty-five minutes. I calculated how far apart we should stand, how I should throw the ball and how many tosses I could comfortably fit into one minute, fifteen seconds. When it was showtime, I hitched up the red sidecar to the Phanatic's four-wheeler and plopped Air Bud on Caitlin's lap. We three breezed down the ramp and onto the field. Good old Bud seemed to soak up the warm Philly reception as his tongue was flapping in the wind and soaking me with doggie drool.

We dismounted in front of the visitor's dugout on the third-base side and began our well-choreographed catch. After two tosses, Air Bud got bored. Face it, the dog is Hollywood. He's used to sitting on the couch with Leno and doing stupid human tricks for Letterman. The little star was craving some action! Looking around, he spotted first baseman Travis Lee throwing warm-up ground balls to the infielders, which seemed like lots more fun than what we were doing.

Like a flash, the magnificent golden retriever was off to the races. He charged across the field towards Travis Lee and then chased the ground ball heading

PHANATIC PHILE

towards third baseman Scott Rolen. Rolen snatched the ball up before the playful pooch could get it and tossed it back to Lee. Air Bud was the victim in every kid's schoolyard nightmare: monkey-in-the-middle.

He dashed back over to Lee, then dashed back after the bounding ball that shortstop Jimmy Rollins swooped up. Instead of throwing it back, J-Roll teasingly threw a grounder back over to Travis, sending Air Bud into a tail-wagging fit. Mike Lieberthal's throw down to Marlon Anderson sailed right over Bud's head and down to second base. Second baseman Anderson waved the ball tauntingly in front of Air Bud. Three balls to chase—the dog would have been in doggie heaven if only there had been fire hydrants at every base.

The throw down to second snapped me out of it. I was so busy laughing, I forgot about the game. Marlon flipped the ball over to pitcher Randy Wolf, who stood next to the mound, hands on hips, watching Air Bud dodge his trainers and our own director of entertainment, Chrissy Long. They were all trying to coax his Airness off the field. I was using the time wisely, formulating a defense for when the inevitable phone call from the executive box would come.

"Uh, David, we didn't anticipate Air Bud going after the infield practice ball," I would argue. "But wasn't it great—the perfect scene for a Norman Rockwell painting. A dog runs out onto the field and wants to use the ball to play catch in the middle of a baseball game. That's Americana! That's baseball! That's what we're all about."

And I could picture David saying, "No we're not. That's a violation of Rule # 1. And Rule # 2."

Opening day at Huntingdon Grounds was April 30, 1887, and Philly's new ballpark was an immediate hit with the locals. By the close of the park's maiden season, 253,671 patrons had spun through the turnstiles (although spinning didn't become a craze for another century). That attendance figure is 44.5% higher than Recreation Park's best-ever year. Before Huntingdon Grounds popped up on the scene, the rival Athletic of Philadelphia (yes, that is yet *another* Philadelphia team that went by the name Athletics or more precisely Athletic) in the American Association, the competing professional league in the era, had outdrawn the Phils every year. In 1887 the Phillies reversed that. Ensconced in their new stadium, the Phils outdrew the A's by 52,651 spectators.

Hollywood star Air Bud (with co-star Caitlin Wachs and the Phanatic) caused one of the most memorable delays ever at the Vet.

(Photo: Heddy Bergsman)

STADIUM STUFF

PHILLIES BALLPARKS . . . THEN AND NOW

BAKER BOWL

Rain, not the Phanatic, still is the number one, all-time delay of the game king. At Baker Bowl, groundskeepers used to pour gasoline on standing puddles to burn off the water that would sit on the field.

CITIZENS BANK PARK

At Citizens Bank Park, there are one and a third miles of irrigation pipes under the field and 87 sprinkler heads on the field. They are controlled by a state-of-the-art software package that allows maximum flow rates and a reduction in the amount of time required to irrigate the field. Matches and gasoline are no longer required.

On August 6, 1894, tragedy struck. The Huntingdon Grounds burned completely down (not because they were drying the field). Temporary stands were thrown up for the rest of the season.

While the stadium was being repaired, the Phils played some of their games at University Field at 37th and Spruce—a University of Pennsylvania football field. That represented a role reversal. Usually it was football teams that were forced to use baseball fields, not the other way around. The Eagles kicked off that phenomenon later in the thirties. The Birds played their first three seasons at Baker Bowl (a later name for the Huntingdon Grounds—but we're jumping ahead), thus making Baker Bowl the first dual-use stadium for professional sports in the Keystone State. The Eagles also played several seasons in Shibe Park, a baseball facility.

Now back to the Huntingdon Grounds.The entire ballpark at Huntingdon Grounds was rebuilt and improved—almost in time for the upcoming season. On May 2, 1895 the new structure, which seated 18,800, was dedicated. Historians sometimes credit this structure as the first modern baseball park because it featured revolutionary design elements like cantilevered concrete supports that eliminated or reduced obstructed views. It was also the first ballpark constructed primarily of steel and brick which reduced the hazard of fire.

Over its fifty-one year run, Huntingdon Street Baseball Grounds took on more names than a modern-day bank or utility company. It was often called Philadelphia Park though its official name was National League Park. It appears, however, that Philadelphians referred to it as National League Park less frequently than Chipper Jones is referred to as Larry, even though he's old enough to be Larry now.

More tragedy struck at the ballpark. The stands collapsed in 1903, killing twelve and injuring 232. A fire had broken out in a building across from the third-base stands. Fans congregated to get a better look. The overload caused the pavilion to collapse.

The franchise at that juncture was as unstable as the stands. Original owners Reach and Rogers had sold the team for $170,000 after the 1902 season when the suddenly lackluster Phillies tumbled to seventh place. James Potter was the owner when the stands collapsed but he stayed on only one more season before selling the team to William Shettsline, who had been the Phils' manager from 1898 to 1902. Potter reportedly left in a huff because the city refused to rename the park Potter's Fields.

We're just kidding.

In 1913, William F. Baker bought the Phillies, succeeding Horace Fogel and Alfred Wiler as owner. The former, who had been a writer for the *Sporting News*, owned the Phillies from 1909 to 1912. In the midst of the 1912 pennant race, Fogel accused the NL and its umpires of favoring the New York Giants, and called the pennant race "crooked." Fogel's comments got him banned from professional baseball for life. Wiler owned the club only briefly before Baker took over.

After William F. Baker bought the franchise in 1913, the park's name was changed to the eponymous Baker Bowl. Hopefully, Steinbrenner isn't reading this or it'll be bye, bye Yankee Stadium, hello Steinbrenner Stadium. And God forbid if Trump ever buys the Yankees. The New York Trumps? You're fired.

Baker Bowl was not lacking in amenities. Up until World War I, there was a swimming pool in the basement of the center field clubhouse. The bathroom and shower were also in the center field clubhouse. Fans were treated to the sight of ballplayers trotting (for real) out to center field in between innings because when you gotta go, you gotta go. But, as other cities built up and pressed newer stadiums into service, Baker Bowl went to seed and became a source of embarrassment to the Phils and Philly.

THE GREATEST

In some circles, Phillie Baker Bowl great Lefty O'Doul gets the credit for telling this story first.

At a banquet in the late fifties, someone asked Lefty who was the greatest hitter of all time. Lefty answered without hesitation, "Ty Cobb." Lefty went on to compare Cobb to the pantheon of current baseball greats: Mays, Mantle, Frank Robinson, Berra, Clemente, etc., and concluded that none of them could compare. Cobb was the greatest.

Someone asked: "What do you think Cobb would hit if he were playing today?" Lefty shot back, "About .320." The fan thought he had the best of O'Doul, challenging: "But Cobb's career average was .367. If the ballplayers were better in Cobb's day, why would he only hit .320 today?" "Because," Lefty said, "you gotta take into account, Cobb's a 74-year-old man now."

A STRANGE BALLPARK

The dimensions at the Baker Bowl are fabled. Built on an odd parcel of land, the field featured a 341-foot left field foul line and a 280-foot right field foul line. It was 408 feet to dead center but the right center field power alleys were a cozy 310-320 feet. Throughout the park's lifetime, the Phils tinkered with the dimensions, but right field was *always* close, really close to home plate. The short right field fence, coupled with the Phillies' poor showings throughout the twenties and thirties, undermined the achievements and legacy of Phillie greats like Chuck Klein, Cy Williams, and Gavvy Cravath. Red Smith once observed about Baker Bowl, "It might be exaggerating to say the outfield wall cast a shadow across the infield, but if the right fielder had eaten onions at lunch, the second baseman knew it."

There is some substance to Red's charge. After all, Red sat in the catbird seat. Consider the 1920 season. Left-handed-hitting Cy Williams and his Phillie teammates blasted fifty homers at home versus only fourteen on the road. The last-place Phils' total of sixty-four round-trippers that year topped the NL runner-up in the category by 16 salamis. In 1920, the right-field fence was only 272 feet away from the plate. It didn't take much of a blast with baseball's new jacked-up baseball to crash one over the fence. Or through it. The tin fence in right was so rusted that hard line drives supposedly pierced right through it.

The height of the right field fence was formidable, an attempt to compensate for the short distance to the plate. The fence rose up forty feet in 1895, and was lengthened to sixty feet in 1915. As a frame of reference, Boston's Green Monster is 37 feet high. The outfield walls were strewn with advertisements. Presumably no balls punched through the "Health Soap Stops B.O." sign that was painted on the outfield fence for years. B.O. in those days meant bad odor, not the Baltimore and Ohio Railroad, although really bad odor arguably might stop a B & O train. In the thirties, a big sign in right field informed the world, "The Phillies Use Lifebuoy."

"And they still stink," was the punch line around the city.

But let's return to 1920 and power numbers. Over in the American League a guy named Ruth swatted out 54 homers all by himself. Ruth's total bested every other *team total* in both leagues, except for the Phils. As great as Bonds is, he's not going to accomplish that. He gets too many walks.

In 1920, Ruth was looking out at a right field fence at the Polo Grounds that lay only 257 feet away. The Babe ate hot dogs longer than that. In any event, it was shorter than the right field dimension at Baker Bowl by half a first down. Half a decade later, the Babe moved into the house he built in the Bronx and took pokes at its friendly 296-foot right field porch.

In 1921, the Phils set another National League team record by whacking 88 round-trippers. The Phils led the NL in homers each of the next five seasons and finished last or next to last in each of the standings of those seasons. Baker Bowl's friendly dimensions also helped opponents.

As time went by, Baker Bowl was dissed with tags like the Cigar Box, the Band Box, and the Hump. Why the Hump? The park was situated on an elevated piece of ground with a railroad tunnel running underneath the outfield. By the thirties, Baker Bowl was passé. The Phils had to look to their AL rival crosstown for their next move on up.

JOLTIN' JOLTIN' JOE'S UNBREAKABLE RECORD – TAKE 7 AND 8

It's hard to imagine that Chuck Klein's assist record will ever be broken. Klein is remembered best as a hitter—a left-handed slugger whose exploits have often been questioned because he benefited from Baker Bowl's friendly right field dimensions. Still, the offensive stats Klein put up over a five-year period (1929 through 1933) rival anyone's. Klein won the National League MVP in 1932. He won the Triple Crown the following season, and amazingly did *not* win his second consecutive MVP which went to the NY Giants' meal ticket, Carl Hubbell (before Philly fans rant about another slight to Philadelphia, Ted Williams hit .406 in 1941, and did not win the MVP).

Klein's numbers are fantastic. He broke into the league in 1928 with a .360 average and stroked 11 HRs in only 253 at-bats. From 1929 through 1933, his batting averages were .356, .386, .337, .368, and .368. He banged out 200 or more hits in each of those seasons. His home run totals for the same years were 43, 40, 31, 38, and 28. His RBI totals were 145, 170, 121, 137, and 120. He also led the Senior Circuit in stolen bases in 1932, the year of his Triple Crown.

But all those stats pale to one other record Klein holds, and will most likely hold forever. Klein tallied 44 assists from right field in 1930.

One Phillie outfielder, Gavvy Cravath, nailed 34 runners in 1914. Cravath was the only other Phillie ever to top or equal 30 assists. For comparison's sake, Pat Burrell led the NL with 18 assists in 2001. You have to go back to 1986 for the last time a Phillie reached 20 assists. Glenn Wilson led the NL with 20 that year. Twenty-one years before that, another Phillie broke the 20 threshold when Johnny Callison led the NL with 21 assists.

The 1930 Phils set some other dubious, never-to-be-broken records. The Phils as a team batted .315, tops in the league. They certainly didn't top the league in wins. They finished last, 52-102 (.338), 40 games out of first place, and 7 games out of seventh place. It's doubtful that any last-place team will ever break their record of highest team batting average for a last-place team. It's also doubtful that any team that loses 100 games will ever lead the league in batting. And on the hurling side, the 1930 staff made locals hurl. It's doubtful any other team will put up a higher staff ERA than the 6.71 the 1930 staff recorded. Fourteen different intrepid souls took the mound that season and pitched as though someone had indeed taken the mound and placed it somewhere behind second base.

The only hurler with a winning record was Phil Collins. It was just another day in paradise that year when Phil toed the rubber on his way to a 16-11 record. As for the Phils' other thirteen chuckers, they were throwing it all away. The next-best winning percentage on the staff belonged to Ray Benge, who went 11-15 for a .423 percentage. Even Alexander the Great (Grover Cleveland), who was back with the '30 Phils, pitching in his twentieth and final season, was 0-3 with a 9.14 ERA. It's a sobering thought that Tommy Lasorda—he of the 6.48 career ERA—would have been the ace of the staff. In baseball, all is possible.

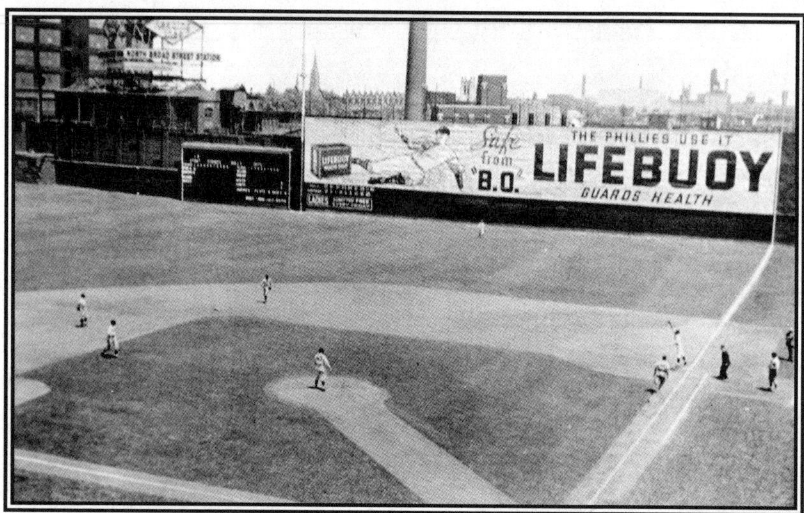

At Baker Bowl, the giant 60 ft. fence in right field loomed only 280 feet from home plate. Phillies left-handed sluggers Chuck Klein and Cy Williams took advantage of the short dimensions.

(Photo: Courtesy of the Phillies)

STADIUM STUFF

PHILLIES BALLPARKS . . . THEN AND NOW

BAKER BOWL

At Baker Bowl, the Phils kept some sheep and a ram in the outfield to keep the grass from growing too long.

CITIZENS BANK PARK

At Citizens Bank Park, there is $500,000 worth of tractors, mowers, edgers, blowers, aerators, and assorted other equipment to keep the field in tip-top shape. The Phillies also spend over $140,000 a year on maintenance for the field, not including labor. Maybe they should bring back the sheep and ram to save a few bucks.

PIGEON DROPPINGS

Speaking of the Zoo . . .

Before Philadelphians had KYW to broadcast Phillies game scores every half-hour, America's first zoo handled the job. Yes, back in 1883, a Philadelphia zookeeper named Jim Murray (not the former Philadelphia Eagles General Manager) provided the Phillies with homing pigeons that were released from Recreation Park every half-inning. The keepers scratched the score on a paper and attached it to the bird's leg. The pigeons flew back to the zoo and kept the zoo workers up to the minute—actually, up to the inning. Unfortunately the pigeons usually brought bad news. That was the season the Phils played at a .173 clip. Other Phillies fans wanted in on this modern marvel. Murray obliged. At the height of the service, as many as six pigeons were dropping updates of the ballgame (and other things) around the city.

STADIUM STUFF

THE CITY SERIES

Philly lost one fun tradition when the A's bolted for Kansas City—the annual city series. Once Connie Mack established his Athletics franchise in the American League in 1901, it was a natural for the crosstown rivals to go head to head. The A's and Phillies played each other in Philly every year prior to the start of the regular season. Many years, they also squared off on the trip north from spring training, opposing one another in exhibition games along the way. But the first city series game was played long before the arrival of Mack and his A's. The first city series pitted the Phillies and the Athletic of Philadelphia of the American Association in 1883. The series was played in the Huntingdon Grounds and drew more than 10,000 spectators.

Once Connie Mack's A's left town in 1954, the Phils never played them again except in spring training. The 2003 series with the Oakland A's at the Vet was the first time the two have played in Philly since the old city series.

PHILLIES BALLPARKS . . . THEN AND NOW

BAKER BOWL

• Baker Bowl never had a public address system. They had a guy who delivered all the announcements via megaphone. It was not Dan Baker, or so Dan claims.

CONNIE MACK STADIUM

• Connie Mack Stadium was one of the first stadiums to use a PA sound system (1930). In the late forties, the late and great Dave Zinkoff, who later was the Sixers' legendary PA man, was the PA man at Connie Mack Stadium (for youngsters, he's the guy they named the Dave Zinkoff Drive after—that's the entrance to the Wachovia Center off Broad Street).

THE VET

• The Vet had one master switch that controlled volume for the entire stadium. If fans in, lets say, section 320 complained that the sound was too loud, the volume had to be lowered for the entire stadium—including the fans in, for example, section 540 who then couldn't hear a thing.

CITIZENS BANK PARK

• The new ballpark's sound system is multi-zoned and computer-operated. Everything is done with the click of a mouse. Not only volume but timbre can be fine-tuned for any particular section of the stadium without affecting any other section. In addition, different audio can play simultaneously in different zones.

PHILLIES BALLPARKS . . . THEN AND NOW

BAKER BOWL

• The term "knotholers" was born at the Baker Bowl. It's a euphemism. Kids were watching the action, but it wasn't through natural knotholes in the wood. People drilled holes through the outfield fence to watch the action at a "reduced" price. Forgive them. It was the Depression, and watching the Phillies in that era only added to their depression.

CONNIE MACK STADIUM

• Ever see the photos of the 1910 and 1911 World Series? You can't miss the army of fans watching from the roofs of houses opposite the right field fence. Connie Mack put an end to that freeloading by constructing his "Spite Fence," the corrugated metal monstrosity that blocked the view from the rooftops.

CITIZENS BANK PARK

• At Citizens Bank Park sightlines are superb. Thanks to computer-assisted design and a century of experience in the art and science of ballpark construction, any seat in the house affords an excellent, unobstructed view of the action. And, with a wink toward Connie, Citizens Bank Park features "rooftop bleachers"—200 seats overlooking Ashburn Alley in right field that return spectators to those thrilling days of yesteryear before Mr. Mack's Spite Fence.

CHAPTER 8

MOVIN' ON UP TO SHIBE PARK

Baseball was the biggest game in town at the turn of the nineteenth century. The Frankford Yellow Jackets, Philadelphia Eagles, Philadelphia Warriors, Philadelphia 76ers, Philadelphia Ramblers, and Philadelphia Flyers wouldn't show up for at least another quarter century (OK, a few years less for the Yellow Jackets). Hard to imagine but back then, baseball vied with horseracing, sculling, and bicycle racing for the spectator dollar.

When the Phillies set up shop for good in the Quaker City in 1883, the National League was surviving—not thriving, but holding its own. By the turn of the century, the Phillies had firmly entrenched themselves as Philadelphia's National League representative.

Up until 1891, Philadelphia had two professional baseball teams, each in a different league. The Phils played in the National League. The Athletic of Philadelphia played in the American Association, the other professional baseball league. The American Association died in 1891, leaving the National League sole and uncontested as the country's professional baseball league.

In 1901, Ban Johnson started another professional baseball league. He called it the American League. Suddenly the long-established National League, forevermore referred to as the Senior Circuit, faced another new rival. This new league, however, was not about to go away. So solid did the American League turn out to be that the eight franchises that played in 1903 remained in place till 1953. Even afterwards, not one of the group perished (though several clubs relocated).

Philadelphia was a fertile baseball market. In those days, Philly was the nation's third largest city. Ban Johnson wanted to seed a team in Philly, even if a National League flag was already planted there (just a flag, not a pennant flag). Enter the Philadelphia Athletics, and this Athletics team *is* the same one they honor in Hatboro.

The father of this new American League franchise was an Irishman, Cornelius Alexander McGillicuddy, Philly's greatest expatriate from New England since Ben Franklin told Beantown to go fly a kite.

As an aside, why is it that *Bostonians* don't ever gripe and whine about losing Ben Franklin and Connie Mack to Philly? Both guys were "wicked hard core." The only one Boston ever whines about is the Babe.

Maybe the Big Dig is Boston's way of plugging their exodus of talent. If you've been to Boston in recent years, every highway everywhere is ripped up. It's easier for light to escape a black hole than a car to get out of Boston. In fact, Franklin and Mack made better time traveling from Boston to Philly in carriages than you'll make today in a BMW.

CONNIE MACK

Connie Mack was born the third of seven children to Irish immigrants in East Brookfield, Massachusetts. He played infield and outfield (but not at the same time) on his hometown team. Finally, he settled on the position of catcher. The year the National League came to be, Mack's team won the state championship, a success that set Connie Mack on the peripatetic portion of his life.

First the young catcher signed with Meriden in 1884 for a contract of $90 a month. The next two years he played for Hartford before getting sold to Washington.

The Players League was starting up at that time and Mack was a rabid supporter. The league was formed in reaction to various National League practices that ballplayers viewed as gimmicks and devices to restrict their salaries. Several big names in the National League jumped over to the upstart league. But only one team turned a profit, so the financial backers backed off and the crusade fizzled after one year of operation.

Next, Mack shuffled off to Buffalo, where he became part owner, and staked his entire life savings of $500 on the team. He lost it all. Undaunted, he moved on up to Pittsburgh in 1891. There, at age thirty-two, he found himself promoted to manager.

In 1897, Mack began managing both on and off the field for Milwaukee in the Western League, the precursor to the American League, with Ban Johnson as its President. The Mack-Johnson connection landed Mack in the City of Brotherly Love, where he would remain the rest of his days. Mack had impressed Johnson, who offered the hardworking Irishman an opportunity to organize and manage a Philadelphia franchise in the new American League. Mack secured the financial backing he needed from Ben Shibe who was Phillies owner Al Reach's partner in Reach's sporting-goods business.

Mack's Athletics immediately became one of the dominant teams in the American League. They won the pennant in the League's second year, and fell just short of taking half the AL's first 14 pennants. They won six.

COLUMBIA PARK

When the A's came to town in 1901, Connie Mack took out a 10-year lease on a vacant lot that was bounded by 29th Street, Columbia Avenue, 30th Street, and Oxford Street in North Philadelphia's Brewerytown section. He called the park he erected on his new slice of real estate Columbia Park, which had a seating capacity of 9,500. The stadium, which cost $35,000 (along with the real estate), was nothing more than two wooden grandstands extending down both sides of the diamond from home plate to somewhere around first and third bases.

The new American League gained talent parity quickly with the established National League. More important, they gained fan popularity. After their maiden season, the A's outdrew the Phillies every year in the first decade of the twentieth century. In 1901, the Athletics drew 206,329 fans. By 1907, that figure had rocketed to 625,581. The early success of the Athletics—they won pennants in 1902 and 1905—hastened their need for a new home. They began looking for more commodious accommodations as early as 1902. In both the 1902 and 1905 World Series, the A's were forced to turn away a multitude of disappointed fans. The technical term for disappointed fans is paying customers. The accounting term is lost revenue.

The Athletics abandoned Columbia Park after a disappointing sixth-place 1908 finish. They contracted William Steele and Sons to design and construct their new palace on a site bounded by 21st Street, Lehigh Avenue, 20th Street, and Somerset Street. For you real-estate magnates, the $457,167.61 bill broke down like this: $315,248.69 for the stadium and $141,918.92 for the land.

At the time of sale, the neighborhood wasn't viewed as overly, let's say, salubrious. The Philadelphia Hospital for Contagious Diseases—a name that outscores terms like swampland, flood plain, and nuclear fuel depository as a real-estate killer—was located at 22nd Street and Lehigh Avenue.

Reputedly, prior to the sale, Ben Shibe caught wind that the city planned to close the hospital, and bought the land while the price was suppressed. Whatever the story, it worked out well for the A's owners. The hospital closed in June 1909 and was razed in 1911. As for any lingering effect the contagious disease facility might have had on Philly players, you can draw your own conclusions.

The new stadium seated 23,000. Given the propensity of us Irish to wax nostalgic about the "Auld Sod," it's touching that sod from Columbia Park was transported to the new park for the playing field. Connie Mack would have it no other way. The motivation was purely economic, however, not sentimental. The structure that rose up at 22nd and Lehigh was opulent and dignified, characterized by the elegant French Renaissance tower and cupola at the entrance. That tower that you see on the cover has become the stadium's signature element, housing the offices of John Shibe, who served as the A's VP, and Connie Mack.

LINEUP FOR FIRST GAME AT CONNIE MACK, APRIL 12, 1909

Philadelphia Athletics	Boston Red Sox
Topsy Hartsel lf	Ambrose McConnell 2b
Simon Nicholls 3b	Harry Lord 3b
Eddie Collins 2b	Jake Stahl 1b
Dan Murphy rf	Doc Gessler rf
Harry Davis 1b	Tris Speaker cf
Amos Strunk cf	Heinie Wagner s/s
Stuffy McInnis s/s	Jack Thoney lf
Doc Powers c	Bill Carrigan c
Eddie Plank pitcher	Frank Arellanes pitcher

On April 12, 1909, the Athletics played their first game in Shibe Park. A Philadelphian named George McFadden was the first fan at the ticket window at 7 AM. The window wasn't slated to open till noon, but George was there early. (Dead Heads are thinking "That's *late* for a *concert*, man—it's too early for a job interview but not a concert!") McFadden later turned down an offer of $35.00 for that first ticket, proving that the sports memorabilia market is not a modern invention. When the turnstile finally stopped spinning on Shibe Park's opening day, 30,162 spectators had packed into the park. Reportedly, 5,000 more crushed inside using courtesy passes, or climbing over the walls, or squeezing through security when crowds rushed the gates en masse. As many as 30,000 more spectators were shut out completely. Unhappy campers too. They got unruly and needed police intervention to restore order.

As for the big opening-day festivities—well, suffice it to say, ours is a splashier age. The Third Regiment Band played. The crowd sang "America the Beautiful" prior to Mayor John Reyborn's throwing out the first ball. The Athletics and the Red Sox marched out to center field behind the bands. Ben Shibe and American League President Ban Johnson hoisted the flag and the band played "The Star-Spangled Banner." Dick Clark may or may not have been in attendance. There were no reported clothing malfunctions.

At 3 PM, "Gettysburg" Eddie Plank, the A's lefty Hall of Famer, trotted to the mound for the A's and twirled a convincing 8-1 complete game victory.

The new park brought the team success. The A's lost out in a close race to the Tigers in the stadium's maiden year before taking the AL flag in 1910, 1911, 1913, and 1914. With the exception of 1914 when the Miracle Braves surprised them, the Athletics won the World Series as well as the pennant every year they played in it.

The A's were a team of extremes. Offsetting that great winning skein from 1910 through 1914, they wallowed in the basement for *seven consecutive years* from 1915 through 1921. In the 1910 Series, they batted .316—a Series batting mark that would endure for half a century, till the '60 Yankees shattered it. In stark contrast to the batting prowess they displayed in 1910, the 1905 pennant-winning Athletics batted a miserable .161, a World Series mark for futility that lasted 61 years till the '66 Dodgers chopped it down to .142. Incidentally, in that very same 1905 Series, the Athletics sealed the Christy Mathewson legend. "Big Six," as Mathewson was known, whitewashed them three times in one Series—another record not likely to be broken.

CONNIE MACK CHARACTERS

Lots of characters—too numerous to mention—passed through Connie Mack Stadium.

MAJE McDONNELL, WHIZ KIDS COACH AND PHILLIES INSTITUTION: "Jim Tabor, a player in '46 and '47, used to like his tea with a shot in it before the game, or between games. He came in really bombed one night before a night game. Benny Bengough and I worked on him for an hour, trying to sober him up. We gave him a cold shower, walked him outside, then gave him another shower. We didn't want the manager to see him like that. You know he went out and got two hits! Same thing happened with Willie Jones. Puddin' Head [Willie Jones] came in feeling really good one morning about 9:30. The other players weren't expected to arrive till about 11:30, so we worked on him—Ted Kazanski and me. Ted was in the clubhouse every day bright and early after mass. He was a devout Catholic. Whatever we did to Willie, it worked. He went 5-9 in the doubleheader. But you know, at that point, Willie was in his thirties. I think he cut two years off his career by not taking care of himself."

Willie's granddaughter, Janine, works for the Phils at Citizens Bank Park.

THE PHILLIES MOVE ON UP TO SHIBE PARK

Baker Bowl was feeling its age as the twenties roared along. On May 14, 1927, there was another collapse in the stands. A section of the upper deck in right field crumbled and hundreds of fans tumbled down, injuring themselves and fans in the lower section. That marked a rare occasion when the Phils could brag that fans were piled on top of each other. The Phils played some of their games in Shibe Park while repairs were made to their rapidly deteriorating home grounds. By 1938, Baker Bowl had become the butt of jokes, much as the Vet did in its declining days. The Phils were anxious to bolt from the Bowl. They finally did, movin' on up for good to Shibe Park on July 4, 1938. Independence Day. For the occasion, the Phils split a doubleheader with the Boston Bees, losing the opener 10-5, and winning the nightcap 10-2.

Unfortunately, for most of the era, the Phils and A's shared mediocrity as well as a diamond. Both franchises hit the skids in the thirties and forties, a bleak period for Philadelphia baseball. In the Phils' first season at Shibe Park, both Philadelphia teams finished last. In each of the first ten seasons that the clubs shared Shibe Park, one of the Philadelphia teams ended up in last place. Forty percent of the time (in 1940, 1941, 1942, and 1946), *both* Philly teams finished last. We've moved on up. The Phils 86-76 record in 2004 was disappointing. But these days, we complain when the Eagles lose three straight times in *the playoffs*, and the Phil's have consecutive second-place finishes.

The Phillies moved into Shibe Park on July 4, 1938. The next year lights were added and night games became common place.
(Photo: Courtesy of the Phillies)

STADIUM STUFF

PHILLIES BALLPARKS . . . THEN AND NOW

CONNIE MACK STADIUM

• Shibe Park was designed with parking for 200 carriages underneath the stadium. That was considered ample at the time.

CITIZENS BANK PARK

• Citizens Bank Park has parking for 15,500 plus another 5,000 where the Vet used to stand. That's 20,500 spaces for cars, not horses.

In its first two decades, Shibe Park underwent several major modifications. By the time the Phils became tenants, the park had reached its ultimate size. Originally it seated 23,000. There were no outfield seats. Fans stood behind ropes in the outfield in the early years. In 1913, left field seats were added. The biggest change took place in 1925. All the remaining grandstands that had not yet been double-decked were double-decked, and the main grandstand was rebuilt. In 1929, a mezzanine was added and the capacity increased to 35,000. Essentially, that remained the capacity till its dying day.

The left and right field walls met at a virtual right angle in center. The original center field wall was a cavernous 515 feet away. It wasn't shortened to less than 440 feet till 1969. In 1956, the backstop fence was replaced with see-through plexiglas. Since owner Bob Carpenter was married to a duPont, that change seems like a no-brainer. The Phils also purchased the mammoth 60-foot-high scoreboard that once hung in Yankee Stadium. Perhaps the Yankees felt that the Phillies could extend its life by giving the scoreboard far less of a workout than the fifties Yankee dynasty gave it. Anyway, they hung the Ballantine Beer scoreboard with the Longines clock in right center on Connie Mack's Spite Fence. Here's a little more spice for the Spite Fence.

Before 1935, 20th Street residents (20th Street ran parallel to the right field wall) could watch games for free by sitting on their rooftops. Great seats, too—nary an obstructed view because there were no light towers for night baseball at that point. Mack smarted from the lost revenue. He filed a complaint but lost the suit—not the suit he wore in the dugout for fifty years (Connie was noted for frugality, but he did have more than one suit). So Mack capped the original twelve-foot concrete fence in right with a 22-foot-high piece of corrugated iron. Philadelphia called it the "Spite Fence."

STADIUM STUFF

CONNIE MACK STADIUM

Shibe Park changed its name to Connie Mack Stadium in 1953, a year before the A's left town and three years before the Grand Old Man of Baseball died. The change was supposed to have taken place twelve years earlier, but Mack put the kibosh on it.

The city honored the longtime A's manager with a "Connie Mack Day" on May 17, 1941 before the Athletics played the Tigers. Fans that day saw a new plaque hanging on the wall at the 21st and Lehigh street entrance to the stadium. For the grand finale of Connie Mack Day, Shibe Park was supposed to be renamed Connie Mack Stadium. But Mack declined the honor out of respect for his deceased partner Ben Shibe.

George M. Cohan entertained at the festivities. The legendary song-and-dance man wrote a special song for the occasion, "The Grand Old Man of the National Game." Here's an extract:

The grand old man of the National game
And every fan of the National game
Has a feeling of pride for Connie
There are cheers far and wide for Connie
The U.S.A. all rooting for him
The big brass bands all tooting for him
Today in baseball's Hall of Fame
Connie Mack is a grand old name

They don't write them like they used to, do they?

When the Athletics moved on down to Kansas City in '55, the Phillies bought the 46-year-old park for $2,000,000. The Eagles also called it home till 1957, when they moved on up to Franklin Field. The Phils hung around till 1970 before movin' on up to Veterans Stadium.

Between April 12, 1909 and October 1, 1970, Connie Mack Stadium left its mark on city and national history. It brushed the hearts of thousands of Delaware Valley residents who found refuge there from two World Wars, the Depression, an extended Cold War,

Viet Nam, recessions, and other apocalyptic horsemen.

After the Phils moved on up to the Vet, Connie Mack Stadium went to seed. It was used as a dump for a while, but for the most part it lay vacant—an eyesore and blight. A huge fire broke out on August 20, 1971 and persistent problems with vandalism made the place a health hazard. The park was eventually razed. Ironically, the wrecking ball struck in 1976, about the same time as the Phils were hosting the All-Star Game and showing off their still relatively new digs at the Vet to the nation. Few vestiges of Connie Mack Stadium found their way into active service at Veterans Stadium, except for home plate.

Today a church occupies the site where Connie Mack Stadium once stood.

STADIUM STUFF

THE BABE'S BEST

Some claim that Babe Ruth hit the longest home run ever hit. He socked it in the early thirties at Shibe Park. Reputedly it cleared 20th Street entirely and landed in Opal Street, the next street over.

6 FOR 8 SEASON FINALES IN PHILLY

• On the eve of the 1941 season finale, Ted Williams was hitting a precarious .400. His average stood at .39955. Rounded up, that officially made Williams a .400 hitter. Bosox manager Joe Cronin told Williams he could sit out the doubleheader scheduled for the next day. Williams said later that he and coach Johnny Orlando walked all over center city Philadelphia the night before the game. Williams resolved to play both games and put his .400 average on the line. He went 6-8 and upped his average to .406.

• A dozen years earlier, Phillie great Lefty O'Doul also went 6-8 in a season-finale doubleheader, raising his average to an oh-so-close .398 and his hit total to 254, the most ever for a National Leaguer (tied with Bill Terry).

STADIUM STUFF

CONNIE MACK STADIUM

Advertising was banned from Shibe Park/Connie Mack Stadium till the Phillies assumed sole ownership in 1955. That's when the signs and billboards that so many Baby Boomers remember went up.

Signs on the Left Field Wall

Formost Hot Dogs, Goldenberg's Peanut Chews, Wise Potato Chips, Boyd's, Alpo

Signs Atop the Left Field Roof

Coca Cola billboard and Philco billboard

Signs on the Right Field Fence

Yellow Pages sign underneath the Ballantine scoreboard, MAB Paints sign

Sign on the Center Field Wall

Philco sign (where the Philco Daily Lucky Number was posted)

ROOKIES WHO DIDN'T GET SPOOKED ON OPENING DAY

• On Opening Day in 1954 at Connie Mack Stadium, the A's Forrest "Spook" Jacobs became the first rookie to get four hits in his major league debut. On Opening Day, 1990, Delino DeShields became the second.

• On Opening Day at Connie Mack Stadium in 1938, Brooklyn rookie outfielder Ernie Koy homered in his first major league at-bat. In the bottom of the first, Phillie rookie Emmett Mueller homered in his first major league at-bat.

STADIUM STUFF

PHILLIES BALLPARKS . . . THEN AND NOW

OPENERS

CONNIE MACK STADIUM

• Robin Roberts holds the major league record for most consecutive Opening Day starts for the same team (12). He started every Opening Day for the Philadelphia Phillies from 1950 to 1961.

• Bob Feller is the only pitcher in history to toss an Opening Day no-hitter. Roberts came close to matching Feller's feat on April 13, 1955, when he carried a no-hitter for 8-1/3 innings before Giants' infielder Alvin Dark spoiled his bid with a single. A side note on Dark—at LSU, all-time Eagle great Steve Van Buren was Alvin Dark's blocking back.

THE VET

• Jim Bunning started the first opener ever at the Vet, beating Montreal 4-1.

• Steve Carlton started 14 of 15 openers for the Phillies from 1972 to 1986, missing only the 1976 tilt when Jim Kaat got the nod.

CITIZENS BANK PARK

• Kevin Millwood has started two straight season openers for the Phils. Randy Wolf pitched the opening game at Citizens Bank Park.

PHILLIES BALLPARKS . . . THEN AND NOW

CONNIE MACK STADIUM

• The scorekeeper's hole at Connie Mack Stadium was underneath the "Ball" sign in the right field scoreboard. The scorekeeper peered out to get the umpire's ball/strike call.

CITIZENS BANK PARK

• At Citizens Bank Park, the scorekeeper sits in the air-conditioned comfort of the press box close by all the goodies in the press dining room.

MASCOT P.I.

Everyone knows the Phillie Phanatic and some of you probably remember colonial-looking mascots Philadelphia Phil and Phillis from the early years of the Vet. But the first Philly "mascots" actually appeared in the early years of Shibe Park. A hunchback by the name of Lou Van Zandt (and later Hughie McLoon) worked as the batboy for the A's. The players used to rub their hunched backs for good luck before the game. Political correctness is a *good* thing.

BASEBALL'S GREATEST INVENTION

The opening of Citizens Bank Park really underscores the approach-avoidance tug-of-war that plays inside the heads of baseball fans. We don't want to see the game changed in any way, yet we can't resist the glitter of innovation. The Phils new ballpark has been praised—and rightly so—for evoking baseball's warm sense of heritage and tradition, even though in reality, the Phils' new gem is about as far removed from old-timey ballparks as the practice of bleeding patients is from modern medicine (except in some HMO's). The wave of nostalgia that gushes into the subconscious upon entering Citizens Bank Park is about as bona fide as reminiscing with a complete stranger.

Baseball hasn't embraced every technological improvement that's come down the pike. Far from it, and thank God for that. You can hit a baseball a whole lot farther with an aluminum bat than a wooden one, but fortunately, the rule book prohibits aluminum bats. The rule book prohibits corked bats too, but apparently the release of the Spanish-language edition of the rule book was delayed. Pitching machines, the "Iron Mikes" of yore, can propel a ball faster than any human arm. So could Steve Austin in his second career. But baseball hasn't allowed a machine to replace a person. We don't think. Actually, it might be wise to check Barry Bonds and Roger Clemens for wires every so often.

DO SOMETHING RELIGIOUS!

The Phils took their first plane ride in 1950. It was a ride that almost made the Whiz Kids the Was Kids.

MAJE McDONNELL, PHILLIES LEGEND AND FIVE-DECADE EMPLOYEE: "I was a coach on the Whiz Kids when we took that first flight. We flew from St. Louis to Boston to play the Braves. Most of the guys on the team had never flown. It was a prop plane. The plane trip took about four hours, versus 26 hours by train, which was the way we normally traveled. Everything was going fine till we got about a half-hour out of Boston. Then the pilot came on the PA and announced we were running into turbulence and fog and we were going to land by instruments. We landed—but we missed the runway. Somehow the pilot managed to get the plane back on the runway, and everything turned out OK. The whole plane cheered when we stopped.

"The funniest part about the whole incident was Richie Ashburn's. Whitey was really scared. So were a lot of other guys. Whitey yelled to me, 'Maje, do something religious.' I said I would. So I announced I was taking up a collection. I don't think Whitey appreciated my humor till the next day.

"We never minded taking the train after that. We weren't too anxious for our next plane trip."

Some baseball inventions and innovations seem obvious and are quickly embraced. For instance in 1887, Robert M. Keating, a ballplayer himself, *invented* a rubber home plate. Up till that time, plates were placed above ground level made of wood, iron, or stone, and players were suffering injuries. Duh. But seven years before the invention of the rubber plate, on September 2, 1880, the first night baseball game was played in Hull, Massachusetts. Two amateur teams took the field that evening. The pros did *not* follow suit quickly behind. It would take another *fifty-five* years before the first major league night game came about. A major league park did host a night game in the interim. On August 28, 1910, a crowd of 20,000 watched Logan Square and Rogers Park play under twenty 137,000-candlepower arc lights in the White Sox's brand-new Comiskey Park.

The first minor league night game was played in 1930. But night baseball didn't happen in the majors till May 25, 1935. The Phils were the visitors that historic day or night against Cincinnati in Redland Park. Even though the game was well attended and hailed a success, it would be another four years before lights were added to Shibe Park in Philly. Unfortunately (but not surprisingly), both of Philadelphia's hometown teams lost their nighttime home-field debuts. Cleveland topped the A's 8-3 on May 16, 1939 and Pittsburgh bested the Phils 5-2 a couple of weeks later on June 1.

That same year, 1939, the Phils played Brooklyn at Ebbets Field in the first major league game ever televised. Almost two decades earlier, Harold Arlin of KDKA had delivered the first radio broadcast from Pittsburgh's Forbes Field on August 5, 1921. In October of the same year, the first World Series (the Yankees versus the Giants) was broadcast.

Though the pace of change has varied, technology in baseball has been movin' on up since 1876. So has attendance. By their second home game in 2004, the Phils had drawn more fans than their entire inaugural season (55,992). By 1920, thanks to a guy named Ruth who was revolutionizing the game, the bar for baseball attendance had moved on up to a million. Those same damn Yankees drew two million in 1946 as the war ended.

In 1991, Toronto upped the bar to four million fans.

Salaries have escalated too. Ruth made $50,000 in 1923. When asked why he made more money than the President of the U.S., Ruth replied, "I had a better year." Hank Greenberg earned $100,000 all by his lonesome in 1947. That's the same price tag they hung on Connie Mack's "priceless" 1911 infield. Mike Schmidt in 1977 was the first ballplayer to hit the half-million-dollar mark. Nolan Ryan upped that figure to a cool million in 1980, although we doubt that Schmidt had any problems with that. Michael Jack used to say the hardest pitch to hit in all of baseball was a Nolan Ryan fastball. The second hardest was a Nolan Ryan slider.

By 1982, George Foster had doubled Ryan's salary, and in 1990, Kirby Puckett tripled it. Albert Belle and Kevin Brown have since escalated those figures into the stratosphere, and space limitations prohibit writing all the zeros in A-Rod's salary.

Speaking of escalators, that's one of the many innovations in ballparks we simply take for granted nowadays. Citizens Bank Park has three escalators to go along with 17 elevators. The Vet had escalators too, but Connie Mack Stadium had none, nor did any of the earlier parks. We've moved on up in so many facets of the game: exploding scoreboards, center field cameras, pitch velocities on the scoreboard, identification of pitches on the scoreboard, fireworks displays, high foul poles with a fair net, comfortable individual seating, 62 restrooms and 20 water stations, with 2 fountains each in Citizens Bank Park, and food—glorious food everywhere.

But all these great innovations pale to one, the greatest invention in the history of a great game. Every 7th inning, fans all over the country stand up and sing "Take Me Out to the Ball Game." The singers implore someone, anyone—whoever the hell they're singing to—to buy them *some peanuts and Cracker Jacks.* Sorry, but those items are outdated and irrelevant. Everyone associates peanuts more with the zoo, or Buffalo Bob Smith, or ex-Phillie coaches (fifties fans will get the reference) than with baseball. As for Cracker Jacks, how many people have actually ever eaten Cracker Jacks at a ball game? For that matter, how many people have ever actually eaten Cracker Jacks anywhere? Cracker Jacks aren't even sold at Yankee Stadium anymore. Besides Cracker Jacks leave your hands too sticky to handle your cell phone and palm pilot.

THE HOT DOG

Some credit Frankfurt-am-Main, Germany, as the place where the hot dog originated. The people of Vienna (Wien), Austria, disagree. They claim that the term "wiener" proves the hot dog was invented in Vienna. Maybe Mozart ate hot dogs between his movements—symphonic movements of course.

The hottest dog-dispute concerns who was the first one to serve a hot dog on a roll. In 1871, Charles Feltman, a German butcher, opened up the first Coney Island hot dog stand. Charley sold 3,684 "dachshund sausages," as they were called, in a milk roll during his first year in business.

In Chicago in 1893, lots of those dachshund sausages were sold at the Columbian Exposition. That same year, sausages allegedly became standard fare at baseball parks. Supposedly a St. Louis bar owner, Chris Von de Ahe, a German immigrant who also owned the St. Louis Browns major league baseball team, popularized the hot dog as baseball game fare.

Another long-standing hot dog story claims that today's hot dog on a bun was introduced at the St. Louis "Louisiana Purchase Exposition" in 1904 by Bavarian concessionaire Anton Feuchtwanger. Legend has it that Anton loaned white gloves to his patrons to hold his piping-hot sausages. Most of the gloves didn't make their way back to his stand. With the glove supply running low, Anton asked his brother-in-law, a baker, for help. The baker improvised long soft rolls that fit the meat—and, presto, the hot dog bun was invented.

In reality, no one authoritatively knows when and where the hot dog as we know it originated. Nor do we know how the term "hot dog" came into being. Some say the word was coined in 1901 at the New York Polo Grounds on a cold April day. Vendors hawking hot dogs from portable hot water tanks shouted, "They're red hot! Get your dachshund sausages while they're red hot!" A *New York Journal* sports cartoonist, Tad Dorgan, quickly drew a cartoon of barking dachshund sausages nestled warmly in rolls. Ted didn't know how to spell "dachshund" so he substituted "hot dog." Good story. Trouble is, no one has been able to come up with the cartoon.

Other culinary historians say that the term "hot dog" started appearing in certain college magazines in the 1890s. At Yale in 1894, "dog wagons" sold hot dogs in the dorms. Many Phillie fans claim the term was coined the first time Willie Montanez made a putout at first base.

No matter what you call it, a ball game is not a ball game without a hot dog. The same does not apply for peanuts and Cracker Jacks.

No, baseball is about hot dogs. Even with stiff competition from Schmitters (you'll read about them later) and cheesesteaks, hot dogs remain the culinary king. And hot dogs have remained essentially unchanged for a century now. Why tinker with ballpark perfection? Nonetheless, something has improved dramatically in the kingdom of ballpark hot dogs. We're talking about the method of delivery which has moved on up to epic heights. We're talking about what many (many only because the Burgoyne family is very large) consider the greatest baseball innovation ever, the innovation that stokes fans more than a ninth-inning rally in a World Series finale. We're referring of course to the hot dog launcher.

PHANATIC PHILE

THE COTTON GIN VS. THE HOT DOG LAUNCHER

Technological advancements? Mmm . . . let's see. Well to be fair, you have to first give kudos to the caveperson who came up with the wheel. I mean, if it weren't for that woman, whoever she was (it pays to suck up with the phemale phans), Vanna White would be unemployed, though not for too long. Any guy would let her spin his wheel anytime. Next, I guess you gotta give it up for Philly's homeboy Ben Franklin. Any guy crazy enough to stand outside in a thunderstorm *trying* to get struck by lightning is definite mascot material (actually, he is/was Philly's first mascot—the Quaker, even though Franklin wasn't a Quaker). And how about Eli Whitney? Every fifth grader in America has it drilled into his or her brain that Eli Whitney invented the cotton gin. However, not a single fifth grader in America can tell you what a cotton gin is. Nor can their parents, though some swear cotton gin tastes great with tonic and a twist of lime.

For my money, the greatest invention known to man has got to be the Phillie Phanatic's own Hot Dog Launcher.

For all you aspiring mascots out there, here is a little advice: to be a good mascot you've got to come up with ideas that are really stupid. But to be a *great* mascot, you have to be the *first* one to come up with the really stupid idea—so my pet rock promotion idea never cut it (besides, rocks are not good things to put into the throwing hands of rabid Phillies fans). But in the winter of 1996, I came up with a unique idea, although admittedly it wasn't as good as the "how about paying the Phanatic $10,000 a game" idea. (I *know* that one was funny. Bill Giles and David Montgomery laughed their tails off when I brought it up. They never did get back to me on it though. Note to self: remember to ask Bill and David about the ten-grand-a-game for the Phanatic idea.)

The idea I came up with in '96 that was accepted was to launch cooked frankfurters, condiments and all, out of a 3-foot, CO_2-powered fiberglass hot dog. Suddenly the traditional stand-in-line-and-miss-an-inning-and-a-half-while-you-buy-a-hot-dog-at-a-hot-dog-stand way of getting a dog at a ballgame seemed as passé as not swinging at a low outside first pitch fastball in the dirt after the pitcher has walked the three guys ahead of you on twelve pitches. Actually, the idea of the Hot Dog Launcher came about after a series of meetings between members of the Phils' crackerjack promotions team and folks at Hatfield Meats. Hatfield had just introduced the Phillie Phanatic Frank, a smaller, sweeter hot dog for kids. We were brainstorming different ways to promote the new dog. I had just finished taping a commercial that featured the Phillie Phanatic and umpire Eric Gregg, a Philly native. In the thirty-second spot, the Phanatic satisfies Eric's appetite by tossing a Phanatic Frank into the wide-open mouth of the rotund ump, sort of like feeding Audrey in the *Little Shop of Horrors*. I've got to kiss up to those umpires if I want them to cut me any slack when I'm slow getting off the field. Besides, the way to an umpire's heart is through his stomach. At least it is with Eric.

The Hatfield commercial flavored our thinking a bit. We thought: "Maybe the Phanatic can throw hot dogs into the crowd." Nah, too boring. Maybe the Phanatic can use a slingshot and sling hot dogs into the stands. Nah, shooting t-shirts into the crowd with an oversized slingshot was the latest fad. Everyone else was doing it. Nope, we gotta do something unique . . . something stupid. Then it hit me. Let's shoot hot dogs out of some sort of gas-powered cannon . . . or something like that.

The guys in Hatfield's fabrication shop took it from there. And at the end of the fifth inning, on Opening Night in 1996, the first-ever, flying frankfurter went sailing through the air at the Vet. As history-making orbits go, it may not have equaled John Glenn's, but hey, it was a *first*. And it certainly was stupid.

The fans ate it up (so to speak). The new invention caught on quick and got lots of local media attention. Then a funny thing happened. It seemed like the whole country started going hot-diggity-dog crazy. Our phone lines started to light up with calls from other sports teams who wanted the same contraption for their promotions. We got calls from teams in professional hockey, baseball, football and basketball as well as minor league and collegiate teams. Jay Leno and David Letterman were including Hot Dog Launcher jokes in their monologues. A CNN reporter was dispatched to the Vet and put a great video piece together on the hot dog launching phenomenon that was causing such a stir at Phillies games. The video footage, which culminated in a spectacular catch in left field by an ungainly female reporter, played on the news and on an endless loop used country-wide in airports. The Hot Dog Launcher was the cover story in the *Frankfurter Chronicle,* a monthly newsletter dedicated to the majesty of the delicacy known as the hot dog. (I'm not making this stuff up!) It's an even greater honor considering that this particular issue was the "National Hot Dog Month Spectacular" edition. That's kind of like nabbing the coveted cover of the *Sports Illustrated* swimsuit issue. OK, it's not, but I thought I might slip it by.

Where can you go after you've been featured in *Frankfurter Chronicle*? It's an intriguing question, but this book isn't titled *Movin' On Up* for nothing. With our move into Citizens Bank Park, the challenge was to make the Hot Dog Launcher bigger, better and yes, *dumberer*. That meant converting one of our new Gator trucks from a grounds maintenance vehicle into the Phanatic's own hot dog-mobile. It meant ratcheting up the pressure needed to fire a wiener into the crowd from 150 psi to 350 psi (doesn't it sound like I really understand this technical stuff?). It meant converting a three-foot cannon into a six-foot monstrosity.

We had some fun joking with the media that the Phanatic was hard at work in his laboratory concocting a launcher that would shock and amaze but was not to be unveiled until Opening Day at Citizens Bank Park. And it was hard work—relatively speaking, for a mascot anyway. In the past we shot hot dogs from foul territory but with this baby, the dogs fly from fair territory in shallow right and left field. The trajectory of the flying doggie is a majestic sight from the outfield but we had to make sure that the wrapper could withstand the extra psi so that it didn't break up in pieces all over the field. That would result in a clear violation of Rule #1 and Rule #2 in the mascot handbook.

We tested shooting hot dogs in just the tinfoil wrappers but that blew the dog up into confetti. We tried wrapping the dogs in plastic bags, but the aerodynamics got screwed up, and the dogs weren't flying far enough. We tried taping them with athletic tape and then with duct tape (adding to the many uses of man's most useful adhesive) but by the time the hot dog reached the lucky recipient, it was mangled and unrecognizable (but of course still edible to a *guy*—but not a lady). We settled on wrapping the dog in its ballpark foil wrapper in paper, folding down the edges and duct taping the ends, making it look more like a miniature missile than a frankfurter.

On April 12, Opening Day at Citizens Bank Park, the Phanatic, dressed in a chef's hat and barbeque apron, roared out onto the field in the makeshift hot dog-mobile with the six-foot hot dog cannon arcing straight into the air. We tore right in front of Bobby Abreu as he jogged out to take his position in right field. Poor Bobby. In Venezuela, he never had to deal with a guy in a pig costume crashing his quad-runner in front of him and he's never had to encounter naked mascots trying to hide behind him during a streaking demonstration. But this was the new ballpark, a new era in Phillies baseball and the Phanatic was movin' on up and getting more and more stupid!

It was a successful inaugural launch that day. Twelve hot dogs were scattered into various levels of the new ballpark. One dog found its way onto the distant Ashburn Alley. The new launcher had come through with flying colors—twelve fans fed, three million and some change to go.

Leave it to ESPN analyst and incurable hot dog gourmet Jayson Stark to sum up all this nonsense. In the nineties, when Jayson was writing a nationally syndicated baseball column for the *Philadelphia Inquirer*, he reported that the original launcher was "launching so brilliantly, we're surprised NASA hasn't called for tips." He ended the article with words that still ring true: "And the rest of us—we're just proud to be living in America."

Yes, Don King, you're right. "Only in America."

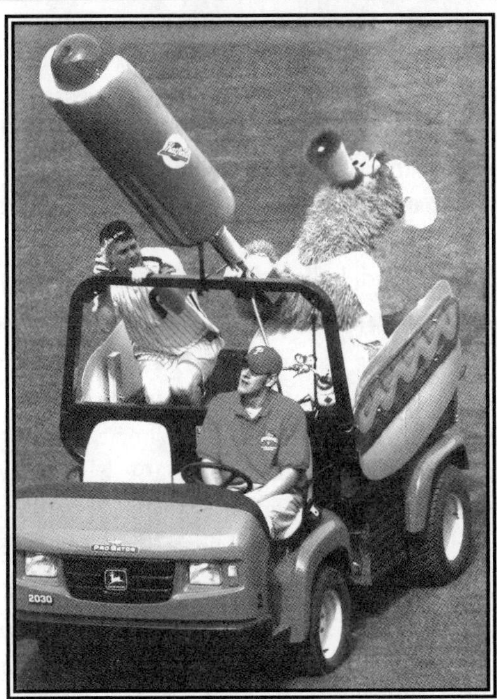

Something Baker Bowl never had—the Phillie Phanatic's world famous Hot Dog Launcher.

(Photo: Rosemary Rahn)

CHAPTER 10

Pocotopaug

"Pocotopaug" was the Native American word for "clear water." The Native Americans chose that name because of the abundant fresh springs along the shore in the area they called home. The non-Native Americans, the group that showed up from Europe a few centuries ago and shoved the Native Americans out of Pocotopaug as well as every other place on their continent, kept the concept but tagged the area with a more Anglo-Saxon name, "Clearwater." The non-Native colonists settled Clearwater in the mid-1830s, but it wasn't until the 1890s that Clearwater gained a reputation as a resort community.

Mention Florida today (or for the past seven decades or so) and every non-Native American in love with our national pastime thinks spring training. To a baseball fan, the Circle of Life begins each year on that glorious, bitter cold, northeast-coast day when pitchers and catchers report to spring training. You read the news in the morning paper, then bundle up and venture out to scrape the ice off your windshield. But you do so with renewed heart. You have the strength to hang in because you know Old Man Winter's days are numbered. No matter what he throws at you, he doesn't have much nasty stuff left. And Old Man Winter has no closer in his April bullpen like Billy Wagner or Eric Gagne.

It took a while for major league baseball clubs to drift on down to Florida and claim it in the name of God and baseball as a spring training haven. Some baseball historians will tell you that spring training got its start in 1886. The Phillies and the Chicago White Sox were allegedly the first pro teams to do spring training. The White Sox went to Little Rock, Arkansas, the Phillies to Charleston, South Carolina. Of course, baseball historians probably dispute that claim because it was hard to distinguish whether a team was barnstorming or training in those days and also because baseball historians dispute everything anyway.

We do know that, by the thirties, most clubs had set up spring-training operations in Florida. Before then, they trained in all kinds of strange places—like Philadelphia. Not that Philadelphia is a strange place—well it is if your only frame of reference is South Street—but in a typical February, Philly is more suitable for ice-skating than base running.

Anyway, in 1901, the Phils and the Athletics both did their spring training in Philly. That one Philly gig was enough for the Phils, although the destitute, last-place A's reprised their 1901 Philly gig in 1919. The Phils did return to Pennsylvania during World War II because of government-imposed travel restrictions. Every major league team stuck close to home during that period, which explains why the White Sox trained in French Lick, Indiana from '43 to '45. Baseball put French Lick on the map long before Larry Bird became its pride and joy. Travel restrictions explain why the rich Yankees trained in Atlantic City and Asbury Park during the war years. As for Philadelphia teams, from '43 to '45 the A's trained either in the balmy climes of Wilmington, Delaware or Frederick, Maryland. The Phils trained at Hershey where at least they had first-class hot chocolate to warm them up.

After the war, the Phils returned to Florida to train at Miami Beach. The following year, 1947, they set up shop for good in Clearwater. They've been there now for 57 years and counting. Only the Dodgers have held spring training in the same place, Vero Beach, longer.

Clearwater is Phillie territory now, although it hasn't always been. Those same Dodgers were the first major league team to colonize Clearwater for spring training. That was way back in 1923. The Bums kept coming back to Clearwater till 1932. After a hiatus of four years, they returned from 1936 to 1940. The Indians (the team from Cleveland, not the rightful original owners of Pocotopaug) showed up in 1942 for spring training and returned again in 1946. Since then, Clearwater's heart clearly belongs to the Phillies.

MAJE McDONNELL, WHIZ KIDS COACH: "Clearwater was two blocks long and two blocks wide when I first saw it in '48. The Beachcomber was the only building in town. We ate there every night. The area was beautiful—the Beachcomber and all of Clearwater. We all loved to go down there every spring. Who wouldn't? Some years, no wives were allowed and they'd all be disappointed. We all looked forward to it so much. In those early years, there was only one bar in town. That's where we went every night. The guy who owned it had a big house outside town. He'd throw a big shindig for all the players when spring training broke every year."

The once-sleepy town of Clearwater has grown by leaps and bounds ever since. The population now exceeds 108,000, and by most accounts, that adds another 108,000 Phillie fans to the rolls. To many, Clearwater is considered Philadelphia South (not South Philadelphia—that's a whole 'nother story).

John Timberlake, Director of Phillies Florida Operations, has been working for the Phils in Clearwater since 1985. John is a Memphis transplant who grew up a Cardinals fan. ("You were either a Cardinal or Reds fan if you lived in that area.") Even more incriminating or at least embarrassing, John became a Braves fan in college in Knoxville. After college, he headed to Clearwater for employment.

JOHN TIMBERLAKE: "I got here in '85 and started working for the Phils in '86. We didn't have the best of teams when I got here. From '85-'90, we never broke .500. We had some good ballplayers come through like Bruce Ruffin, Pat Combs, and Brad Brink but we didn't put winning teams on the field. I loved the job though, loved the people. We had some great times, especially when Granny Hamner was manager here. There are hundreds of Hamner stories. There's even a few I can tell.

"One day I walked in the clubhouse and Granny says to me, 'You pick the lineup today. It doesn't matter who I put in. It doesn't matter what order they bat in and putting Bustamonte at third base is like going to war with a popgun.' Then he starts to complain to me about 'that freakin' pigeon.' What are we gonna do about that freakin' pigeon? I thought he was talking about the pigeons at the park. He kept saying, 'You know the one I mean.' I said, 'No, honest Granny, I don't.' Turns out he was talking about the San Diego Chicken who was performing at the park that night.

"Granny was one piece of work. I don't know how many times I had to call him at the pool hall when he didn't show up at the park. In one way it was easy. We always knew where he was.

"We started to turn things around here in '91 when Lee Elia came to town as manager, although Lee was quite a character himself. But he was the first major league manager we had and you could see the difference."

Quality players like Mike Lieberthal and Kevin Stocker started infiltrating the roster as the operation started movin' on up. Then in 1997, Timberlake started to give oomph to the initiative that really got Clearwater movin' on up.

JOHN TIMBERLAKE: "Clearwater got a new city manager that year. The guy's name was Mike Roberto and he seemed like a dynamic guy. The first week he was in office I met with him about building a new ballpark in town. Our lease was about up with the Phils and one of the big issues in Florida politics at the time was keeping the pro baseball teams that came down here for spring training in Florida. In recent years, we've seen a big exodus of teams to Arizona. We didn't want the Phils to ship out. So in 1999, a Spring Training Retention Bill was passed in Florida and we secured our financing for the new stadium with that bill. Mike Roberto and the city of Clearwater partnered with the Phillies and us. And I'll tell you, Bill Giles and David Montgomery have been great. The Phils, the city of Clearwater, and the state put up money and we couldn't be more pleased with the result."

The result was Bright House Networks Field, which opened in spring, 2004. As Director of the Phillies Florida Operations, Timberlake was wrapped up almost exclusively in new stadium issues for the past few years.

JOHN TIMBERLAKE: "Essentially the way it worked out, the city hired the

Threshers to build the stadium. Building the stadium became my main focus for a few years. I couldn't be happier with the way things are turning out. In the old Jack Russell Stadium, our top year for attendance was 97,000. We sold out all our spring training games this year with the new park. We had 8,000 people here every game. The ballplayers love the new park too. So do the fans. We're leading the Florida State League in attendance this year, averaging about 2,000 people a game. We're expecting to hit about 140,000 for the year and feel that we can reasonably reach 200,000 in the near future. The ballpark has been a great thing for the city, the baseball fans, and the organization."

Bright House Networks Field is something to be excited about. It's a showcase with a Florida feel. Fans can walk along the concourse at the park and never miss the action on the field. Sounds a lot like Citizens Bank Park.

JOHN TIMBERLAKE: "We *are* like Citizens Bank Park. The field has the same dimensions as the new field in Philly. The only difference is the height of some of the fences. And yes, like Citizens Bank Park, Bright House Networks Field turned out to be a hitter's park. Balls have been flying out down here."

"As for our park hot spots, there's a place called Frenchy's Tiki Pavilion that has really caught fire with the locals. Frenchy's has a Happy Hour every Wednesday, game or no game. It seats about seventy people around the bar, and there are five tiers. Besides Frenchy's, there are three party suites upstairs. They've been getting a lot of action too. And the berm is great."

The berm is the grassy area beyond and above the left and right field fences.

JOHN TIMBERLAKE: "College kids come in, throw beach towels down, and catch rays while they watch the game. The berm area is about 14, 15 feet wide. Older people love it too. It's a relaxing way to watch a game and it adds another dimension. It gives that laid-back Florida feel that the whole Clearwater area has. And the berm goes right up to the concourse so everyone there has access to it. You can walk 1/3 of a mile all around the park and never lose sight of the game."

Now that Bright House Networks Field is completed, what does John Timberlake do to fill his day?

JOHN TIMBERLAKE: "I have to organize spring training, our draft mini-camps, our Gulf Coast League activity, and the fall instructional leagues. I manage the Carpenter Complex (there are four fields at the Carpenter Complex named after Mike Schmidt, Steve Carlton, Robin Roberts, and Richie Ashburn) and I'm still involved with the daily operation of the minor league team."

That minor league team is the Threshers. Yes, Clearwater has moved on up in 2004 in every way. New stadium, new name, new manager—new attitude. The team no longer calls itself the Clearwater Phillies. It's now the Clearwater Threshers.

JOHN TIMBERLAKE: "The name change has done wonders. To be honest, we hadn't been very successful over the years, so we wanted to change our name to something that had more pop. I guess we really wanted a new start and with the new stadium, it seemed like the time to make changes. It worked. It's amazing what the name change has done for our concessions and sales. We sold more merchandise in a half-year than we ever sold in a full season. We had a lot of fun coming up with the name Threshers too, although I can't pinpoint one path that led to that name. We held fan contests. We hired a firm called Plan B Branding from San Diego to work with us. They insisted that it's much more effective for branding to have a single name for a team. They were right.

"As for choosing the thresher shark for a nickname, we liked the name. So did many of our fans. It has a good sound. We also found out the thresher is the third most popular shark in the Caribbean [we didn't ask John what the most popular one was, but we suspect it's the loan shark, at least in Miami]. The thresher slaps its prey with its tail, then comes around and eats it. The thresher just seemed like a good choice."

In case you're wondering, the thresher is not a man-eater, which makes them more lovable than lawyers. It's a cool-looking shark with a tail as long as its body. The tail is shaped like the scythe that the Grim Reaper carries. The Clearwater Threshers have designed a cool logo that is multi-colored with red, a couple of blues, sand, and peach. The Threshers' motto or catchphrase for the season is "Can you survive the attack?"

You can survive anything in Clearwater. The Phils have survived almost six decades down there and they look to be settled in for many more. Phillies players, past and present, have developed an allegiance to the city that rivals what many Philadelphians feel for Ocean City (NJ of course), Wildwood, and Cape May. Many of them buy second homes or condos there, or they relocate entirely. The list includes Robert Person, Lenny Dykstra, Jim Fregosi, Larry Andersen, and others. Curt Schilling had a place and later sold it. If you spend time boating in Clearwater, you might see the "Two In the First" floating somewhere in the waters. You probably guessed that's Von Hayes' boat, named for his June 11, 1985 feat when he became the first major leaguer in history to wallop two homers in the first inning.

The Clearwater Threshers have done as Von did, figuratively. In the first inning of their existence, they've hit a home run or two with Bright House Networks Field. Clearwater Chamber of Commerce head Mike Meidell estimates that visitors to the Clearwater area have increased 10 to 15 percent because of the new stadium complex so there's no reason to believe Clearwater and its Threshers won't be movin' on up for a long, long time to come.

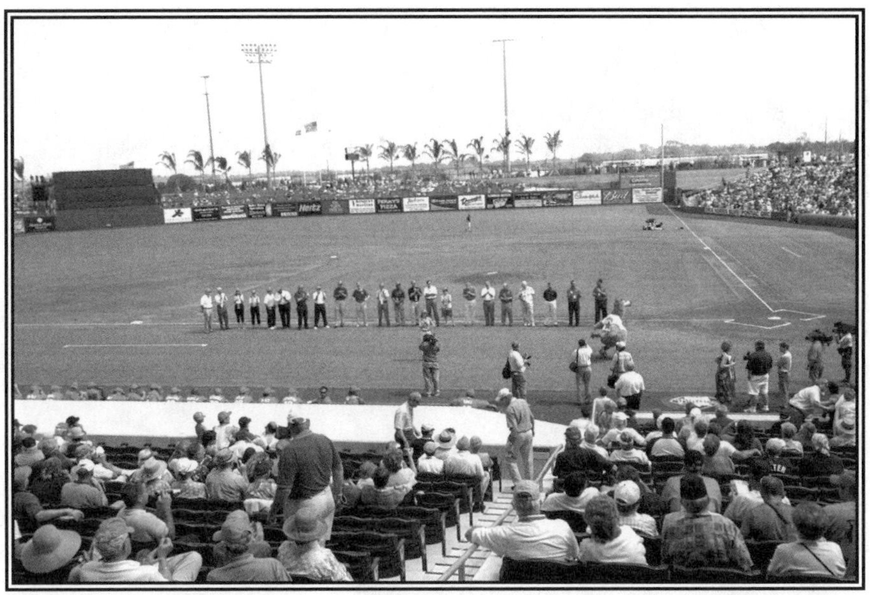

The Phillies played their first game at Bright House Networks Field in Clearwater on March 4, 2004 against the Yankees. Clearwater has been the spring training home of the Phillies for 57 years and counting.
(Photo: Courtesy of the Clearwater Threshers)

PHILS SPRING TRAINING SITES SINCE 1901

1901	Philadelphia, PA
1902	Washington, NC
1903	Richmond, VA
1904	Savannah, GA
1905	Augusta, GA
1906-08	Savannah, GA
1909-10	Southern Pines, NC
1911	Birmingham, AL
1912	Hot Springs, AR
1913	Southern Pines, NC
1914	Wilmington, NC
1915-18	St. Petersburg, FL
1919	Charlotte, NC
1920	Birmingham, AL
1921	Gainesville, FL
1922-24	Leesburg, FL
1925-27	Bradenton, FL
1928-37	Winter Haven, FL
1938	Biloxi, MS
1939	New Braunfels, TX
1940-42	Miami Beach, FL
1943	Hershey, PA
1944-45	Wilmington, DE
1946	Miami Beach, FL
1947-	Clearwater, FL

LENNY'S

Head down bustling Highway 19 in Clearwater and you spot Lenny's. Every Phillie and Phillie fan spots Lenny's at some point and ends up going there frequently. The place specializes in belly fillers—old-fashioned breakfasts that keep cardiologists in Cadillacs. They've been serving chowhounds from the Phillies since 1980. Everything at Lenny's relates somehow to the Phillies. The walls are sagging under the weight of gobs of Phillies photos and memorabilia. Most of the staff are diehard Phillies fans. Of course there are exceptions, like waitress Melodie Sorenson. Melodie didn't know baseball and soon found that knowledge of the game helps enormously in relating to the clientele. Dutifully, she put herself on a crash baseball course by reading *Baseball for Dummies* last spring (the IRS allows her to deduct the cost of that book as a job-related expense), just so she could make intelligent conversation with her customers. With the fanatics that frequent Lenny's, she'd better study hard. In fact, next time you visit Lenny's, ask Melodie what a grand slam is. If she directs you to the nearest Denny's, tell her she needs to re-read the book.

PHANATIC PHILE

MASCOT SURVIVAL GUIDE TO CLEARWATER

Clearwater and Clearwater Beach have changed a lot since the days when Maje McDonnell was throwing BP (batting practice, not gasoline) to the Whiz Kids. Here's one mascot's opinion of the Best of Clearwater. Feel free to tear out this page as a survival guide for your spring training adventure and don't forget to pack the suntan lotion.

Best Breakfast—Lenny's—You gotta love the free pastry basket and the Phillies stuff hanging on the walls.

Best Grouper Sandwich—Frenchy's—They've been catching their own grouper and serving it up grilled, blackened, Cajun and Caribbean-jerk style since 1981. With four locations on Clearwater Beach, there's no excuse not to try one!

Best Sunset (Happy Hour style)—The deck at the Palm Pavilion—With live music humming in the background and pretty bartenders catering to your every whim (that's reasonable whims), you'll think you died and went to Margaritaville.

Best Sunset (Family style)—Pier 60—With a nod to Key West's famous Mallory Pier, this nightly celebration features arts, crafts, and street per formers. The kids love the playground, too.

Best Buffet—Shephard's—You might need to be wheeled home after a dinner at the impressive, all-you-can-eat spread at this local landmark on the beach.

Best Local Bar—Tommy Duff's—Need a little taste of a South Philly taproom? This unassuming bar on Island Way Estates fits the bill and will fill your Frank Sinatra fix too.

Best Surf and Turf—Create your own at the **Island Way Grill**. They'll fire up your filet and roll your sushi right in front of your eyes.

Best Place to Go Dancing—The Wave—Twenty-something crowd? Check. Techno dance music? Check. Flashing lights? Check. Disco ball? Check. Looking for a hip club scene? It's all here.

Best Family Restaurant—Leverock's—At the base of the bridge that leads to Sand Key, this huge family restaurant will make you feel you're back in Somers Point at the Crab Trap.

Best Restaurant that Oozes Phillies History—Bob Heilman's Beachcomber—Just about every Phillies player, manager, owner, and scout has walked through the doors of this legendary establishment—and walked out a few pounds heavier.

PHANATIC PHILE

SC-AIR JORDAN

It was love at first sight. I loved Clearwater since the first time I laid eyes on it. What's not to like? I'll admit it. I do everything possible to wangle Clearwater junkets, short of begging. Well, OK, it depends on how you define begging. Maybe I do a little begging too. Begging seems to work for those kiss-ups on *The Apprentice*. Truth is, I love to perform in front of the Clearwater crowds. To be honest, everyone at the Phillies loves Clearwater and Clearwater crowds. That's why, when the Phillies brass sat down with the architects who designed Citizens Bank Park, they gave the architects clear-cut instructions: give the new ballpark an intimate, old-time feel and sight lines that make fans feel like they're part of the action no matter where they are in the park. In other words, make the Phils' glittery new baseball temple minor league-ish. Funny how things come full circle, isn't it? Folks who love minor league baseball have long been preaching that the down-home feel in their smallish stadiums is

PHANATIC PHILE

what baseball is all about.

I agree with all that. But on the other hand, I also loved performing at the cavernous Vet. I loved standing on the home team dugout and getting 60,000-plus in attendance to scream at the top of their lungs and make the earth shake as a game stood in the balance. But I've gotta admit, there *is* something special about a minor league atmosphere.

For years, I've been traveling around the country visiting minor league teams from small towns. I've Phanaticked for teams from the Pacific Coast League to the Cape Cod League, to the Carolina and Gulf Coast Leagues and everywhere in between. These towns really get jacked up for a visit from the Phanatic. They promote my appearance on the local radio and TV stations. Highlights of the Phanatic in action often air as the lead sports story that night. Admittedly, in some of these places I'm competing for the headlines with cow-milking contests, so back in Philly it would be considered a "slow moos" night. But some of the minor league promotions are big league. On a four-city tour of the Mexican League one year, one newspaper's front-page headline read: *"Presentacion De La Mascota Màs Popular De Las Grandes Ligas—Fil-Fanatico!"* I'm not sure what that means, but, since I didn't see the word gringo anywhere, I figured I was OK, or at least safe. En route to the game that night we passed a car with a giant megaphone strapped to the roof blasting out to all within earshot (which stretched from skiers in Utah to penguins at the South Pole) to come and see "*el loco Fil-Fanatico*!" Apparently, Mexico does not have Philly's "PH" problem..

In the minor leagues, when I come zipping out onto the field, there's a no-holds-barred mentality that doesn't exist in the big leagues. Heck, I could burn the stadium down and not worry too much because I'd be on to my next gig in another town. The players get into the act big time down in the bush leagues by taking turns wrestling the Phanatic. Sometimes the whole squad charges the Phanatic and leaves me a little wobbly. Of course, I take retribution to a whole new level down there. I may steal a glove and toss it over the fence or into the crowd. Sometimes I'll turn the grounds-crew hose on the bench and soak down the guilty parties from head to toe. I might heist a player's cap and return it to him only when he bows down and kisses my sneaks. Somehow I'd never be able to get any of that to happen with Barry Bonds, unless we were making a commercial, in which case Barry would get a Mercedes full of cash and I'd get Arby's coupons (buy a sandwich and get a free Coke), Greyhound tickets back to Philly, and an official thank-you letter from the sponsor.

The umps in the minor leagues are a lot looser too. They give me more time between innings so I can kick some extra dirt on home plate or dish out an extra goose as needed. I even "assist" the third base coach giving signs, another big-league no-no.

The laughs from the minor league crowds seem more light-hearted. So do the players. These guys endure long summers with little pay. They spend weeks at a time in cramped buses at all hours of the day and night. Many have no shot at making it to the Show. Many more get tantalizingly close and have their hearts broken. A visit by the Phanatic brings a little bit of the big leagues to these guys. They've told me that and it's gratifying to hear. They ask questions about life with the Phillies. They have their pictures taken with the Phanatic, and sometimes they even ask for an autograph.

On June 4, 1994, a night I'll never forget, it wasn't me who was signing autographs. I was one of the thousands hoping to *get* an autograph. Whose? Why the Birmingham Barons' very own Michael Jordan. You remember that little detour in Mike's basketball career, don't you? Bored with being the best basketball player on the planet, Michael announced his desire to play baseball and soon had major league teams jockeying to ink him to a minor league contract. That's right—a minor league contract. In our heart of hearts, most of us knew it was a million-to-one shot that Jordan would make it to the big leagues. BUT what a windfall it would be for the minor league franchise that did land Jordan! Michael finally signed with the White Sox and jetted off to their Class AA Birmingham Barons squad, along with half the paparazzi in professional sport.

Michael Jordan wasn't moving on up. He was moving on *down* to the minor leagues. The Barons clubhouse that I walked into that night was unlike any I had ever seen. These guys were practically giddy and having more fun than a human being, well baseball player (not that they're not human beings—you know what I mean), should be allowed to have. Here they were in baseball's version of purgatory, scraping along with their $15-a-day meal money on the one hand. But on the other hand, they were playing baseball with the most recognizable athlete in the world and enjoying the perks that went along with it. They played to a packed house every night. Every night the national media would air Jordon. Players that previously couldn't get a free Happy Meal at McDonald's were suddenly being interviewed by the ESPN's and CNN's of the world on a nightly basis. Michael had reached into his own pocket (not too deep either) and bought a luxurious bus for the team. That bus was the envy not only of every team in the Southern League, but also of half the rock bands on tour. The Barons players were surrounded by celebrities—no, I'm not referring to me. But as a for instance, the night before I arrived, ex-Philly b-ball star Charles Barkley stopped in the clubhouse to see his longtime friend and to sign autographs for the players.

Even though my partner, Mr. Gordon, keeps me grounded by reminding me: "Phanatic, you are *no* Charles Barkley," I was stunned that the players gathered around me like I was a rock star.

One guy reached for a pen and handed it to me.

"Hey, Phanatic, I've been a big fan of yours for a long time. Can I get you to sign a baseball for me?"

My heart (and ego) swelled with pride. Imagine! This guy, who might be a star in his own right someday, was asking me for my autograph. I'm thinking, "He'll probably put my John Henry right next to Michael's and other celebrities on his mantle. Some day I too can bid for it on e-Bay."

"Sure," I said as I reached for the pen. Suddenly, my hand was shocked with a charge of electricity, sending voltage ripping up my arm and right shoulder. The hairs on my arm were standing at attention. I had fallen for the old electric buzzer/pen gag.

The players who had gathered around me—and set me up so perfectly—erupted into laughter.

"Gottcha! Barkley fell for the same gag last night!" the player taunted.

Barkley . . . They did *that* to Barkley and the clubhouse is still standing? I mumbled something about paying a hospital visit to the survivors and headed out to the playing field.

Out on the field, I paid the obligatory homage to King Michael as he was introduced before the game. I got down on my knees and bowed down to him in my best Wayne and Garth "I'm not worthy" pose and quivered like a nervous teenybopper at a Justin Timberlake concert (that's *Justin*, not *John* Timberlake—John Timberlake would never perpetrate a clothing malfunction like Justin did) while Michael was shagging pre-game flies (for Melodie, the waitress at Lenny's—that doesn't mean the insects were bad that night—read your book). As His Airness trotted back to the dugout, I held out a piece of paper and a pen to him, and mimed a big rejection.

But I saved the best for later. When Michael was warming up in right field in the top of the sixth, the opening chords of Mariah Carey's hit, "Hero," blared over the loudspeakers.

I zoomed onto the field on an ATV from just behind first base—not as the Phillie Phanatic, but as Phyllis Phanatic. This is pretty technical stuff, but I'll do my best to explain the sophisticated process of transforming into Phyllis Phanatic. I realize most of our readers are not in show biz, so I'll try to go slow.

Step one: take the Phillies jersey off the Phanatic. Step two: throw on a black-and-white checkered dress. Step three: add a matching baseball cap with a long blonde ponytail and *Voilà!* I'm Phyllis. Yes, I know. Pretty clever, pretty sophisticated stuff—and yet they give the Oscar for best makeup to *Lord of the Rings* for a ham-and-egger like Gollum!

Phyllis made a beeline to Michael. Now, it has always been my policy not to tell the intended "victim" before the game that he is about to be "Phanaticized" (maybe I should have waived that guideline in the case of Tommy Lasorda . . . nah, I don't think so). It's better to ambush somebody to get his true reaction rather than stage something and get a phony reaction. Besides, if the Barons' bigwigs knew I was planning a *tête-à-tête* with Michael between innings, they would have put the kibosh on it real fast. Come to think of it though, they haven't asked me back.

When Michael caught his first glimpse of this green, cross-dressing mascot loping towards him, his shoulders dropped. A look of resignation came across his face. He was toast and he knew it. With nowhere to run, the great Michael Jordan stood there in his knee-high socks and black pinstripes and took it like a man.

I jumped off the bike as Mariah crooned, "*and then a hero comes along / with the strength to carry on . . . .*" What a sight! Michael Jordan, the epitome of "No Fear," was scared. Phyllis Phanatic twirled and spun around Jordan until she was dizzy. Phyllis stood behind His Airness and rubbed up and down his body, finishing off the light petting session with a pinch to his derrière. Then Phyllis grabbed his leg like an obsessed female stalker. The stoic Michael Jordan just let me go through the whole ordeal.

Completely embarrassed, Michael took a deep breath as Phyllis' furry snout smothered his face. It was the signature Phanatic smooch and it brought the house down. I fell to the ground with a thud, overcome. Then I staggered to my feet to give Michael one last gift. I raised Phyllis' skirt up high for a full monty flash—*Girls Gone Wild*—Alabama style!

A month later, Michael announced that he was hanging up his spikes for good. It was back to the hardwoods, where mascots are not as free to walk, but basketball megastars are—they can walk all they want without an infraction as long as they finish with a spectacular dunk (I'm kidding, Mikey).

Pound for pound and inch for inch, Phyllis Phanatic proved Michael's toughest challenge, doing what Shaq and other NBA behemoths never could. Phyllis brought out the quit in Michael Jordan. She was just too much mascot for him.

CHAPTER 11

PHILLY KIDS MOVIN' ON UP

According to Philly writer Rich Wescott's research, 350 ballplayers from the Philadelphia area have moved on up to the big leagues. We appreciate Rich's efforts and don't intend to add to his opus. You can read about each of those Philly natives in Rich's book, *Native Sons—Philadelphia Baseball Players Who Made the Major Leagues.*

Philly has produced some monster diamond talent. Just say Roy Campanella and you've proved your point. But throw in Cheltenham's Reggie Jackson and the area's heritage is irrefutably established. Then add Eddie Stanky, Bucky Walters, and Jimmy Dykes for good measure. And to show the area is still pumping out talent, mention Hall of Famer in waiting Mike Piazza.

But neither Campy nor Reggie nor (alas) Mike Piazza played for the Phils. And in this book, we're celebrating Philadelphia and the Phillies and the inscrutable bond between the two. So we'll talk about a few cases where Philly kids have moved on up to their hometown team. As always, we're not trying to cram 122 years of history into 250+ pages (which is why we don't specifically cover the 1980, 1983, or 1993 Phils—and they certainly moved on up! However, there's a great body of work already written on them). So in this chapter we'll look at two Philly kids who moved on up. We'll also look at a local wellspring of major league talent. And we'll reach way back to Ty Cobb's era. Some unwitting Philly kids moved on up to the big leagues for one day thanks to the Georgia Peach. Eat your heart out, Moonlight Graham, or is it Maharg ("Graham" backwards)? You'll find out about that shortly.

Movin' on up to the Phillies—for any Philly kid, you'd think it couldn't get better than that—feeling the love from your brothers in the City of Brotherly Love. But that's not always the case. The sometimes baffling bond between this city and its teams at times can morph a kid's dream into a nightmare or at least a restless night or two. Wilt Chamberlain found that out. So did Del Ennis.

DEL ENNIS

The name Delmer Ennis doesn't sound like a Philly name. Maybe that's why Del Ennis and the Phillie fans never struck a comfortable peace. Occasionally the Phillie faithful loved him—after a three-homer day like he had on July 23, 1951, for example. Or on any of the nine occasions when he socked two or more homers in a game. Or on August 28, 1948, when he blasted three round-trippers in a doubleheader. Otherwise, Del got booed lustily on those approximately seven out of ten occasions when he—and every other great hitter who ever lived—failed. Mike Schmidt knows a little about the love/hate relationship with the hometown customers. Mike Schmidt is a name that *does* sound like a Philly name. It even sounds like a Philly brew. But Schmidty is a Dayton, Ohio native.

No, it wasn't his peculiar first name that did Del in with the locals. Del was a Philly guy. Everyone in Philly knew that all too well. He was a bruiser. He had a powerful physique. He *looked* like a power hitter. Therefore he was expected to succeed . . . every time.

There weren't many bona fide, homegrown, Quaker City stars who played for the Phils before Del's arrival. That would seem to make him the toast of any town—just not Philly town.

Del Ennis starred at Olney High School at Front and Duncannon Streets. He was scouted and signed by Phillies scout Jocko Collins in 1942. Ennis was raw when he came up through the system. He was raw when he got to the Bigs.

PAUL ROGERS, WHIZ KIDS AUTHOR: "Del told me he was really naïve and really unschooled in baseball when he was signed. That's an understatement. He was a young kid when he was signed and he was still a real homebody. The Phils arranged for him to play for Trenton. It wasn't a Phillie minor-league affiliate, but the Phils struck a business relationship with them so Del could play there and live at home. The club sent a driver to pick him up and take him home each game. Hard to believe, but Del told me he didn't even know what a batting average was when he first broke in. Military service helped to season him. He played a lot of baseball in the service, and learned how to play the game."

Ennis learned the game well enough to cop the 1946 Rookie of the Year Award. (It wasn't the same Rookie of the Year Award that's recognized today. That award was first presented in 1947 and Jackie Robinson was the first recipient.) Del burst onto the National League scene that year, batting .313 with 17 homers and 73 RBI's.

His RBI totals moved on up steadily the following two seasons as he plated 81 and 95 respectively. In 1949, he broke the century mark in RBI's for the first time. He would fail to reach 100 RBI's only one season between 1949 and 1955. He was traded to the Cardinals after the '56 season, and drove in 100 for them.

Philly native and Onley High School product Del Ennis is the only Phillie who appears in the team's all-time top ten list in singles, doubles, triples, and homeruns.

(Photo: Courtesy of the Phillies)

Going into 2004, Del Ennis still ranks in the Phillies all-time top ten in games played, at-bats, hits, runs, RBI's, singles, doubles, triples, and home runs (where he places second behind Mike Schmidt). It may surprise his detractors (if any remain) that Del Ennis is not in the all-time Phillie top-ten for strikeouts.

Del occasionally came across to some fans as dour. His fifties teammates insist he was anything but. He was one of the team's top practical jokers. His favorite target was coach Benny Bengough, a Yankee catcher in the twenties. Bengough was a roly-poly guy who loved his cigars. Ennis was forever booby-trapping Benny's cigar box with exploding cigars. Ennis also made a habit of taping over the number 11 on Bengough's uniform. Benny used to wander onto the field till fans pointed out that he was out of uniform, or in but out of uniform.

Whiz Kid fans remember three popular uniform numbers on the team. Richie Ashburn's number one is the most recognized and revered. Richie, who was born in Tilden, Nebraska, became a Philly boy by extension. He settled in Philly during his playing days and never left. After his playing career, he boosted his hometown popularity rating with a few decades of broadcasting. Robin Roberts wore number 36—a well-chosen number in that it approximated the complete games he'd turn in each year. Del Ennis wore number 14. All three jerseys are retired. The hitch is that number 14 is retired in honor of Jim Bunning.

If you head out Lancaster Avenue to Villanova's Pavilion, you'll notice that jersey #54 hangs from the rafters. Howard Porter wore number 54. Porter starred on the '71 Wildcats who came oh-so-close to winning a national championship. Ten years or so later, Ed Pinckney wore number 54. Pinckney did succeed in leading his team to a championship. The jersey is retired in *both* their names.

The Phils ought to consider double-duty honors for jersey #14. Few Phillies have matched Ennis' production over a 10-year span. Not many Phillies have even *had* a 10-year span. The guy's achievements are compelling. Ennis is one of only two Phils to win the *Sporting News* Rookie of the Year Award, and one of only seven Phillies who *ever* won a Rookie of the Year Award. He was chosen to three All-Star teams and started twice. Only Schmidt, Roberts, and Luzinski have started more. Ennis is the first Phil ever to start in left field and the last Phil ever to start in right field. He's the only Phillie to start at two different positions in the All-Star Game as a Phillie. We think of Ennis as a power hitter, yet in three of the nine seasons that he and Richie Ashburn were teammates, Ennis hit for a higher average than Ashburn. Whitey is the only Phillie outfielder in the franchise's history who played more games than Ennis. The most convincing statistic, however, is that Del Ennis is the *only* Phillie who appears in the team's all-time top ten list in singles, doubles, triples, and home runs. Mike Schmidt, Ed Delahanty, Chuck Klein, and Sherry Magee do not. Only Del Ennis.

Despite those impressive numbers, the hometown fans never embraced Del Ennis. His widow Liz says Del never understood why.

LIZ ENNIS: "Years after he retired, people used to come up to him and say, 'Hey Del, I used to boo you all the time when you played!' Richie Ashburn heard a guy say that to Del one night and he couldn't believe it. Del told Richie it happens all the time. Del never understood why people booed him like they did. An old friend of ours named Stu told us that people used to gamble during games at Connie Mack Stadium. They'd bet on everything. So if Del didn't hit a home run when they bet he would, they'd boo him. We don't know if there's any truth to it, but it helped Del deal with the booing. I can tell you that the booing really bothered him."

Philly can be a tough stage for any performer. Del played here in front of rough crowds for ten years before being traded to St. Louis for Rip Repulski and Bobby Morgan.

LIZ ENNIS: "Del drove in more runs than Stan Musial that first year after he was traded. Stan was Del's best friend in St. Louis. They roomed together. But Del never wanted to play anywhere else but Philadelphia. He was crushed when he got traded. He had no inkling it was going to happen. He was at dinner at Wis Randolph's house. Wis was a VP with the Phils and a good friend of Del's. In fact, Wis is the one who helped Del get a job at the Philadelphia Stock Exchange in the off-season. When Del came home, the phone rang. It was a sportswriter telling him he was traded. Del said, 'No, that can't be. I was just over Wis' house.' The writer said he read it on the AP wire. Del couldn't believe it. It really hurt him. And it had to be one of the worst trades the Phillies ever made. Del was never happy in St. Louis. He wanted to be in Philly so he rented a place in St. Louis and never even considered relocating there."

As it turns out, Del played only two more seasons. He hung it up after getting fewer than 100 at-bats with two different teams in 1959. After retirement, Ennis built a 36-lane bowling alley in the Hollywood section along Huntingdon Pike near Rockledge. He operated the lanes for several years.

LIZ ENNIS: "Del was a Philly person. He stayed here his whole life, and never wanted to live anywhere else. He coached the Penn State Ogontz team from '75 to '78. In fact, he took the team down to Florida one spring and they played Robin Roberts' team. Robbie was coaching the University of Southern Florida at the time. Del was proud. His team won. He couldn't believe they did because the Florida kids had been playing baseball all winter long. But no, Del wanted to live here in Philly. We raised our six children here: Del Jr., Donna, Liz, David, Debbie, and Darlene, and they all still live in the area."

Del did enjoy his treks to Florida. What Philadelphian doesn't in mid-winter?

LIZ ENNIS: "Del was part of the Phillies Phantasy Week from the beginning. They started the whole thing in 1983 and Del was one of the first ex-players who was part of it. He loved it. We both did. He was there every year till 1996. In fact we were preparing to go when Del passed away in February."

The Ennises had other reasons to go to Florida besides Phantasy Camp.

LIZ ENNIS: "We used to love to go to the dog races. We got so interested we decided to buy some dogs ourselves. We found out that a lot of people are against dog racing because the animals are sometimes mistreated and discarded after they can't race anymore. So we talked to a number of people down there and located a reputable trainer. Then we purchased a dog. We promised we'd find a good home for the dog when he couldn't race anymore. Well, the dog had a litter of four puppies. One of them turned out to be a champion. We bred that dog and had a litter of ten. We named each one after a Whiz Kid. The guys got a real kick out of 'their dog,' especially Bubba Church and Richie Ashburn. Richie was always calling to find out how his dog was doing. When Del died, I got out of dog racing entirely. I made sure I found good homes for each and every one of our dogs."

Del Ennis died of complications associated with diabetes in February 1996.

JOE KERRIGAN
HERE'S TO OUR CRUSADERS

Here's to our Crusaders
Onward to victory
We're out to win, boys
Ever loyal, ever loyal we will be
—Father Judge High School Fight Song

Detention. They call it "jug" in Philadelphia Catholic high schools. At least they do at Father Judge High. Jug is supposed to straighten kids out, give them time to get their head on straight instead of spinning like Regan's. Basically when you do something wrong, a priest or teacher tosses you in jug. When the school bell rings for dismissal that day, you can't do your normal after-school routine like hanging out at the Yard or Summerdale or Rhawnhurst Playground. Instead, you go and sit quietly for an hour and twiddle your thumbs. Occasionally you might grab a book and read something that changes your life.

JOE KERRIGAN: "At [Father] Judge, jug was usually held down in the cafeteria in the basement [we noticed that Joe seems to know a lot about jug]. For some reason, they held jug *in* the library this particular day. I looked around and picked up a book by Bob Feller on how to pitch. One of the pitches he covered was a forkball. I started to mess with it and wound up using it, adding it to my repertoire. Eventually it became one of my big pitches. That book gave me a big start. Actually I never returned it to the library. How much do you figure I owe them at this point?"

We're not sure, Joe, but we are sure the fine Oblate fathers at Father Judge would gladly knock out a quick estimate for you.

The Oblates and everyone else at Father Judge knew the Kerrigans. The school was filled to the rafters in that era. There were about 4,000 boys, give or take a hundred. Joe's brother Eddie played football and baseball for the Crusaders. Eddie, a member of the class of 1957, was good enough to merit induction into the Pennsylvania Sports Hall of Fame. Unfortunately, he passed away not too long ago. Another older brother, Tom, was a star catcher for Judge. But it was his arm that wowed the scouts.

JOE KERRIGAN: "Tommy played in the minors after his Father Judge career, and yes, he was best known for his arm. There used to be an annual pitchometer contest in the city. Tommy won it his senior year. The finals were at Connie Mack Stadium. Bobby Wine was one of the Phillies involved in the contest. He threw something like 88 mph. But Tommy hit 93 mph in one of the heats.

"Tom played in places like Spartanburg and Bakersfield for about three years in the

Phillies organization. Andy Seminick was one of his managers. When he came back from that experience, he taught me so much. I benefited from the transfer of knowledge. I was a young teen at that point, and the things he taught me gave me an advantage in my early career."

Joe Kerrigan grew up in St. Martin's Parish and played basketball and baseball for the Frankford Boys Club. He credits some of the good coaching he got there for his move on up in baseball.

JOE KERRIGAN: "I was active at that Boys Club. They were great with the kids. As a young kid, basketball was my best sport. I can still remember my first midget A baseball game in Philadelphia's old Sandlot Sports Association. We played at Juniata Park. I was nine, I played center field, and I struck out three times on nine pitches."

Kerrigan blossomed into a topnotch hurler at a young age. He pitched on the varsity all four years at Judge, where he played under manager Henry King (*not* Hank King, the Phils' major league advance scout). Joe also played basketball for Judge under legendary Philadelphia coach Hank Greenberg.

JOE KERRIGAN: "We played in the Palestra in the Catholic League championships in front of huge crowds. We also played at places like North Catholic where the spectators were right on top of the court. Those games helped me to not be intimidated by major league crowds. In 1971, Judge played St. James for the championship at the Vet. Our game was scheduled before the Phillies game. It was Helmet Day, so the fans started arriving early. We got locked up in a tie game and it went into extra innings. They had to call our game so the Phillies game could get started. So by the time we cleared the field, there must have been 30,000 people in the stands. All those experiences prepared me to play in front of major league crowds."

The Father Judge-St. James game was an historic first for the Vet—the first non-professional event ever staged there. Unfortunately for the Crusaders, St. James won the championship the next day.

JOE KERRIGAN: "We played an entire game the next day. Our coaches campaigned to push it off a few extra days so I could pitch again. But it didn't happen and we lost."

Kerrigan's successes at Judge earned him a scholarship—half baseball, half basketball—to Temple. At Temple, he played basketball for the freshman team and pitched for the varsity.

JOE KERRIGAN: "I really got noticed when Temple made the College World Series, and I won two games. I ended up getting drafted eighth in the country, so I turned pro at that point."

Kerrigan played in the minors till 1976 when Montreal brought him up,

JOE KERRIGAN: "I was fortunate to come up with Montreal. They had some older players who taught younger guys like me what to do, how to act—all those things. You don't see that much in today's game. It was a great period in my life and a great period for baseball. My big thrill was pitching at the Vet against the Phils. I struck Dick Allen out to end the inning. I walked back to the dugout and felt like king of the world. Allen and Johnny Callison were my childhood idols. The really amazing thing though was that, when I pitched in that Catholic League championship game in '71, Woody Fryman was a Phillie. He happened to be sitting in the dugout watching the game. I'd come back to the dugout after pitching each inning and he'd be encouraging me, saying 'Good job, kid.' Then five years later when I struck Allen out, Woody was in the Montreal dugout at the Vet. We were teammates. And he was still encouraging me."

Joe played four years in the majors. He finished with an 8-13 record, 3.89 ERA, and 15 saves.

JOE KERRIGAN: "Basically I just ran out of bullets before I was thirty. I threw too much. I think it comes down to that. I used to play catch with anyone who wanted to throw the ball. That's *not* the way to do it. I'll tell you this much, I learned that lesson the hard way. I try to pass that experience and knowledge on to our young guys now and hope they listen.

"I wanted to stay in the game after my active career. I was prepared to take a $12,000 a year job as a minor league coach. I was only 29 at the time. I was actually doing more catching than pitching down in spring training. I learned a lot more about pitching from that vantage point. But Bill Virdon brought me on as bullpen coach in Montreal in '83."

Joe stayed on till 1986 before taking a series of assignments as a minor league pitching coach in different cities. He returned to Montreal as a pitching coach from 1992 through 1996, then he headed to Boston where he served as pitching coach till 2001. Near the close of the 2001 season, he was promoted to Bosox manager—only to be ousted the following spring training. He finished out the 2002 season outside the lines. Joe was the post-game analyst for Phillies games on Comcast SportsNet. Occasionally he served as color commentator.

On October 11, 2002, Joe accepted Larry Bowa's offer to become the Phillies pitching coach. Joe has the key assignment of bringing along a promising set of young Phillie arms.

Joe Kerrigan is another Philly kid and Phillies fan who moved on up to the hometown team. Joe's now moved on out from the Phillies and there's a rumor going around that a librarian from Father Judge has been dunning the Phillies pitching staff for a long overdue book and a pretty sizable late fee.

WILDCATS MOVIN' ON UP

Major League (Maje) McDonnell, former Phillies coach and seven-decade employee, isn't the only Villanovan to go major league. The Wildcats have sent 53 of their own into professional baseball. No one made it real big. They have no Howie Long in the baseball program. No one made it big, but 53 pro baseball players movin' on up from a local program isn't shabby.

They've been playing baseball a long time at Villanova. On May 2, 1866, Villanova played its first-ever game. By any reckoning, it was an auspicious start—a 74-9 trouncing of the Central Club of Philadelphia. Prominent on that first 'Nova roster was a guy named Dennis McGee. He was listed as catcher and president of Villanova B.B.C. (Baseball Club). Dennis McGee changed his surname to Mack, even before Cornelius McGillicuddy did. McGee/Mack was Villanova's first baseball player to turn pro. In fact, he was the first Villanova athlete to turn pro. McGee played for the Philadelphia A's (not Connie Mack's A's), the St. Louis Browns, and a few other clubs between 1871 and 1883, the year the Phils arrived in the Quaker City.

Amherst and Williams are credited with playing the first intercollegiate game a decade or two after Abner Doubleday (as lore has it) invented the game. Villanova played its first true intercollegiate game a few decades after the Amherst-Williams tilt. Following their first game against the Central Club in 1866, Villanova had been playing local, non-collegiate clubs from Philadelphia and the Main Line. In its first intercollegiate scrape, Villanova walloped Haverford 66-21 in a lopsided affair. McGee hit a home run in that contest.

Way back in 1905 or so, Villanova took baseball seriously. They had a paid baseball coach, Frederick J. Crolius, whose career record was an impressive 108-65-5.

Art Mahan, who played for the Phils briefly in 1940 (pitching one inning would be considered brief by all but Moonlight Graham), was another Wildcat who made the majors. (By the way, Villanova didn't adopt the Wildcats name till 1929.) Mahan coached from 1950 to 1973. He compiled a 236-169-5 log and sent several players to the majors, including Frank Kreutzer, Bruce Howard, and Frank Fernandez.

JOLTIN' JOLTIN' JOE'S UNBREAKABLE RECORD – TAKE 9
A ST. JOE HAWK MOVES ON UP

New York fans usually rub Philly fans the wrong way. And vice versa. Ty Cobb shared Philly's sentiments about the Big Apple. Actually, Cobb shared those sentiments about the whole world. On May 16, 1912, Cobb's Detroit Tigers took on the Highlanders in New York (the Highlanders changed their name to the Yankees shortly afterwards).

One of the New York fans that day was working Cobb over brutally—so much so that the Georgia Peach sought out the Highlanders' manager, Harry Wolverton. Cobb warned old Harry that he was running out of patience with the heckler. Cobb reminded the NY skipper that the home team has the responsibility of maintaining order in the ballpark. Wolverton didn't take care of matters to Cobb's satisfaction.

Cobb decided to take matters into his own hands. When the heckler acted up again, Cobb went Randall "Tex" Cobb on him, and sprinted to the stands where he pummeled the guy. American League President Ban Johnson suspended Cobb indefinitely without a hearing.

The rest of the Tigers sent Johnson a telegram protesting his action and refusing to play "in another game until such action is adjusted to our satisfaction. He [Cobb] was fully justified as no one could stand such personal abuse from anyone. We want him [Cobb, not the heckler] reinstated or there will be no game. If players cannot have protection, we must protect ourselves."

Detroit's next scheduled game was in Philly against the A's. Johnson threatened the whole Tiger team with suspension if they didn't play. He threatened to fine the Tigers $5000 for each game they didn't field a team. That made the Detroit owners figure they needed to field a team. The day before the game, Detroit passed the word around to Philly-area colleges and semi-pro teams that they were recruiting a standby squad immediately. Consequently on May 18, the morning of the Detroit-Philadelphia game, a motley crew of local ballplayers showed up at the Aldine Hotel, the Tigers' headquarters in Philly. Detroit manager (and one-time Phillie) Hugh Jennings recruited eighteen "ballplayers" for possible service.

That afternoon, the Tigers suited up while their team spokesperson Jim Delahanty (Ed's brother—the Delahantys are the largest baseball family in the game's history; five brothers played big league ball) spoke to the umpire-in-chief. Delahanty was told Cobb's suspension was not lifted. When so informed, the Tigers removed their uniforms (in the clubhouse, not on the field—this was no Madonna concert) and returned to their hotel.

GROUCHING TIGERS, HIDDEN DRAGONS

More like Hidden Hawks, actually. Enter the Tiger replacement squad. There were no Drexel Dragons on the Detroit Tigers emergency squad, but there *was* a flock of St. Joe's Hawks. There was also a boxer named Graham, who would not use his real name (no it wasn't "Moonlight") on the lineup card. He insisted on performing under the mirror image of his name, Maharg. So besides the Tiger rebellion, the game even featured a boxer rebellion of sorts.

Bill Leinhauser, a Philly cop, took Cobb's place in center field. He went 0-4. A guy named Ed Irvin, a local sandlotter, blasted two triples in three at-bats. The A's rapped 25 hits off substitute pitcher Al Travers. Jack Coombs, who went on to win 21 games that year, was the A's starter. Boardwalk Brown, who won 13 in 1912, gave him a breather, and also surrendered the substitute team's two runs. The game ended 24-2.

After the game, the question, of course, was, "Now what?" Cobb saved the day. He convinced his teammates, who had resolved to stick to their guns, to play. A New York newspaper, *The Daily American*, conducted a poll. Fans overwhelmingly supported Cobb's reinstatement, 3,013 to 1,167. Johnson relented and showed good faith by reducing Cobb's suspension to ten days and his fine to $50. The Tigers returned to the diamond. The emergency squad returned to their Quaker City routines. Only Maharg ever played again. Four years after the debacle, he resurfaced with the Phillies for one more at-bat. That gave him a career total of two at-bats. And no hits.

Travers was the big story, however. He set a major league record that day—a record that no one is shooting for, a record that will be very hard to break. Travers, a St. Joe's theology student at the time, yielded all 24 runs—14 of them earned. Not surprisingly, that's the most runs ever given up by one pitcher in a complete game. If Travers was looking for a sign that day to show him what to do with his life, to show him his true calling, the Almighty's message could not have been clearer if he had parted the Delaware and shown the shell-shocked pitcher (of sorts) the way to the Camden Riversharks (nine decades before they arrived). The Almighty could not be that cruel to Camden, however.

Travers heeded the Almighty's message and moved on up to a greater calling. He became a Roman Catholic priest. Father Travers died in Philadelphia on April 19, 1968. He was just short of his 79th birthday.

CHAPTER 12

WHIZ KIDS

At the dawn of the forties, the Phils had a *long* way to move on up. They were one of the major leagues' poorest franchises. Poor as in poor performers. Poor as in no money. Too often, the Phillies had to sell off good players for cash just to stay afloat.

That practice went way back to 1918 when the Phils dealt Pete Alexander to the Cubs. From 1915 through 1917, Alexander had won 94 games. That was *19* more games than the next highest total in baseball, and 29 more than the third best. You may have heard of the two guys he topped: Walter Johnson and Babe Ruth. That gives you an idea of Pete's stature when he packed his bags for the Windy City.

A parade of stars continued to exit Philly as the likes of Chuck Klein, Kirby Higbee, and Lefty O'Doul followed in Alexander's footsteps. O'Doul used to tell the story that, after he led the NL in batting with a .398 average and set the still-standing NL record of 254 hits in a season, Phillies owner L. Charles Ruch offered him a $500 raise—modest, well chintzy, even in the early throes of the Depression. Ruch was only around a couple of years before Charles Nugent took over. Nugent continued the penury program with such moves as dumping Dolph Camilli off to the Dodgers after Camilli posted back-to-back .300 seasons. Camilli went on to win an MVP in 1941.

Nugent sold the club to William Cox in 1943. Cox lasted less time than a Britney Spears marriage. Baseball Commissioner Judge Kenesaw Mountain Landis unceremoniously deposed him for betting on games. Cox wanted to be a hands-on owner. He insisted on getting involved with the daily operation of the team. The Phils manager was future Hall of Famer Bucky Harris. Bucky bucked the owner and Cox resented it. The Steinbrenner Rule worked even then: when a feud brews between an owner and a manager, bet on the owner. Cox fired Harris. Harris, however, scuttled off to the press and ratted on Cox, saying the Phils owner was betting on games, *Phillies* games. Cox soon joined his deposed manager in the ranks of the unemployed.

At that point, Bob Carpenter Sr. purchased the club. Carpenter, a successful businessperson, was married to a duPont. For the first time ever, the Phillies organization had some cash. Bob Carpenter Sr. put Bob Carpenter Jr. in charge of the ball club.

The young Carpenter developed a business plan and set a direction for the previously rudderless franchise. He instituted things that had been lacking for decades. The heart of Carpenter's plan was to develop a Phillies minor league feeder system. To do so, Carpenter opened up his checkbook to woo young phenoms the Phillies' way. If you pay them, they will come.

Under Nugent, the Phils didn't have any minor league affiliates. Hard to believe, Harry . . . but true. Carpenter adopted a sound, businesslike approach to building and sustaining a successful franchise. Carpenter was committed to scouting, signing, and developing young talent in the minors. He brought the single-A, Eastern League Utica club into the Phillie fold. Utica enjoyed some superb seasons during Carpenter's halcyon years. Stan Lopata, Granny Hamner, Richie Ashburn, and Putsy Caballero all played for Utica. They should have been playing in AAA, but Utica was basically the Phils' only option at the time.

By the late forties, the Phillies started to reap dividends from their aggressive scouting operation. Del Ennis was the 1946 *Sporting News* Rookie of the Year. Richie Ashburn copped the same award two years later. Robin Roberts signed for a hefty (for its day) $25,000 bonus. (ROBIN ROBERTS: "That was the best offer I got. That's how I became a Phillie. I lived in Illinois and didn't grow up as a Phillies fan. But the Phils offered me the most money.") Curt Simmons was even more highly sought than Robin. All but one team in baseball was wooing him but the Phils outbid them all and inked the lefty with the herky-jerky motion for a $65,000 bonus.

LITTLE EGYPT IS QUEEN FOR A DAY

PAUL ROGERS, WHIZ KIDS AUTHOR: "The Phillies went all out to get Curt Simmons. Curt told me the Phils scheduled a game in his hometown when they were trying to sign him. It was probably the biggest day in the history of Egypt, Pennsylvania (a little town not far from Bethlehem and Nazareth, Pennsylvania). Fifteen of the sixteen major league clubs were bidding for him.

"Simmons pitched against the Phils in the exhibition game that day and his high school almost won the game. I think Curt said one of his outfielders misjudged a fly ball and the Phillies scored and won. After the game, the Phils and the whole town went back to the school for a barbecue."

And Aunt Bee cooked some apple pie . . . . Yes, a baseball team dropping into a sleepy little town for an exhibition game is as unlikely these days as Roger Clemens dropping in for Sunday dinner at the Piazzas. In any event, the ploy worked. Curt Simmons became a Phillie, and a great one at that.

MONEY MATTERS

Robin Roberts was still attending Michigan State when the Phils signed him. Classes were in session and Robbie was allowed to report late to spring training. He had been playing basketball for Michigan State at the time. When he got to spring training, he experienced some leg problems, and got off to an unimpressive start. One day he was walking behind owner Bob Carpenter, unbeknownst to Carpenter. Robbie overheard Carpenter lamenting: "Yeah, looks like I blew another $25,000." Robbie knew Carpenter was referring to Robbie's bonus. Roberts was distraught.

Cy Perkins, Phils coach and Robbie's mentor, reassured Robbie: "Don't worry. They'll get their money back ten times over by the time you're done." And so they did.

Cy Perkins was an ex-A's catcher who played for the Athletics for virtually his entire 18-year career. He was Mickey Cochrane's backup on the '29 and '30 A's. Cy wasn't a star, but he related well to young ballplayers.

A few years after Roberts' first spring training, the Phils were planning to get rid of Perkins. Roberts pleaded his mentor's case and was told the Phils couldn't afford Cy's $7,500 salary. Robbie offered to pay it himself, but the offer was declined.

Carpenter hired Herb Pennock, former Yankee pitcher and Hall of Famer. Pennock was one of the Bronx Bombers' top pitchers in the Murderer's Row era. His nickname was the "Knight of Kennett Square," where he was born and raised. Pennock started his 22-year career as a Philadelphia A in 1912, before being shipped off to Boston in Connie Mack's colossal 1915 talent sell-off.

Pennock was a seasoned, well-respected "baseball man" in the late forties. He hired Eddie Sawyer, a longtime coach and manager in the Yankee farm chain. At one time, Sawyer had been a promising player himself. Unfortunately, he hurt his shoulder in the minors. The injury forever hindered his throwing so Sawyer was promoted to player-manager while still a young player. When Pennock lured him from the Yankees, Sawyer was assigned to Toronto, a Phillies farm club in the International League.

In mid-season 1948, Phillie pilot Ben Chapman was axed. The Phils named their trainer, Dusty Cooke, as interim manager. Trivia buffs toss that one out as the first and last time a trainer ever managed a big-league squad. Robin Roberts says it wasn't quite that way.

ROBIN ROBERTS: "The league limited you as to how many coaches you were allowed to have. Dusty was actually a coach, but I think we called him a trainer because we would have had too many coaches."

Cooke did well in his brief stint. He "retired" with a 6-6-1 record before being replaced in another unconventional move. Eddie Sawyer was brought in as manager despite having no previous major league experience either as a player or manager. Sawyer took over the reins but kept Chapman's entire staff.

PAUL ROGERS: "Richie Ashburn told me that Chapman got the players together and read them the riot act. He told them if things didn't improve, they'd all be looking for a job. It was only a few days afterwards that Chapman was looking for a job himself."

Ben was an old-timer, notorious—no embarrassing—for his lack of racial tolerance. Chapman was the key culprit in the Phillies' abominable treatment of Jackie Robinson when Jackie came up to the majors. Suffice it to say, Ben lacked the wherewithal to handle young ballplayers. And the Phils had plenty of young players in 1948.

In 1948, the Phils were showing some flash for the future. Rookie Richie Ashburn hit .333, finishing second to Stan Musial (though a distant 43 percentage points behind). Del Ennis walloped thirty homers. Granny Hamner and Andy Seminick were establishing themselves as solid performers. Curt Simmons and Robin Roberts were about to blossom. The Phils climbed out of their perennial basement and finished sixth in 1948.

FOUL BALLS

Pitchers weren't the only ones hurt by Richie Ashburn's storied prowess at hitting foul balls. On August 17, 1957, Alice Roth, the wife of Philadelphia *Bulletin* sportswriter Earl Roth, was sitting in the press box along third base. Ashburn slapped a foul into the press box that broke her nose. The game was interrupted momentarily as they attended to Mrs. Roth and started to carry her off on a stretcher. On the very next pitch, Ashburn hit her again in the thigh. Richie visited Mrs. Roth in the hospital several times during her stay.

That's not the most bizarre story Richie told about hitting fouls. Whitey was playing pepper with Robin Roberts one morning before the gates to Shibe Park opened. Robbie lobbed one in and Ashburn took a full rip at it. One of the ushers had let his friend in before the gates opened. They were both sitting in the first row where the box seats ended. The ball caught the guy flush in the eye. They put him in an ambulance and they told Ashburn later they couldn't save the fan's eye. There was a lawsuit and the guy was awarded a big settlement.

The next year, Richie was going into the park and the guy approached him wearing a patch over one eye. As Richie used to tell the story, he was expecting the guy to pull a gun on him. Instead, the guy shook Whitey's hand and said, "Mr. Ashburn, I just wanted to thank you. I got more money than I ever would have seen in my life. Plus I get a helluva monthly disability check. I'll never have to work again and I see just fine with one eye. God bless you!"

The '50 pennant winners had what may have been considered their epiphany in 1949. The Fightins were foundering at 19-21 on June 2. They were down 3-2 when Del Ennis opened the eighth inning with a first-pitch home run. Andy Seminick stroked the following pitch out of the park. The fireworks had just begun. Before the third out was recorded, Seminick had homered again, and Willie "Puddin Head" Jones and pitcher Schoolboy Rowe had each added round-trippers. The Phils had set the record for most home runs in an inning.

What the record book does not show, however, is that both Granny Hamner and Willie Jones just missed home runs in the same inning. Jones did connect for one homer, but in another plate appearance in the same inning, a shot off his bat fell short of a four-bagger by inches. Puddinhead was "held" to a triple. Granny Hamner also missed a circuit clout by a foot, and had to settle instead for a two-bagger.

The Phils chased former teammate Ken Raffensberger from the mound that inning. Raffensberger was far from an easy mark in 1949. He went on to win eighteen games that year, third best in the NL. When the final scorecards were turned in on June 2, 1949, the Phils had roared to a 12-3 blowout.

Seminick's two-homer inning was a seminal moment for the Whiz Kids of '50. The June 2 power surge jettisoned a suddenly confident Phillie juggernaut into an unexpected third-place finish.

The young 1950 squad reported to Clearwater, Florida feeling like they were contenders. Their '50 lineup was essentially the same as '49 with the exception of first base. A deranged female admirer shot first baseman Eddie Waitkus during the 1949 season. Miraculously, Waitkus returned to full duty in 1950 from his rehabilitation, batting .284 and winning the AP Comeback Player of the Year Award.

WAITKUS AND McNABB

The chilling events of June 14, 1949 shaped Eddie Waitkus' life and inspired a best-selling book that became the classic movie, *The Natural.*

Eddie Waitkus had been out to dinner that evening with a few teammates. When he returned to his room at the Edgewater Beach Hotel in Chicago, he received a note from a Ruth Steinhagen. The note pleaded with the Phillie star to come immediately to her room as a matter of extreme urgency. The note indicated that she was from Waitkus' hometown. When Waitkus showed up at her door and entered her room, she blasted him in the chest with a secondhand .22 she purchased the day before. Steinhagen was dangerously obsessed with the Phillie first baseman—an obsession that started while Waitkus was playing for the Cubs. She had decorated her bedroom with articles about him, studied his every move, and made his uniform number, 36 (Waitkus' number with the Cubs—Roberts, of course, wore 36 for the Phils), her lucky number.

After she shot Waitkus, Steinhagen, in effect, saved his life. She immediately called the front desk and informed them that Waitkus had been shot. Waitkus was on the brink of death but managed to hang on. He underwent four subsequent operations and then went to Florida in the off-season to rehab with Phillies trainer Frank Wiechec.

Eddie Waitkus had come up briefly as a 20-year-old with the Cubs in 1941. He left for World War II, returned to the diamond in 1946, and rolled up three consecutive solid seasons as a Cub, hitting .304, .292, and .295 respectively. He was traded to the Phils in 1949 and was batting .306 when the shooting occurred.

Eddie came back the following year and manned first base the entire season when the Phils won the flag, batting an astounding .284 after being almost fatally wounded. He was honored as "Comeback Player of the Year" at the Philadelphia Sportswriters Banquet. From then on, Eddie's fortunes declined. He spent a few uneventful years with the Phils before a short stint in Baltimore. He returned to the Phils briefly before hanging up his spikes for good in 1955.

After his playing career, Eddie worked in Philly for a while at Wanamaker's department store in the men's clothing section. He later suffered an emotional breakdown and ended up living alone for several years near Harvard University in Boston.

Eddie was not the first ballplayer to be shot by a deranged female fan. On July 6, 1932, Billy Jurges, a second-year shortstop for the Cubs, was shot at the Carlos Hotel, also in Chicago. Jurges' would-be assassin was a showgirl, Violet Popovich Valli. Valli was freed on bail and the case was dismissed for want of prosecution.

Jurges recuperated that same year and helped his team win a pennant.

Both Waitkus and Jurges played key roles in helping their teams win pennants. Waitkus' pennant came the year after the shooting. Jurges' was the same year.

In the World Series, both Waitkus and Jurges stroked three singles and a double. Their teams both squared off against the Yankees and both lost four straight. Jurges, however, went on to play fourteen more years in the big leagues, splitting time between the Cubs and Yanks.

Chicago is a toddlin' town. They ought to write a show about it.

Postscript on *The Natural*: Eddie Waitkus' shooting inspired author Bernard Malamud to craft his story about Roy Hobbs. A Boston Brave named Bama Rowell provided another inspiration for the story. Rowell was the first player at Ebbett's Field to smash the Bulova Clock on May 30, 1946, an incident which morphed into exploding lights in the book and movie. Rowell started for the 1939 Boston Bees (the Braves were called the Bees in '39 and '40; they went back to being Braves in '41). He only hit 19 homers in his career, and batted .240. He was a Phillie in 1948. When Waitkus arrived in '49, Bama was gone, so the two inspirations for one of baseball's greatest epics just missed being teammates.

THE UNNATURAL SHOOTING OF EDDIE WAITKUS

Lyrics by Chuck Brodsky

Ruth Ann Steinhagen, who was an office typist
Went to a baseball game at Wrigley Field
With a couple of her girlfriends, it was innocent enough
Ruth Ann's future though that day would be revealed

Some girls she didn't know were yelling, "Hey you, funny face"
To a player who was within shouting distance
And there stood her Adonis in the form of Eddie Waitkus
Who was blissfully unaware of her existence

It was April 27th of 1947
Ruth Ann blew a circuit in her brain

The 27th of every month would be the anniversary
Of the time she first saw Eddie Waitkus play

Every Saturday & Sunday she would ride the El to Wrigley
Sit halfway up the line behind first base
'Cause that was his position and those were the closest seats
Where she could have the best view of his face

Ruth Ann collected articles & photographs of Eddie
She slept with pictures of him in her head
She learned some Lithuanian, to better understand his roots
Made a shrine to him beside her bed

Ruth Ann's world was shattered the day Eddie was traded
To Philadelphia & for many days she cried
She wrote him letters often and she phoned & left him messages
But never once did she get a reply

On the north side of Chicago, the Edgewater Beach Hotel
When the Phillies came to town that's where they stayed
Ruth Ann made her reservation a month ahead of time
On her calendar she ticked off every day

A room service daiquiri & a couple of whiskey sours
All three of which she nervously consumed
While waiting up for Eddie who was out late having dinner
After starring in the game that afternoon

Ruth Ann bribed a bell hop to leave a note for Eddie
Urging him to come up to her room

1297-A, Ruth Ann wrote on hotel stationery
That had the faintest trace of her perfume

"It's extremely important I see you as soon as possible...
It would be to your advantage to let me explain"
It was very nearly midnight and the Phillies had a curfew
Eddie just kept staring at the name

Ruth Ann was the same name of the woman Eddie dated
But what on earth would she be doing in town?
She surely would've phoned first before coming to Chicago
Eddie rang the elevator down

A tall girl answered the door, said Ruth Ann stepped out for a minute
Eddie sat down by the window in a chair
Ruth Ann said, "I've got a surprise for you"—it was a pawn shop rifle
Eddie stood up & said "Baby, what have you got there?"

"Baby, why'd you do it?" asked a bleeding Eddie Waitkus
Over him a lifeless Ruth Ann stood
"You've been bothering me for two years," Ruth Ann said to Eddie
"And if I couldn't have you then nobody could"

Ruth Ann phoned the desk clerk to say she had shot Eddie
That's probably why he didn't bleed to death
"Baby, why'd you do it?" he kept asking from the stretcher
Struggling for every precious breath

Ruth Ann told the detectives how she'd planned on stabbing Eddie
And how then she would've taken her own life

But when Eddie sat down in the chair a stabbing was impossible
So she used the rifle instead of the knife

Ruth Ann did three years in a mental institution
They set her free when they said she was cured
And after four operations Eddie Waitkus did recover
At least you see his name in all the old boxscores

But Eddie took to drinking . . .
He turned into an angry man
People often wondered, and there were a bunch of rumors
Just how well he knew that crazy star-struck fan

Mike Goliat was pressed into duty as a second baseman in 1950—his only complete year as a starter in a brief 4-year career. Goliat, who, like Andy Seminick, passed away early in 2004, rose to the challenge. He surprised everyone by hitting 13 homers (out of a career total of twenty) and contributing a lot of clutch hits. The pitching staff reinvented itself. In 1949, the Phils' top pitchers were Ken Heintzelman and Russ Meyer, each of whom won eighteen. In 1950, these two staff aces of the previous campaign accounted for only 12 wins—against *20* losses. Robin Roberts and Curt Simmons, the greatest pitching tandem in Phils history, assumed the role of staff aces. Roberts won 20—the first of six consecutive seasons he won 20 or more. The year 1950 was also the first of six consecutive seasons that Robbie or Curt Simmons started the All-Star Game. Simmons won 17 in 1950 before getting called up for the Korean War.

Rookie Bob Miller looked like the Whiz Kid with the most whiz. He started the season with 8 straight wins. Unfortunately, he hurt his back hauling a suitcase at 30th Street Station and finished the campaign 11-6. Miller was never again the same. He fluttered and flashed till 1958—all in a Phillies uniform—before calling it quits.

The other pitching hero of course was the bespectacled Jim Konstanty, who came out of nowhere (he was 9-5 in 1949, but no one expected the big season he had in 1950) to win the NL MVP as a reliever. Konstanty pitched 152 innings, went 16-7, and saved 22 games. Konstanty's 22 saves were not unheard of. Joe Page tallied 27 in 1949. Page saved 17 and 16 in 1947 and 1948 respectively. But aside from Page and the legendary Firpo Marberry, who saved an unprecedented 22 games in 1922, no one else had ever topped 20 in one season.

TONIGHT'S STARTING PITCHER AND TOMORROW'S AND NEXT DAY'S . . .

Phils manager Gene Mauch took a lot of heat for starting only Jim Bunning and Chris Short during the disastrous end-of-the-season skid in 1964. Eddie Sawyer made Mauch look like a piker in 1950. Sawyer found the cupboard bare of pitchers at the end of the '50 campaign. Curt Simmons had been called up to duty in the Korean War. Bob Miller had hurt his back carrying a suitcase at 30th Street Station. Bubba Church was struck by a ball off the bat of Ted Kluszewski and was injured and ineffective. The Phils were down to Robin Roberts. The future Hall of Famer pitched three of the last five games and five of the last eight as the Phils won the pennant.

SOME RUSS MEYER LEGENDS

They called him the Mad Monk. After listening to Paul Rogers, Maje McDonnell, and other Whiz Kids tell Russ Meyer stories, we're convinced the Phillies' Mad Monk might freak out Rasputin himself.

The "Mad Monk," or "Rowdy," grew up in the little Midwest town of Peru, Illinois and came up to the major leagues with the Cubs in 1946. He was traded to the Phils along with Swish Nicholson and Eddie Waitkus in 1949, and immediately became the ace of the staff with 17 wins. Russ got hurt in 1950 and his stats slipped to 9-11, and a 5.30 ERA. He rebounded nicely in '52 with 13 wins and a 3.14 ERA. The rest of the staff overshadowed his comeback, however. Led by Robin Roberts' 28 wins, the staff compiled a glitzy 3.07 ERA. Three of four starters had ERA's under 3.00. Meyer found himself in Brooklyn the next year and responded with a 15-5 mark. He stayed with the Boys of Summer a couple of summers before bouncing from Chicago to Cincy to Boston and finally to KC.

The Mad Monk notched 94 career wins, but is remembered more for his temper than his stats.

ANGER MANAGEMENT

The Phillies lost doubleheaders to the New York Giants on Wednesday and Thursday in the final week of the '50 season. Following those back-to-back *off days*, the Phils had a much-needed *day off* on Friday. A group of Phils, including the Mad Monk, took a busman's holiday that Friday and headed to the ballpark. Some photographers noticed the group of Phils and started taking shots—photos that is. Meyer took offense and went Sean

Penn on them. He ended up punching a photographer and smashing his camera. Cops had to break up the fracas. Meyer got out of it. He had to pay for a new camera. (Sean Penn paid a greater price. He had to continue living with Madonna.)

WAITING FOR THE SHOE TO DROP

PAUL ROGERS, AUTHOR: "Russ told me he was knocked out of a game early one day. He stomped into the clubhouse and went ballistic. He took his baseball shoe, and fired it skyward. The shoe stuck in the ceiling. 'Best fastball I threw all day,' Meyer recalled years later. Anyway, he stood on a chair and tried to pull the shoe out of the ceiling."

It was wedged in like a cleated Excalibur. Unlike King Arthur, Meyer couldn't pull it out.

PAUL ROGERS: "When the Phils came into the clubhouse after the game, the guys got a big laugh. Someone or some ones eventually pulled the spike out, but the clubhouse guys couldn't get the mud and grass stain off the ceiling. It stayed up there all season long."

PLUNKING RICHIE

Richie Ashburn used to tell a story about the Mad Monk as a Dodger. Facing Ashburn one day with the bases loaded, Meyer stewed as Whitey fouled off about eight pitches. Finally, Meyer plunked Ashburn on purpose, forcing in a run. Ashburn said Meyer later told him, "We had a big lead. That run didn't matter." To Meyer's credit, the Dodgers did win the game.

Whitey had his problems with other pitchers too. He used to tell a funny story about Sal Maglie, or the Barber as Maglie was tagged. Sal used to shave batters close with his pitches. Ashburn said the Barber was so notorious that Maglie once threw at him in the on-deck circle. Richie said: "I was just watching him warm up and getting my timing down. Maglie threw one at me and growled, 'No one times my pitches.'" Sal was more barbarian than barber.

THE MEYER RULE

It was the "Game of the Week." Russ Meyer was on the mound for the Dodgers and . . . it just wasn't his day. Umpire Augie Donatelli had just called ball four. Russ disagreed. Actually, he went Lou Piniella on Augie. Rushing up to the plate, he jawed at Augie and bumped into him before the chest bump became part of pop culture.

Donatelli ejected him immediately, which only ticked the Mad Monk off more. Meyer stood his ground on the mound, refusing to leave. Dodger manager Charley Dressen sauntered out to the hill and convinced Meyer to leave. As Russ exited, he tossed the resin bag high in the air. What goes up must come down. And so it did. Right on Meyer's head. The crowd howled. Feeling foolish didn't help Meyer's frame of mind. He stormed into the dugout, where a camera had been positioned.

Players weren't used to cameras in those days. Nowadays, players like Curt Schilling (the '93 Phils called Schilling "Camera Curt") know where the cameras are better than the show's video technicians. But on this day, neither Meyer nor anyone else was cognizant of the clunky camera in the corner of the dugout. Not that Russ would have changed his behavior if he had known, however he grabbed his crotch in defiance—or whatever grabbing your crotch is for. The viewing audience witnessed it—in an era when TV forbade a man and woman sitting on the same bed. Audiences today would not be shocked. They'd simply think they had mistakenly tuned in a rap or Michael Jackson video.

Meyer's grab ended the placement of cameras in dugouts and became known as the "Meyer Rule."

RED ROSE FOR A DODGER BLUE KILLER

PAUL ROGERS: "Dick Sisler told me a strange story about that last game of the '50 season. Sisler and Maje McDonnell and a few others were in a cab headed for Ebbet's Field for the game. Some guy pulled up next to them at a red light and recognized them. The guy was a Phillies fan, an Italian from South Philly. He got out of the cab, walked over and handed Sisler a rose. Then he said to Sisler, 'I went to church and got this from the altar today. Take it for good luck.' Sisler put it on his locker as soon as he got to the clubhouse. Of course, he went on to hit the big home run that won the pennant for the Whiz Kids."

LOADING THE GUN FOR THE SHOT HEARD ROUND THE WORLD

Robin Roberts was a starter who closed. Robbie led the league in complete games from 1952 through 1956. He led in innings pitched for five straight years too, from 1951 through 1955.

But Robbie was a season closer as well, as the Dodgers were aware. For three consecutive years—1949, 1950, and 1951—he pitched the season finale against the Dodgers. Each game was crucial. Of course, only the 1950 game was crucial to the Phils. That's when Robbie beat the Dodgers 4-1 with the help of Dick Sisler's home run and Richie Ashburn's perfect throw to the plate. In 1949, Robbie was on the hill when the Dodgers won a 9-7 tenth-inning victory to eke out a pennant by one game over the Cardinals.

In 1951, Roberts was on the mound in the season finale against the Dodgers. The Dodgers needed a win to force a playoff with the Giants, who had overtaken the Dodgers in one of baseball's greatest pennant races. The Giants won 39 of their final 47 games to erase the 13-1/2 game deficit they faced on August 12.

The Phils jumped out to a 4-0 lead, but the Dodgers battled back and narrowed the gap to one. Robbie entered the game in the eighth to try to preserve the Phils' one-run lead. However, Carl Furillo, the first batter he faced, tied the game with an RBI. The game went to the fourteenth when Jackie Robinson hit a game-winning homer. What the statistics do not show is that the game should have been over in the eleventh, and the Phillies should have won.

ROBIN ROBERTS: "I got a base hit in the eleventh, and I was sacrificed to second. The next guy hit a low liner that Jackie Robinson dove for. I crossed the plate and we thought we had won. But the ump ruled Robbie caught the ball. So the game wasn't over and we had to go out and play some more."

In the fourteenth, of course, baseball's immortal #42 hit the homer that put the Dodgers in a playoff. But the Phils' Robbie remains convinced that the Dodgers' Robinson didn't catch the ball.

ROBIN ROBERTS: "I ran into Jackie in the off-season at a banquet. I asked him if he had really caught it. He answered, 'Ask the umpire!'"

Had the game ended in the eleventh in a Phillie victory, the playoff game where Bobby Thomson hit the Shot Heard Round the World wouldn't have happened.

Chapter 13

Maje

Three kids are playing in the street. A stranger walks up and asks one of the kids, "C-c-c-an y-y-you t-t-t-t-ell m-me how t-t-to g-g-get to T-t-tulip St-street?" The kid looks straight at him and shakes his head no. The guy turns around and leaves. The kids' two friends run over and ask him, "Tommy, you live on Tulip Street. It's only two blocks away! Why'd you say you didn't know where it is!" Tommy looks at his buddies and says: "D-d-d-do y-you w-w-want m-m-me t-to g-g-get the c-c-crap k-kicked out of m-m-me?"

That's a Maje McDonnell joke. He's got a million of them. Of course, that one really happened, sort of. Whiz Kid Dick Sisler, the hero of the Phillies' 1950 pennant-winning final game against the Dodgers, had a slight speech impediment. He stuttered. One day in the early fifties, Sisler stopped at a gas station. The attendant there happened to stutter. When the poor guy finished stuttering "Hello, can I fill it up?" Sisler came back with "F-f-f-f-ill 'er u-u-u-up."

Sisler said he remembered the attendant yelling "s-s-s-m-m-art ass" at him as he pulled out.

"Dick was anything but a smartass," Maje McDonnell recalls today. "He was the nicest guy you'd ever want to meet."

Seems like Maje meets nothing but nice guys. He's got that Will Rogers I-never-met-a-man-I-didn't-like syndrome running 24-7. He's as unlikely to badmouth a Phillie player or the Phillies organization as Curt Schilling is to turn down an interview. Maje bleeds Phillies red. He can tell a million stories about practically every ballplayer who ever waved a bat in this town. That's not surprising, The Maje is in his *seventh* decade with the Phils organization. He's been gathering Philadelphia baseball material since the Truman Administration (for youngsters, that would be President Harry Truman, not the character Jim Carrey played in *The Truman Show*).

I'm so old I remember when the Dead Sea was just sick.

—Maje

Maje was a pitcher for Villanova University back in the late forties. The day after Villanova's graduation, he became a Philadelphia Phillie. How'd that happen? Well, the Phils happened to play Villanova in an exhibition game in the spring of 1947. This may surprise the legions of Philadelphians who have met Maje over the years. They might have roared as Maje brought down the house from a banquet podium. They might have met him at a civic function or a Phillies event. But when the Phillies faced the Wildcats in that exhibition game, Maje McDonnell, all 5′5″, 127 pounds of him, was on the hill for Villanova. Maje McDonnell was the Wildcat's stopper. Right, Maje?

MAJE McDONNELL: "I was one of our top pitchers. I had fought in the Big War, got a Bronze Star too, landed at Omaha Beach—all that. I graduated from Northeast High in 1938—played basketball and baseball for them. I was the captain of the basketball team—great team too—4200 boys, biggest school in the country back then. I went to Brown Prep at 15th and Race for a year. Brown had great teams—I played with Max Patkin. Ever see Max in action? Clown Prince of Baseball. Max was a good ballplayer, got drafted by Cleveland. Lots of our guys got drafted. I went to Villanova after that—first guy from St. Anne's who ever got a sport scholarship. I grew up in Port Richmond. Anyway, I was supposed to pitch and play basketball too. My scholarship was for basketball. Then they switched it to half-and-half—half for baseball and half for basketball. You know why? Both the baseball and basketball coaches got another scholarship that way."

I'm so old when I order a 3-minute egg, they tell me to pay in advance.

—Maje

"Herb Pennock called me before I graduated, told me he'd like to work with me and make me a big-league pitcher. I pitched the whole game against the Phillies when I was at Villanova. I lost 7-6, but they were impressed the way I threw strikes. I had a good curve. Herb said they'd work with me on velocity and help me develop a new pitch. My hands

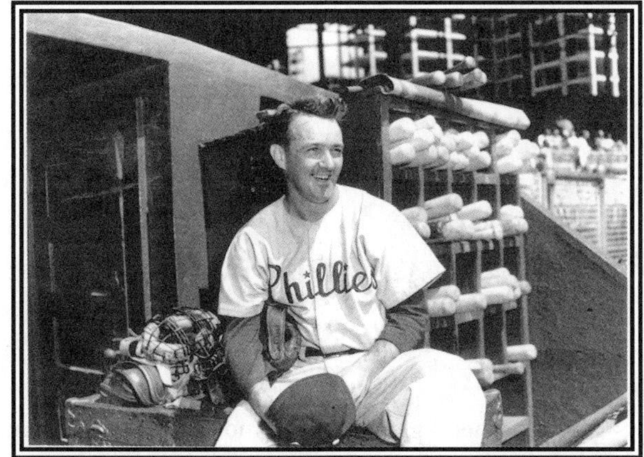

Maje still works with the Phillies in the Community Relations Department. On the speakers circuit, Maje always leaves 'em laughing.

(Photo: Courtesy of the Phillies)

were too small though. I couldn't master a screwball or knuckler, so Herb told me to pitch batting practice. So that's what I did, every day!"

I'm so old my back goes out more than I do.

—Maje

Maje never made that quantum leap to the majors. He did get a few shots at pitching for the Phils. Actually he couldn't have done better when he did appear in Phillies flannels. Not many guys go out with a glittery 0.00 ERA for their career, but Maje did.

MAJE: "I pitched against Waterbury, Connecticut for six scoreless innings in '47. Then I pitched three more scoreless innings in '48 in New Haven, and a couple more scoreless innings in Wilmington. The Phils were going to put me on the roster in '51, but two days later, they brought up some kid from the minors. It was a contract thing. The Phillies would lose him if they didn't bring him up. So that was it for me. I had three appearances and never gave up a run."

I know a guy who's so ugly every time he goes to the zoo he needs two ticketes—one to get in and one to get out.

—Maje

Maje stayed on as a coach though. He was also the assistant basketball coach at Villanova for over a decade. Maje believes he's the only one who ever coached in both a World Series and an NCAA Tournament ("Make that four NCAA Tournaments at Villanova," he winks).

MAJE: "I coached the freshman teams at Villanova for ten years. My teams had a 117-18 record, and I had one team that went 22-0. I had Larry Hennessey on that team. Larry played in the NBA after Paul Arizin."

We had a pitcher. His wife gave birth to eight straight girls. Finally she had a boy. I asked him what happened. He told me he took a little off his fastball.

—Maje

As for the Phils, Maje wound up coaching from 1948 to 1958. That stretch, of course, encompassed 1950 when the Whiz Kids won the pennant. Interestingly, Sawyer never played a regular season game in the majors either. He hadn't even coached at the major-league level.

MAJE: "Remember I was twenty-seven when I graduated Villanova (Q: What are the best ten years of a Port Richmond kid's life? A: Either third grade or sophomore year at Villanova. Just kidding, Maje). I was an Army vet, so I was older than the ballplayers—not much older, but older. Ben Chapman, the Phils' manager, called me into his office after the '47 season. I had worked my butt off as batting practice pitcher! I did everything they wanted. I worked pitchers out, hit fungoes, led calisthenics, whatever. So Chapman told me, 'Maje, you do everything I ask and more. I want you to be one of my coaches.' That's how it happened. The Phils were kind enough to make me a coach so I would be eligible for a pension. I lasted ten years as a coach so I did get a pension."

Maje changed his assignment in 1958, becoming a scout in western Pennsylvania. After scouting for a few years, he left the Phils for a position with Ballantine Beer, where he toiled for seven years. Meanwhile, he coached baseball at Chestnut Hill Academy, a Philadelphia-area prep school.

I know a ballplayer whose wife is so ugly that, when he sits at a bar, he looks at her picture every fifteen minutes. I asked him why. He says, "When she starts to look good, it's time to go home."

—Maje

MAJE: "Bill Giles came over to see me one day when I was coaching at Chestnut Hill Academy. He asked me to come back to the Phils. Bill grew up around the game in the fifties with his father, Warren. His dad was with Cincinnati before he became President of the National League. Bill would be in the dugout or out on the field before the game. Bill remembered me from when I was a coach. He's a sentimental guy anyway. He told me, 'You've got all those years with the Phils. That's where you belong.' He offered me a job so I came back in 1973, and I've been back ever since. God's given me a good life—baseball and God."

Maje has always been deeply religious. With tears in his eyes, he relates how Mildred Mary, his wife of fifty-seven years, battled and beat cancer three times. He unabashedly confides his conviction that the Miraculous Medal he wears and the novenas he made helped the cause. Maje has faith.

PAUL ROGERS, AUTHOR: "Maje told me that, after the Phils beat the Dodgers to win the pennant in 1950, while the rest of the team was in the locker room celebrating, Maje was kneeling down in the Ebbett's Field runway thanking God: 'If you never give me anything else for the rest of my life, thank you for giving me this moment.'"

I'll tell you my nationality. I'm half Scotch and half soda.

—Maje

The McDonnell family hasn't wandered far away from Philly. Mildred and Maje have

three daughters. One trains horses in Maryland, another is an Assistant DA in Philly, and another is the restaurant manager at Stephen Starr's Rouge on Rittenhouse Square.

And at eighty-something, Robert A. "Maje" McDonnell can still be found daily at the Philly offices—chipper and enthused, just as he was when he was serving up batting practice to the likes of Richie Ashburn and Del Ennis. Maje McDonnell is in the Pennsylvania Hall of Fame, the Philadelphia Hall of Fame, the Villanova Hall of Fame, and the Northeast High Hall of Fame. That's impressive, real major league. In fact, that's where the "Maje" comes from.

MAJE: "I was 'Maje' as long as I can remember. I was always dribbling a basketball or playing baseball. They started calling me 'Major League' McDonnell when I was still a little kid in Port Richmond. Then it got shortened to 'Major,' then 'Maje.' I was just born to be around sports."

A guy's riding shotgun on a stagecoach. Outlaws swoop down from the hills and the stagecoach speeds up. The driver asks the guy riding shotgun how close the outlaws are. The shotgunner replies, "I can't tell, but they look this big" (he spreads his hands apart about eight inches). The driver says, "Don't shoot till they're closer." A minute passes. The driver says, "How close now?" The shotgunner says, "Can't tell, but they're this big now" (he spreads his arms apart about two feet). The driver says, "Hold your fire till they're closer." Another minute passes. The outlaws catch up. They're riding alongside the stagecoach, shooting. The driver screams, "Shoot 'em! Shoot 'em!" The shotgunner says, "I can't. I've known them since they were only this big" (spreading his hands apart eight inches).

—Maje

PHILLY INSTITUTIONS

Philly has a pair of them—walking sports institutions who didn't become institutions via their exploits on the field. Too bad every city doesn't. Philly has Maje McDonnell and Jimmy Gallagher. We can't imagine Philly's sport scene without them. These are two guys who worked for their respective hometown professional sports organizations *forever*—Maje with the Phillies, Jimmy with the Eagles. They give their heart and soul not only to the hometown team but to the hometown fans, the lifeblood that some organizations bleed.

These two guys know *everyone* in the Philly sport scene. They're jacks-of-all-trades. They're ambassadors for their team and city. They smooth out the problems the higher-ups can't. They open doors and open hearts the suits can't. And the whole scene benefits from their underappreciated and unrequited love.

For the most part, people like Maje McDonnell and Jimmy Gallagher went out of style when expressions like bottom-line started getting tossed around more than thank you or nice job. We don't shed a tear for some things that vanish—things like the Cold War, telephone party lines, Nehru jackets, and smoking in the office. But we do shed a tear when cherished things vanish, like nickel candy bars, real soda fountains, and grand old movie theaters. Some things enrich life regardless of the era. Some people do the same. They remind us that friendliness, cooperation, cheerfulness, and loyalty never go out of style. They just get harder to find.

Those traits are not hard to find in McDonnell and Gallagher. What you see is what you get. They give everything they have to their organization, their community, and every person they deal with. They do it all with a smile.

Maje is still doing his thing for the Phils at Citizens Bank Park—same as he's done since 1947. Maje bleeds Phillie red. It's safe to say there will never be another who'll match his longevity and visibility as a Phillie ambassador. Hard too to imagine anyone matching his personality, conviviality, candor, approachability, and spirit.

His kindred spirit with the Eagles, Jimmy Gallagher, bled Eagle green for forty-seven years. Unlike Maje, Jimmy never coached for the Eagles. But he was the go-to guy for access. He smoothed out ruffled feathers, Eagle feathers and others. He mediated tiffs involving the franchise and ballplayers or sportswriters. He helped Eagle insiders and outsiders alike. At one time or another, Jimmy held every position in the Eagle front office except President. Maje can't match some bullets on Jimmy Gal's résumé, but he can match his loyalty and goodwill. Not surprisingly the two are long-time friends.

Jimmy Gallagher was recognized twice at the annual Philadelphia Sportswriters Banquet. In 1995, he was honored with the "Good Guy Award." In 2004, he sat on the dais with sport legends like Dr. J, Billie Jean King, Mario Andretti, Tommy Lasorda, Chuck Bednarik, Paul Arizin, and other sport icons who were recognized at the one-hundredth annual Philadelphia Sports Writers Banquet.

Philly has an awe-inspiring sport heritage. But the sport scene—the players, the managers, the front office, the ticket takers, the sportswriters—is so much bigger than just athletes on a field. Even the greatest athletes strut and fret only an hour on the stage. The clock ticks them into oblivion. Body and bravado inevitably betray even the best who must surrender their celebrity to the new kid on the block. Humility and loyalty endure. That's why Maje McDonnell and Jimmy Gallagher lasted so long. They exemplify the values we *want* sport to embody.

It would be fitting to see Maje get the "Good Guy Award" like his buddy Jimmy Gallagher. Like Jimmy Gal and the nickel candy bar, we're not likely to see the likes of Maje McDonnell again.

MIL-WALKING

Maje was Robin Roberts' confidant in Robbie's heyday. Robbie took losses hard and couldn't sleep after a tough game. Maje used to hang around with Robbie while the future Hall of Famer wound down after a loss. Sometimes the wind-down took all night. Once after a tough defeat in Milwaukee's County Stadium, Maje and Robbie hung around the clubhouse late, then decided to walk back to the hotel room.

ROBIN ROBERTS: "Eddie Mathews hit a homer to tie the game in the eighth. Then in the thirteenth, Chuck Tanner hit one to win the game. I was really keyed up after that game."

The hotel was a long distance away from County Stadium, but they could have walked back by way of Chicago. They walked for hours. By the time they got to the hotel, it was 6:30 AM. The two walkers hoofed it over to the hotel coffee shop, where they ran into manager Mayo Smith. Smith thought they were starting the new day, not finishing the old one. Looking back on his ambulatory method of coping, Robbie quipped, "The more games I lost, the better shape I was in from all that walking!"

Maje (pictured with Director of Ballpark Operations Mike DiMuzio) has been with the Phils for seven decades.

(Photo: Courtesy of the Phillies)

CHAPTER 14

GROOVIN' ON UP

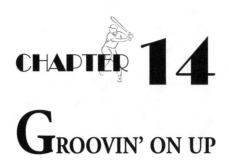

You know if you break my heart I'll go
But I'll be back again

—The Beatles

Being a Phillies fan is all about bleeding Phillies red forevermore. We're bleeding again after the 2004 season. But, like Rocky after his blood bath each round, we'll be set for the next round in 2005. Sorry, Tommy Lasorda, but Phillie red is deeper than Dodger blue. People in LA are more attached to diets, fads, spinning, yoga, tanning, and those kinds of things than their baseball team even if their team is a lot more successful.

Few cities west of Boston can match the cradle-to-grave allegiance the typical Phillie fan feels toward his teams, his city, and his heritage. We are profiling just a few ex-Philadelphians with special Phillies tie-ins who have grooved on up in the world of music and the arts. They may have left Philly but they never left their city or their Phillies behind. We'll also groove on up the Philly food chain in this chapter. Eating at the ballpark certainly has moved on up these days.

RADIO

You can never take the Philadelphia out of a Philadelphian.

—Chuck Brodsky

The once-a-Phillies-fan-always-a-Phillies-fan theme/syndrome/phenomenon keeps groovin' along. Curt Schilling tells us that Phillies-love moves on up from generation to generation, a genetically encoded passion entangled hopelessly in Philadelphians' DNA along with a love of soft pretzels, cream cheese, and cheesesteaks. (Authors' Note: Sorry, but even as diehard Philadelphians, we can't bring ourselves to include scrapple in that list. Rather than passing a love of scrapple on to your kids, arguably it's kinder to pass on male-pattern baldness, even to your daughters.)

Sometimes Philadelphians are a little unreasonable and intolerant about things that don't originate in Philly. How many Philadelphians tote Tastykakes around in their suitcase when they venture into *foreign* territory? (Foreign territory is any place where locals think *Wawa* is baby babble for *water*, or in Phillytalk, *warter.*) Philadelphians typically turn their noses up at inferior packaged-baked goods that pollute grocery-store shelves outside the Philly area. That same nobody-does-it-better Philly snobbishness holds for cheesesteaks. No true Philadelphian ever admits to finding a decent cheesesteak outside the shadow of Billy Penn's hat. Yo.

But nowhere is that Philadelphia-forever fervor embedded as deeply as it is in the hearts of native-son sport fans. Why else would a successful Hollywood producer-director dress his five-year-old as Jim Thome to trick-or-treat on the mean streets of *Beverly Hills*? We'll tell you why. Because the five-year-old *demanded* to go out as Jim Thome. The kid is a carrier of that Philly-forever gene.

The producer-director in this story is Mike Tollin. Tollin's list of movies includes *Radio, Summer Catch, Big Fat Liar, Hardball, Burger,* and *Chasing the Dream* (the documentary on Hank Aaron). Mike might reside in Dodgerland, but his blood is red, the kind that hemoglobin-toting humans carry rather than the oxygen-deprived blue variety. (Are you reading this, Tommy Lasorda?)

MIKE TOLLIN: "When I moved out to Los Angeles, I told my fiancée, 'There's something you've got to know if you marry me.' She was bracing herself, afraid I was about to dredge up some huge skeleton from my past. I didn't. What I told her was, 'Look honey, you're marrying a rabid Phillies fan. We *have* to raise our kids to be Phillies fans, not Dodgers fans. If you have problems with that, we'd better call it off now.'"

Robbie (Roberta Rowe) is now Mike's wife. Their children, eleven-year-old Georgia and five-year-old Lucas, are rabid Phillies fans. Lucas' first two words were Harry Kalas' "Outta here!" (Is that three words?) There's that Phillies genetic encoding again.

Mike Tollin was raised a dyed-in-the-wool Phillies fan. He hails from Haverford. He was a good-field-no-hit shortstop, long on aspirations but short on big-league talent. He and his father hustled out to Phillies games every chance they got. One of Mike's biggest childhood thrills was the day in 1964 when his father came home and whipped out World Series tickets for the whole family.

MIKE TOLLIN: "I couldn't wait to see that Series game! I'll never forget going to bed with a little transistor radio under my pillow. Basically I cried myself to sleep every night when they lost all those games in September. I couldn't bear to look at the Philadelphia *Bulletin* when it was delivered in the afternoons that September. Normally, my brother and I fought to grab it soon as it hit the doorstep, but not while the Phillies were folding."

Mike left Philly for college but returned and landed a job with MLB (Major League

Baseball) Productions, which later became Phoenix Productions. He worked a lot with the Phillies video department. He did the 1980 Phillies highlight film and *Centennial—100 Years of Phillies Baseball.* That piece of work established his relationship with David Montgomery and the Phils brass. In the mid-'80s, he did *Phanatic Phillies*, featuring Tug McGraw and the Phillie Phanatic. Video Dan updated that one in 1998 with *Channel Surfin' Phanatic*, considered by many (of Video Dan's closest friends) as the best surfing movie since *Beach Blanket Bingo*. In 1993, Tollin did *Whatever It Takes, Dude*, narrated by the Dude himself—no, not Mike Tollin, Lenny Dykstra. Even though he's a coast away and years removed from those videos, Tollin remains close to several people in the Phillies organization.

MIKE TOLLIN: "My daughter Georgia was oh-for-life when it came to seeing the Phillies win a game at the ballpark. I took her out to the ballpark two or three times a year for about five years and the Phils never won! Last year (2003), the Phils were playing a four-game series at Dodger Stadium. We decided we'd go to *every* game till the Phils won. If the Dodgers swept, we were going to follow the Phils down to San Diego.

"The first game we went to, Brett Myers is pitching a gem. He gets into trouble in the late innings and Jose Mesa comes in. Little did I know that David Montgomery back in Philadelphia had phoned Ed Wade who was on the bench with the Phils in LA. I had spoken with David earlier in the day and told him what Georgia and I were up to. So David told Ed I was at the game, and asked him to get Brett to sign the game ball for Georgia.

"We got out of the park that night without picking up the ball. David [Montgomery] called me and told me the Phils had the game ball. He told me to pick it up in the clubhouse. So I did. This time I had my son Lucas with me. We were out on the field and I turned to talk to Wheels and Kruk who were setting up for the pre-game show. That's when Lucas decided to toss me the ball. He plunked me right on the cheekbone and gave me an enormous shiner. Naturally, Krukker laughed, thought it was the funniest thing he ever saw. [Phils trainer] Jeff Cooper gave me an ice pack. Normally I wouldn't have cared. But this was the week that *Radio* was being released and I was scheduled for a series of interviews. I had to pay makeup artists to travel everywhere with me so they could cover up my shiner."

Mike Tollin has a recognizable Hollywood mug, not bad for an ex-Philadelphian who loves his Phillies. Mike did a lot of great work for the Phils. He also started the 1980 series *The Baseball Bunch* hosted by Johnny Bench (MIKE TOLLIN: "I made sure we got some Phillies on the show, like Schmidty and the Tugger"). Tollin also produced a string of Hollywood films including the documentary on Hank Aaron, *Chasing the Dream*.

MIKE TOLLIN: "I was a big Richie Allen fan as a kid. Little did I know the two of us would become good friends years later. I asked Richie to come to a school in

Germantown to show the film to some inner-city kids. I introduced him but the kids of that era didn't know him. I told them he hit 351 home runs, won the Rookie of the Year Award, won an MVP, won a home run title, was an All-Star several times—all those things. Richie is a quiet man. He didn't say much or react when I highlighted his career. While the film was airing, I noticed he had left the room. I went outside and saw him standing alone on the step. He told me the film was too emotional to watch. He said, 'That's what we black players went through back then—the hate mail, not being able to eat with the team, getting turned away at hotels, all those hurts. I just couldn't watch it.'"

PHILLIES TROUBADOUR

Folk singer Chuck Brodsky does considerable globetrotting in his profession. He's done some USA-trotting outside his profession too. Chuck grew up in the Philly area in Bala Cynwyd. He and his dad were fixtures at Connie Mack Stadium and the Vet. Chuck was tiny when he made his first trips to Connie Mack Stadium, but those visits bonded him with baseball and the Phils for a lifetime. Even though he was a young child, he recalls the last game ever played at Connie Mack.

CHUCK BRODSKY: "My dad's company had season tickets, and no one was using them much in those days. My dad and I would go a lot because the seats were free—and we loved the Phils. That last game at Connie Mack, I'll never forget. Yeah, like everyone else, we knocked the seats off the hinges and carried them home. I still have them."

Chuck attended Haverford School where he played baseball. His teammate was Richard Ashburn, Whitey's son. After graduation, Chuck went to Penn State for a year before hitchhiking out to California in search of the things twenty-year-olds are in search of. Chuck took jobs as a deliveryman—worked them for years, all the while perfecting his guitar playing, soaking up life experiences, and honing his performing skills. Eventually he became a full-time musician, playing gigs in and around San Francisco, appearing at clubs like East Bay, the Owl and Monkey, and Albion. In 1993, he went on tour for the first time, playing in Ireland and around the States. He also recorded his first album.

While his career was movin' on up after that first album, Chuck added some unusual riffs to his repertoire.

CHUCK BRODSKY: "In the late eighties, I wrote a song, 'Lefty,' that was loosely based on Steve Carlton. It was about a great pitcher who stayed in the game too long. I was kind of shy about playing it at first. I didn't think audiences would like a baseball theme. I played it for some friends around a campfire at a festival, and everyone gave me the thumbs up, so I added it to my show. It's become a favorite, especially with the Phillies rooters—and there are plenty of them everywhere. Wherever I perform, there are Phillies fans in the audience, and now they all request my Phillies songs."

Philly guy Mike Tollin directs Dick Allen on the set of *Summer Catch*.
Summer Catch ©Copyright 2000, Warner Bros. (Photo: Michael Tackett)

Chuck's "Lefty" composition started a trend. He's gone on to write nine baseball songs—and counting. Almost half have a Phillies connection. He became "the baseball singer" to some people when he put all the baseball songs on one album, *The Baseball Ballads*, one of his best-sellers.

The album cover shows an open locker where Phillies uniform #28 hangs. His dad wore that shirt at a Phillies Phantasy Camp in Clearwater. The baseball equipment in the locker was his dad's at Overbrook High where the senior Brodsky played a few years before Wilt Chamberlain.

That's not the end of the baseball connection. A friend of Chuck's put him in touch with Tim Flannery, former Padres player and coach. Flannery is a serious guitarist. Chuck and Flannery started corresponding and got a chance to jam together when the Padres came to Philly. Flannery left game tickets for Chuck and his dad. Brodsky and Flannery wound up hanging out playing guitar till 3:00 AM after the game. They finished the evening with a cheesesteak at Pat's.

Flannery wound up touring briefly with Chuck, doing four shows with him. Chuck also did a benefit in San Diego called "Tim Flannery and Friends." The proceeds were used to buy Padres tickets for underprivileged kids.

Chuck has another strong baseball connection—this one from Philly. Chuck wrote the lyrics to the title song in Mike Tollin's movie *Radio*, starring Ed Harris as Coach Jones and Cuba Gooding Jr. as Radio.

CHUCK BRODSKY: "My dad sent me the *Sports Illustrated* article about *Radio*. Gary Smith, another ex-Philadelphian, wrote it. My dad knew it was the kind of uplifting human-interest story I love. So I wrote a song about it. When the movie came around, Mike used it as the title track.

"I got to be good friends with the real Coach Howard Jones. That's how I met Mike Tollin. Coach Jones called Mike from his office and said he had a guy with him who had written a song about *Radio*. Then he handed me the phone. When I got on the line and said I was Chuck Brodsky, Mike cut in, 'I know you. You're the guy who writes the baseball songs.' Mike and I struck up a good friendship. He actually put me in the film. He put the real Coach Jones and Gary Smith in too. Mike tried to get everyone who had something to do with the real *Radio* story into the film. We were all in the banquet scene at the end."

As a folk singer, Chuck has appeared on nationally syndicated radio programs like NPR's "Mountain Stage," the "Acoustic Café," and "River City Folk." He has performed in Denmark, and in festivals in dozens of states, including the Philly Folk Fest. But his greatest kick was performing at the Hall of Fame in Cooperstown, not once but three times. Tim Wiles, the Director of Research at the Hall, writes this about Chuck: "Chuck is baseball's poet laureate. He combines his gift for lyrics and melody with his love for baseball history and culture, and in the process creates a new chapter in the folklore of our national pastime."

Heady stuff. But the bottom line is that Chuck's just another guy whose roots are in Philadelphia, no matter where he's planted or transplanted. He lives down in Asheville, North Carolina now. Up in the Blue Mountains, Chuck used to tune in all the Phillies games and cheer the Fightins on. When Richie Ashburn died, Chuck wrote a song about those days, "Whitey and Harry" (see the lyrics in Chapter 15). You can check out all his songs at www.chuckbrodsky.com and buy all his albums online.

Here's a song he wrote about his and Mike Tollin's childhood hero, Dick Allen. Allen was so troubled by Philly booing that he took to writing messages in the dirt at first base at Connie Mack Stadium.

Letters in the Dirt

Lyrics by Chuck Brodsky

Me & you, we never booed Richie Allen
I never understood why people did
He hit a homer every time he stepped up to the plate
That's what I remember as a kid

Richie in the field out there by first base
The target of some mighty foul words
With his shoes he'd scrawl between the pitches
"B-O-O" in great big letters in the dirt

Philly fans, they've been known to get nasty
When Joe must go, they'll run him out of town
I saw Santa get hit by a snowball
And then get hit again when he was down

Me & you, we never booed Richie Allen
Even if he did sometimes strike out
I was too young to read the papers
To know what all that booing was about

That big collapse of '64 was ugly
They blew a lead of 6 and one-half games with 12 to play
Some might say their fans were justifiably angry
World Series tickets printed up in vain

Philly fans, they've been known to get nasty
When Joe must go, they'll run him out of town
I saw Santa get hit by a snowball
And then get hit again when he was down

Going back to old Connie Mack Stadium
You teaching me the rules of the game
We root-root-rooted for the home team
Those other people shoulda been ashamed
This was before the days of the million dollar contracts

Before the days of the artificial grass
He stood a bit outside the lines which made him fair game for those times
Richie Allen never kissed a white man's ass

Me & you, we never booed Richie Allen
No, we'd pound our mitts & we'd yell, "We want a hit"
How could they call a guy a bum after he'd just hit a home run?
That didn't make any sense to a kid

Now I've since found out all these days later
Now I know a lot more than I did
And if back then you knew, Daddy, why all those other people booed . . .
Thanks for letting me have my heroes as a kid

PAUL RICHARDSON

Trivia question . . . Quick, who's the only guy who ever played for the Phillies and Eagles in the same year? Answer: Paul Richardson.

Paul is the longtime Phillies organist, who has played his keyboards for Phillies games since 1970, the last year at Connie Mack Stadium. He also played for the Eagles at the Vet. Paul used to set up in the lower box-seat section behind first base and was named "Rookie of the Year" by the Phils. When the club moved on up to the Vet, he set up in the Vet's control room.

Now for the nasty part. From 1978 through 1982, Paul also played the organ for the New York Yankees while the Phillies were on the road. He's a friend of Yankees owner George Steinbrenner (an organ-music lover) who has his own organ in his New York home. But Paul moved on up, or as Billy Joel puts it, he moved out of the Yankee gig and came back exclusively to the Quaker City.

For the past several years Paul was a fixture behind third base on the 300 Level concourse at the Vet where fans could see him sitting behind his Roland organ, belting out tunes to stir up the hometown fans. Nowadays he sets up in Ashburn Alley behind Richie's statue at Citizens Bank Park.

You never know what songs are going to drift across the ballpark. Paul plays everything from the Rolling Stones to Britney Spears.

PAUL RICHARDSON: "I have about 400 songs in my repertoire. But I've made my living from six notes (with that, Paul plays da-da-da-daaaaa-da-daaaaa—the six notes that finish with the crowd screaming, 'Charge!')."

Paul has cut four albums. His latest, *Frisky*, features the Phillie Phanatic on the jacket. You can check them all out on his website www.paulrichardson.com. You can also purchase them online. How? Da-da-da-daaaaa-da-daaaaa—charge!

SKIP DENENBERG

On March 21, 2004, spring roared in like a lion. The sound of tumbling concrete and steel deafened South Philly for several seconds. The sound moistened eyes all around the City of Brotherly Love, same as the last time the sound of "Concrete and Steel" was heard at the Vet. That was on Sunday, September 28, 2003. "Concrete and Steel," the Skip Denenberg song, wafted across the Field of Memories at the Vet's finale that day. Skip wrote the ode especially for the occasion.

SKIP DENENBERG: "Video Dan [head of the Phils' video department] thought the song I wrote for Tug McGraw was too long. He didn't think baseball fans would listen as attentively as they did. But people are so into the Vet and so into baseball in this town, they did listen. When I did 'Concrete and Steel,' I think it moved some people."

Singer songwriter Skip Denenberg wrote a song for the Phillie Phanatic and performed it at the Phanatic's first birthday party at Citizens Bank Park.

(Photo: Heddy Bergsman)

I heard "Concrete and Steel" next at the Theater of the Living Arts on South Street. Skip was opening for a group called Sun Kil Moon. The playbill should have been reversed.

"Concrete and Steel" is Denenberg's tribute to the town and the team he loves most. Skip's another Phillie boy. He left Quaker City years ago to make a new life a whole coast away. He has since found his way back to his old town and his old haunts.

Back in the late seventies and early eighties, Skip was a bartender at Doc Watson's Pub in Philly. Doc Watson's had an impressive lineup of employees for a Center City tappy. Randall "Tex" Cobb, Dom Irrera, and Carl Cherkin all worked there. In case you don't know this crew, Tex Cobb is a boxing legend who fought Larry Holmes and many other big names. In the ring, Tex ate leather like Popeye ate spinach—the more he ate, the stronger he got. Tex also became a legend, sort of, of the silver screen. He's appeared in numerous films. Dom Irrera is a South Philly native and popular stand-up comedian who has had his own HBO specials and is best known for his "Badda-bing, badda-boom" shtick. Carl Cherkin is recognized around Philly as the former Fox-29 sports anchor.

Then there's Skip Denenberg.You might not recognize that name but you've heard his music. Skip has scored theme music and soundtracks for numerous documentaries like *Remember When, Things That Aren't There Anymore, More Things That Aren't There Anymore, South Philly Italian Style, Workshop of the World,* and *It's a Mitzvah*, to name a few. He also wrote the theme music for Channel 10's *Time Out* when John Bolaris was host. Skip wrote the music for the Phanatic's 2004 birthday party too. He's well established in the music industry. However, he got his start as a songwriter in a way that was pure serendipity.

SKIP DENENBERG: "We were hanging around after a night at Doc Watson's Pub, a bunch of us over at a friend's apartment house. It got to be really late—maybe three, four in the morning. We were passing the guitar around and singing songs. All of a sudden, this gorgeous woman walks down the steps and comes to our door. We thought she was going to scream at us to shut up. Instead she says, 'Mikey is really sick and we keep hearing your music upstairs. He wants to know if you could please come up to our room and play for him.' So we did. Mikey turned out to be Miguel Piñera, and the girl who asked us to come up and play was his girlfriend Sherry. I played some songs I had written myself for Miguel. He listened and told me, 'I like your music. I want you to write something for my movie.' We didn't believe anything about a movie, but it turns out he had written the movie *Short Eyes.* [The movie starred Bruce Davison, whom you may recognize as Senator Kelly in *X-Men* and *X-Men 2.* What you may not realize is that Davison too is a native Philadelphian.] I wrote the song 'Break It Down' for him and he used it in the movie."

After that, doors opened and Skip headed to California where he started writing music for documentaries and commercials. He was enjoying California life. But he was also missing Philly. (SKIP: "And I missed the food big time.")

Denenberg met his beautiful wife, Ann Marie, a University of Pennsylvania grad, and the two decided to settle back in Philly. They now have two lovely daughters, Allison (11) and Erin (7). Alison is Skip's precocious partner on some of his projects like the Phanatic's birthday song. ("Don't forget to say I helped my dad write it.")

SKIP: "I missed the sport scene here in Philly—the people, the teams, the food. I liked LA, but ultimately this is my home and this is where I want to be."

Skip was raised an avid Phillies fan—a love that's lasted all life long. While he was playing guitar in the restaurants in Fairmount—the London Grill and Rembrandt's—as well as several other spots, Skip met and befriended several Phillies.

SKIP: "Tug McGraw used to come in to hear me play. And when I was at J.C. Dobbs, 3rd & South, I met Don Lee Van Winkle, Maje McDonnell's son-in-law. He heard me play there and asked me into his band, The Wanderers. Later he was in the group The American Dream and he did the song, 'You Can't Get to Heaven on the Frankford El.' J.C. Dobbs was an amazing place. The Stray Cats, Robert Hazard [the guy who wrote Cyndi Lauper's 'Girls Just Want to Have Fun'], and George Thorogood started there. In fact, Thorogood slept there. He offered to play on Friday, Saturday, and Sunday for $300, and the owner said, 'I don't know, George. That's a lot of money.'"

Skip had another thrill when he got to meet Willie Nelson.

SKIP: "Tex Cobb and I became really good friends, and of course, he and Willie were good friends. So I got to hang out and play guitar with Willie. He liked my music, and I wound up appearing with him onstage at Farm Aid '99. I wrote 'Don't Bet the Farm' for Farm Aid and got to play it onstage with his backup band.

"Anyway, back to Tug—that was one of my big thrills, introducing Tug to Willie Nelson. Tug and I and some other Phillies were at a Willie Nelson concert and Willie played 'Pancho and Lefty,' which was one of Tug's favorite Willie Nelson songs. Tug went crazy. Here's a guy who starred in two World Series, had this huge baseball career, and he's like a little kid when Willie starts playing a song he loves. That's what Tug brought wherever he went—enthusiasm that lifted everybody around him.

"So one day I'm playing at North Star which is around 24th or 26th and Poplar, and Tug walks in with his son Tim. Tim asks me if he could play. I had this old Gibson SJ guitar I had just bought. I loved the sound—sounded like the acoustic guitars the Beatles used on *Rubber Soul.* Tim comes up and plays like five songs. And he says to me, 'I'm going to Nashville and I'm gonna be a country & western singer.' I told him, 'That's great, but it's tough down there. I was there and it's tough to break in.' Next time I heard Tim McGraw's name, I'm riding along the West River Drive and the DJ says, and here's the number one song in the nation by Tim McGraw! I almost drove off the road."

Skip, as mentioned, did the *Hero* video about Tug McGraw—the clip that showed on the video board on August 30, 2000—Tug's birthday and the day Tug was inducted into the Philadelphia Wall of Fame.

SKIP: "Unfortunately I couldn't be there that day. I was performing in North Carolina, but Ann Marie [Skip's wife] was there and said it was terrific. I was at Tug's fifty-ninth birthday party. His son Hank and I played Tug's favorite Willie Nelson songs for him. We sang 'Pancho and Lefty' and 'Seven Spanish Angels' and a bunch of other songs that the Tugger loved. I'll tell you this much, Tug really lived to the max his final year. He died young but he didn't get cheated out of anything."

You should catch Skip's act around Phillytown. He appears frequently at the Tin Angel and the TLA. He has engagements at the Keswick and the Pontiac (that's the former J.C. Dobbs) too. He's a good singer-songwriter—just another ex-Philly boy who does Phillies songs—except Skip is now an ex-ex-Philly boy. He came back home—he's grooved on up to Philly—back where a friend is a friend and a cheesesteak is a cheesesteak.

PHANATIC PHILE

CHEESESTEAKS

Let's groove on up the Philly food chain now. But first a little lead-in so we can give you the full flavor.

Every year I get a call from our PR office to fill in the Phillie Phanatic's bio for the upcoming Phillies Yearbook. Questions range from "What's your favorite movie?" (*Rocky*) and "What's your favorite song?" ("Take Me Out to the Ballgame") to "Who would you like to have dinner with?" (Kermit the Frog). Trying to come up with a clever response every year (OK, I'd like to come up with a clever response just *one* year) can be a real challenge. Inevitably each year, the Phanatic has to say what his favorite food is and each year the Phanatic gives the same response—Tastykakes, scrapple (a food not fit for man nor beasts, and certainly not for mascots), soft pretzels, and of course, cheesesteaks.

A couple years back, some national magazine (we will not grace them by naming such Philly detractors) fingered Philadelphia as the fattest city in the country. (Hip-hoppers—that's *f*attest, not *ph*attest—like they dissed us, you know what I'm sayin'?) With my waistline bulging in at a flaccid ninety-eight inches, I suppose the Phanatic could be a poster child for our rotund reputation. That poster would show the Phanatic lounging on Ashburn Alley with a cheesesteak in each hand and the headline "Philly's Better When You *Eat* Over"—or "Overeat."

Fans attending Citizens Bank Park have been spending more time on Ashburn

PHANATIC PHILLE

Alley than in their seats. That's because two Philly cheesesteak institutions—Geno's and Tony Luke's—are located in the outfield entertainment zone. These two places consistently have the longest food lines in the park, not that I have time to notice because I'm working so hard. Thanks to Citizens Bank Park's open-air design, fans can catch the action on the field while they wait for their sandwich. Actually, that little stretch along Asburn Alley could have cost us a pennant in '93, had the '93 team been playing at Citizens Bank Park. Fans in line would have been stepping aside all night for the likes of Kruk and Inky rushing in off the field to scarf down a cheesesteak between innings.

That's just a joke. Not that the '93 team would *not* have headed for Geno's during the game—it's just that they wouldn't have to. The players at Citizens Bank Park have Swanny's Kitchen to satisfy all their gastronomic needs. (How's that word for a mascot?) Never heard of Swanny's? It's the name of the players' lounge located across from the home team's clubhouse. Joe Swanhart is Swanny (duh). Joe runs the show. He's a clubhouse assistant turned master chef. Step aside, Alison Barshak and Georges Perrier.

Before we talk about Swanny's, let's back up for a minute. When Maje McDonnell took an employees-only tour of Citizens Bank Park in March, he was bowled over by the full-sized, industrial kitchen built for the players *right inside the clubhouse*. Times sure have changed from the old days back at Connie Mack Stadium, right Major League?

MAJE McDONNELL: "Back in the day, the only thing you could get at the ballpark was a hot dog and a box of popcorn. Oh and Dixie Cups too. There was a bar on the corner of 20th and Lehigh Avenue called Quinn's. Down in the bullpen, if a player got hungry during the game, he'd either get somebody to go to Quinnie's to bring him back a sandwich or he'd sneak over there himself. He'd probably have more than a sandwich too—know what I mean?"

LARRY SHENK: "We didn't have the variety of food at Connie Mack that we have today at Citizens Bank Park. That goes for the press box as well. I remember Dick Young from the *New York Daily News* ordering a hot dog in the press box. The guy behind the counter handed him a hot dog on a plate with no roll. Dick said, 'Where the heck is the roll?' and the concession guy replied, 'You didn't *ask* for a roll.' Dick had a fit!"

So much for the flashback. Now, back to Swanny's. Joe Swanhart started as a clubhouse attendant for the Cardinals during spring training in St. Petersburg, Florida. When the Devil Rays came to town in 1997, Joe switched teams and wound up as the visiting-team clubhouse assistant at Tropicana, the Devil

Rays' home field, the following year. That's when Swanny started dabbling in the culinary arts.

SWANNY: "I was running the food area there and began experimenting. The main meal was catered but I started cooking breakfasts for the guys—you know, like eggs made to order, pancakes, and waffles. Then I started offering them grilled sandwiches after batting practice. We didn't have a kitchen so we had to use electric, plug-in skillets and butane burners. It was a makeshift kind of thing."

In 2002, Phillies clubhouse manager Frank Coppenbarger started using Swanny in Clearwater during spring training. In 2004, Swanny moved on up to Citizens Bank Park and staked his claim in the lounge by hanging a bright, neon sign bearing his name on the wall right next to his kitchen.

SWANNY: "My family had that sign made for me and I brought it all the way up from St. Pete. I feel fortunate that, at a relatively young age, I've already opened up two new ballparks [although technically Tropicana Field was already being used before the Devil Rays moved in].

"The players really enjoy the service. We use different outside caterers for dinner. I'll offer a beef product, some kind of chicken or pork dish and a seafood dish. I'll also put out a starch, a vegetable, salad, dinner rolls, and dessert. I generally don't do pastas post-game because of the whole low-carb diet thing that everybody's into at the moment but I do offer pasta for lunch. I call it *Swanny's pasta* and it's made with one of my own special sauces. I make it to order with your choice of tomato-basil sauce or alfredo sauce. Then I mix in chicken or grilled veggies, whatever the guy wants."

Low-carb diet notwithstanding, the Phillies want cheesesteaks. In Philadelphia, somehow it always comes back to the cheesesteak.

I walked around the clubhouse one day and asked the players what they felt was the perfect cheesesteak. Marlon Byrd may have been born in Boynton Beach, Florida and may reside in San Diego, but when it comes to cheesesteaks, he's an old-school Philly-cheesesteak purist. He likes his cheesesteaks from Pat's or Geno's, Whiz wit. (Translation for you non-Philly folks: Whiz is Cheese Whiz and "wit" means you want fried onions *with*, or *wit* your cheesesteak.) Speaking of Pat's and Geno's, here's some more advice for out-of-towners. Watch the *Seinfeld* episode with the Soup Nazi. When you order from Pat's or Geno's you'd better not hesitate giving your order or else the guy or lady behind the counter will make the Soup Nazi seem as warm and fuzzy as a greeter at a time-share presentation.

Mike Lieberthal prefers his cheesesteaks from Jim's on South Street. Lieby prefers them plain, with nothing on them (wimp—sorry Lieby, I didn't mean that). Billy Wagner, new to the whole Philly cheesesteak thing, explains: "I enjoyed the barbeque when I was in Houston all those years but I like cheesesteaks, too. I like 'em with a little tomato on top and that's it."

"I try not to eat cheesesteaks, especially before a game or late at night," Jim Thome laments. "When you're my size, you can't eat many of them and that's hard to do because they're so good."

Placido Polanco tries to stay away from cheesesteaks. Instead he yearns for the delicacies from his homeland. "In the Dominican Republic, we eat 'chimichurras.' They're sort of like hamburgers with special sauce on them. They're delicious."

Fellow Dominican Amaury Telemaco interrupted: "Don't listen to Pollie [Polanco]. Eating chimichurras will make you sick."

Tomas Perez overheard the disagreement and chimed in: "No, no, no, in Venezuela we like to eat 'pepitos.' They're like steak sandwiches with cheese, tomato, sauce and special sauce. You can't get them around here."

Actually, Tomas might be in business soon because (to keep the Spanish-speaking players happy) Swanny has started to cater food from some of the local Latin restaurants.

Of all the Phils, Kevin Millwood and Jason Michaels sing Swanny's praises the loudest ("*Swanny, how I love you, how I love you, my dear old Swanny . . .*" Sorry again).

"I'll go in and order a cheesesteak with the works and he'll cook it right there for me," said J-Mike. "You can't beat that for service or taste. Swanny's are the best."

"Yeah," added Millwood, "with Swanny, you get it exactly the way you want it. It tastes great."

SWANNY: "We use meat from the Philadelphia Cheesesteak Company and we always use the freshest rolls. I use a special type of seasoning but I can't really tell you what it is or I'd have to kill you. [Scrapple makers don't make that threat when they refuse to divulge their ingredients. They don't have to. The scrapple'll kill you all by itself.]

"The clear favorite with the team is cheesesteaks. Eric Milton especially loves them. Before his first start with the Phillies, Milton ordered a cheesesteak and

PHANATIC PHILE

then won the game. Ever since, he's ordered a cheesesteak from me every day he's pitched."

Yo, Eric, what's up with that? Didn't they have cheesesteaks in Minnesota?

ERIC MILTON: "Are you kidding? No way, only here in Philly. But it's true. I've started eating cheesesteaks before each start, even when I'm on the road. I try to order it the same way wherever I am—with provolone cheese and onions. I'll even order one *for breakfast* before day games. I started the season 5-0 and when we went to New York, I couldn't get a cheesesteak at our hotel. Wouldn't you know, I took my first loss of the season."

That's alright, Eric. A Philly cheesesteak in New York is sacrilege. But Eric's story debunks another myth New York likes to spread about itself. New Yorkers always say you can find *anything* you want to eat at any hour of the day or night in the Big Apple. Apparently you can't. In fact, I know first-hand you can't. I went into a restaurant that advertised, "There's *nothing* you can order that we don't have. If we don't have it, your meal is on us." I ordered a kangaroo pouch on toast. Sure enough, I got a free meal. Their toaster was broken.

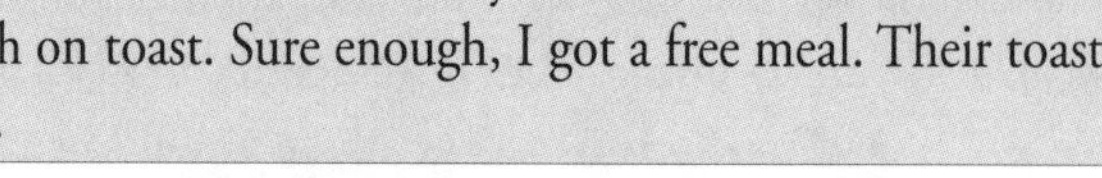

PHANATIC PHILE

SOUTH STREET

One thing that just about all the Phillies players agree on is this, if you want a *real* Philly cheesesteak, there's only one place to get it.

In Philly.

Phillies outfielder Doug Glanville grew up in North Jersey before movin' on up to the University of Pennsylvania. Doug has learned a thing or two about the power of the cheesesteak in Philadelphia.

DOUG GLANVILLE: "When I attended Penn, I went to Abner's [in University City] for cheesesteaks all the time. I'm convinced Philly's the only place you can get a real cheesesteak. All those places around the country that advertise Philly cheesesteaks on their menu just don't cut it. Eating a cheesesteak outside of Philadelphia doesn't count as the real deal."

"Smitty" would definitely take issue with that. Smitty (he's been known as Smitty since he was six years old) is a Philly sports fanatic who moved to Los Angeles the day after the Phillies won their only World Series in 1980. He worked as a marketing executive with Twentieth Century Fox and later started his own business, In Sync Advertising. His new company took off. They helped put together trailers and TV commercials for movies such as *Home Alone, Terminator 2, Castaway*, and *A Beautiful Mind*. Everything in his LA life was perfect, almost, except for one nagging vacuum. No matter where he went in Tinseltown, Smitty couldn't get a decent cheesesteak.

SMITTY: "I used to drive all my friends crazy complaining about how bad the cheesesteaks were in LA. Finally they said to me, 'Instead of bitching and moaning all the time, why don't you do something about it?' And I did!"

In January 2002, Smitty, along with his partner Mitch Goldman, opened up their first authentic cheesesteak shop in Westwood Village. They named it "South Street." The phone rang in my office before the grand opening. It was Smitty and he wanted to invite the Phanatic out to LA for a week's worth of ribbon-cutting events and private parties to celebrate the new Philly restaurant on the block. A week's worth of free Philly cheesesteaks! It was an offer I couldn't refuse.

SMITTY: "We had to have the Phillie Phanatic out here in LA for the grand opening. We wanted to go all out. Listen, I grew up in Cheltenham [just outside Philadelphia] and went to William Penn Charter High School. I got started in the business of video and advertising in Philly by helping to produce the Sixers and Flyers year-end highlight films. I did Penn State football highlights, too. I got a big break to come to LA and take a job with Twentieth Century Fox, but I had a hard time saying goodbye to Philly. They wanted me to come out and report to the new job at the beginning of September in 1980, but the Phils were in the middle of a hot streak so I told them I'd come out after the World Series. I went to every post-season game at the Vet that year. I left the day after the Tugger struck out Willie Wilson to win it all."

South Street opened in the heart of UCLA's campus to rave reviews. Just listen to how the Los Angeles *Zagat Guide* describes Smitty's oasis of Philly food:

"The next best thing to a visit to the City of Brotherly Love, this Westwood Village American café attracts Philly fanatics [hey, they forgot the "ph"!] with deliciously decadent, authentic cheesesteaks, not-for-the-novice spicy fries and even TastyKakes, served in a cute, brick-walled room so evocative you can almost hear the *Rocky* theme while you eat—oh, wait, they *are* playing it in the background."

When I arrived for South Street's grand opening, I felt right at home. Phillies, Sixers, Flyers, and Eagle highlights run on a continuous loop on a high-definition, flat, wide-screen TV. And yes, the trailers for *Rocky* and other Philly based movies play as well. There are Philly newspaper clippings on the walls and sports memorabilia celebrating the city's teams throughout the little shop. There are seats from Connie Mack Stadium and photos of notable Philadelphians like Frank Rizzo, Betsy Ross (I know, they didn't have photos in Betsy's day), Jerry Blavat, and Larry Fine. They also have a copy of our book, *More Than Beards, Bellies, and Biceps—The Story of the 1993 Philadelphia Phillies and the Phillie Phanatic Too,* in their display case. What an eclectic collection of Philly's finest. They hung a picture of the Phanatic on their Wall of Fame before I left.

South Street offers other Philly regional treats too. They order their soft pretzels from Federal Pretzel Baking Co. in Philly and sell Hank's soda, Goldenberg's Peanut Chews and of course, Tastykakes. You can finish off your meal with an Italian water ice. But the main deal is the cheesesteak.

SMITTY: "In Philly, they pile the steak real high on the grill and it tends to dry out. We cook our sandwiches to order. We only use rib-eye, the best cut of meat. And you can't have a good sandwich without the right roll. That's one of the reasons they have a hard time making good sandwiches out here. We fly in half-baked Amoroso rolls from Philly everyday and finish the baking process in our ovens at the shop. The cheese is important, too. In Philly, they usually drop the cheese right on top. But here we use a blend of white American and provolone cheese that we mix in with the steak. And yes, you can order it with Cheese Whiz if you want, too."

Phillies shortstop and California resident Jimmy Rollins is a believer in South Street and a frequent South Street visitor just like Will Smith, Kevin Bacon, Mike Tollin, and other Philly expatriates.

JIMMY ROLLINS: "That place is awesome. I'm a big fan of Jim's Steaks on South Street in Philly but *South Street* in LA beats Jim's—no question about it. They really take their time when they make a cheesesteak and you can taste the difference. When I go in there, they treat me great. I've given them signed balls and pictures that they hung up in the shop and they never charge me. Smitty did it right out there. If you're going to open up a restaurant in Hollywood or LA, it *better* be good or it won't make it."

South Street has caught on in Tinseltown. Since their opening, they have two more shops, one on Hollywood Boulevard and the other in Burbank. Even more exciting, South Street is the official cheesesteak at the Staples Center and there are plans to supply arenas around the country with their version of the Philly classic.

SMITTY: "It's been great to see this place do so well. We get Philly people in here all the time and they can't believe we've been able to replicate the bona fide

Philly cheesesteak. Mike Tollin comes in our shop all the time. That guy might live in LA, but in his heart, he's still living in Philly. He resents the fact that I have Lakers season tickets. I live and die with all the Philly sports teams but I've been going to Laker games for so long now, I'm a big fan. I'm surprised that Mike's still talking to me."

And the natives? Yes, LA people are being won over. Some of them are being bowled over. We asked some natives who have become South Street regulars. One guy, a lifelong Dodger fan named David Bronow, who goes to South Street about once a week, has this to offer: "I'm on a roll (no pun intended) with Philly stuff. These sandwiches taste delicious. When I'm hungry at lunch, I crave them. Not only that, I'm doing terrific with Phillies ballplayers on my fantasy-league baseball team. So I say, 'Go Phillies!' . . . until they play the Dodgers."

But Smitty still gets the biggest kick from the Philly people who stop in.

SMITTY: "There's nothing like people from Philly. I see something that takes me back home every time I stop by the restaurant. If two people from New York meet, they usually chat for a minute or two. You know. They small-talk with things like 'What part of New York are you from?' that kind of thing. But when Philadelphia people run into one another, they'll talk for hours about *everything* happening back home.

"This big guy came into the shop one day. He took one look around at all the Philly stuff on the walls and he took one big whiff and said to no one in particular, 'I'm home.'"

And when he's buzzing around *South Street* on a busy Saturday night, so is Smitty.

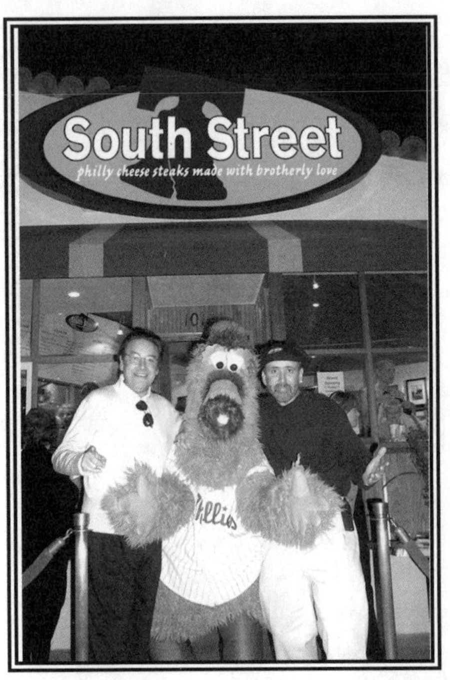

In January 2002, the Phanatic helped open South Street, an authentic Philly cheesesteak joint in Westwood Village. Partners Mitch Goldman (left) and Smitty have since opened up two more South Streets in the Los Angeles area. (Photo: Courtesy of South Street)

PHANATIC PHILE

THE SCHMITTER

Speaking of Smitty—in a related story . . .

One of the main attractions at the new ballpark (besides squinting to catch Thome bombs disappearing into the right field bleachers and watching the radar gun tilt every time Billy Wagner throws a pitch) is the official arrival at the ballpark of one of Philadelphia's legendary culinary masterpieces—the Schmitter sandwich. It's a sandwich that was born in McNally's, an old tavern in Chestnut Hill. It's so delectable it consistently wins the best sandwich award in the annual Best of Philly edition of *Philadelphia Magazine*.

Now before I go on, when Bob Gordon and I were researching legendary sandwiches around the country that might compare with the Schmitter (by the way, researching sandwiches is great work if you can get it), we posted an inquiry on the Pittsburgh Pirates message board about a sandwich in Pittsburgh called the Primanti. Bob had tried one on a visit to Pittsburgh's new park last year. (Forgive him, we were kicking off a convention in the city and he stayed on for the game. I didn't. The Pirates have Randall Simon.) Anyway, a fan of the Primanti sandwich (who elected to keep his identity secret for fear of starting a cross-state civil war) posted the following response, which we have duplicated word for word.

Some documents, like the Gettysburg Address, need no word-smithing:

Our Primanti sandwich is a complete meal between 2 slices of Italian bread. All basic food groups are represented: Grains (bread and french fries), meats (Capicola, steak, or turkey), fruit and vegetable (tomato and cole slaw), and dairy (cheese).

Layered carefully and eaten sloppily, a Primanti sandwich has its perfect companion in a sour pickle, which is served alongside. Prepared and eaten properly, a good sandwich requires about 4 napkins for post-meal face and finger wiping.

Shocking when first looked at, the first bite leads to a savory second, then with lips licked and taste buds still wanting, the mind wonders, "Can I handle another?"

Can your Schmitter top that?

In answer to his first question, it looks as though—judging from the waist sizes in Pittsburgh—most Pirate fans *can* indeed handle more than one Primanti sandwich. Steeler fans can handle four. In fact, most Pittsburgh fans don't get around to asking themselves the question, "Can I handle another?" until they have consumed a quantity that corresponds with their ring finger (on either the first or second hand) in the Pittsburgh sandwich-counting process. But I also have a hard time trusting a guy who roots for a team that provides safe haven for mascot batterers. (I still wake up in a cold sweat at night, visualizing Randall Simon swinging a baseball bat at a sausage with scrawny legs. But in my dream, the sausage has a Phanatic head on top. Speaking for mascots everywhere, Pittsburgh is one place where playing "Simon says" is scary.)

But the answer to the big question this Pirate rooter poses, "Can your Schmitter top that?" is: "Well, uh, yeah, with one arm tied behind our back."

OK, class, let's go to the lab and dissect a Schmitter. At the core, you'll find prime roast beef smothered in cheese, sautéed onions, tomato, and grilled salami—yes, grilled salami, a touch of class if ever there were one. You'll find that whole scrumptious ensemble lathered in a special sauce that somewhat resembles Russian dressing, but is far better than any Russian dressing anyone in Pittsburgh ever tasted. Round Kaiser rolls slightly toasted serve as bookends on a sandwich that's guaranteed to drip all over your shirt. (Note to that anonymous Pirates fan: please notice that nowhere is cole slaw to be found, or better yet tasted, on the Schmitter.)

Now that it's obvious which sandwich packs more artery-clogging pop, lets examine the history of this great sandwich.

JOE PIÉ, MANAGER, McNALLY'S: "The Schmitter was invented about thirty years ago by a guy named Dennis Krenich. Dennis worked up the road at Chestnut Hill Hospital. He came here all the time to shoot the breeze with 'Pops' [tavern owner Huey McNally] and drink [Philadelphia's own] Schmidt's beer. One day, they decided to experiment with a new sandwich that went so well with Schmidt's beer they called it the Schmitter.

"As fate would have it, Dennis moved to Pittsburgh and worked as a steel worker. He was called back down to Philly to work on the Citizens Bank Park construction project. He helped put up the big Phillies sign over the scoreboard in left field."

Dennis' sandwich made its debut at Citizens Bank Park at the start of the season and has proven to be a big hit. Working at the ballpark has not been without its challenges, however.

JOE PIÉ: "Feeding so many people at one time is the biggest challenge. McNally's is a small neighborhood tavern. Normally we'll sell about 50 Schmitters a week. In the first two months of this season alone, we sold over *15,000* sandwiches. Our biggest day was in April. We sold *1,197* Schmitters in one day. We were running out of room on the grill that day. As a result, we've added a second grill, which has helped a lot. And we can't make the special sauce ourselves in such mass quantities so we have another food company replicating it. It tastes just like the sauce we use at the bar, plus we can order 400 gallons of it at a time.

"It's been so exciting for everyone associated with McNally's to have this relationship with the Phillies. A lot of people from the Phillies come to McNally's. David Montgomery comes in all the time. David's a down-to-earth Philly kind of guy.

"The guy who's most choked up about this great partnership with the Phillies is Pops McNally. His grandmother started a luncheonette at the top of Germantown Avenue back in 1921. That's what evolved into McNally's. Back then, Chestnut Hill was mostly rich folks. The trolley drivers who rode up and down Germantown Avenue never had a place to go for a sandwich. Pops'

PHANATIC PHILE

grandfather was one of those trolley drivers. His trolley was the number 23 that ran from Chestnut Hill all the way into South Philadelphia, exactly two blocks from the new ballpark. When Pops visited Citizens Bank Park for the first time and looked two blocks north to where his grandfather worked every day, his emotions got the better of him."

We don't know how the Primanti sandwich got started. We figure it happened one day when the garbage disposal broke and someone yelled, "Hey, what should I do with all this cole slaw and french fries?"

Joe mentioned he'd be happy to pit the Schmitter against any sandwich in the country including the Primanti: "We'll gladly go to war with anyone. Maybe Governor Rendell, who's no stranger to the Schmitter, could be the judge."

Ed may as well. As Governor, he's used to being sandwiched between Philly and Pittsburgh.

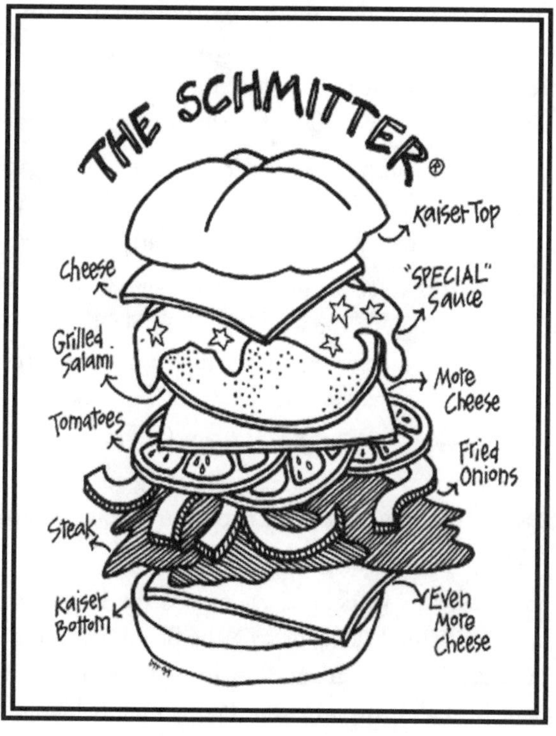

The legendary Schmitter sandwich can now be found at Citizens Bank Park. Napkins required. (Illustration: Courtesy of McNally's Tavern)

CHAPTER 15

HARRY THE K MOVIN' ON UP TO COOPERSTOWN

Philadelphia didn't know Harry Kalas when he breezed into town from Houston in 1971. Harry was a stranger to Philly, a fresh figure brought in specially to ring in a new era that featured a brand-new stadium and a whole new cast of promising ballplayers with unfamiliar names like Schmidt, Luzinski, Bowa, and Boone. Harry also swept out the old—or at least the good-riddance old. Harry arrived in town on the heels of a rough decade for Phillies fans. The hometowners trotted some great players out to the diamond in the sixties, talents like future Hall of Famer Jim Bunning, pitcher Chris Short, outfielder Johnny Callison, outfielder Tony Gonzalez, and others. Unfortunately, they assembled a strong cast at a time when some of the more talent-laden squads in the game's history were competing. Consequently, the Phils managed only three first-division finishes in the decade, including the heartbreaking second-place finish after the 1964 collapse.

Harry Kalas was introduced to the Philly faithful when he emceed the Opening Day ceremonies at the Vet. Over the ensuing decades, he formed a bond with the fans and with broadcast partner Whitey Ashburn that touched the heart of a blue-collar town.

And arguably—no, categorically—Harry's voice became more recognizable than any other Philadelphia personality. Harry was the man on the scene in 1980 when those "new" names—Carlton, Schmidt, Luzinski, et al.—blossomed into national prominence to accomplish what no other Phillie team in history had ever done; win a World Series.

Harry added color and Philly flavor to everything he did. He expanded to other sports and became one of the more recognizable voices in football as well, doing voice-overs for NFL Films. In addition to broadcasting Big Five basketball and Notre Dame football, Harry has voiced-over several national commercials.

Kalas has reaped numerous honors for his work. He was named the Pennsylvania Sportscaster of the year 18 times. In the year 2002 alone, he won the Board of Governor's Award at the Mid-Atlantic Emmy Awards, the Ken Garland Lifetime Achievement Award at the Philadelphia AIR (Achievement In Radio) Awards, and the Lifetime Achievement Award from the Philadelphia Sports Congress. In 2004, he was the recipient of the inaugural Legacy of Excellence Award from the Philadelphia Sports Hall of Fame and was one of 19 charter inductees.

All in all, Harry the K has moved on up to a respected position in the Philly sport scene and an enviable position in the hearts of Phillies fans everywhere.

PHANATIC PHILE

HARRY AND ME

My neighbor Steve Gillin is a cop. He's a great guy. Steve loves his own job but he's always telling me, "Tom, *you* have the greatest job in the world." I hear that comment everywhere, from lawyers, doctors, students, housewives, househusbands, accountants—everybody. I guess that feeling stems from the notion that the Phanatic gets to live out every sports-obsessed kid's fantasy by working for the hometown team (thankfully my employer considers donning a furry, green costume and acting like an idiot "work"; your employer might not).

Growing up in Jenkintown, Pennsylvania in the northern suburbs of Philadelphia, I ate, drank, slept, and breathed Philly sports. In the mid to late-seventies there was a lot to cheer about too. The Broad Street Bullies were bullying on up to two Stanley Cups. Year after year, the Sixers excited the city with one of the most electric teams in the NBA. And the Phillies and Eagles combined to provide monster moments at the Vet year round.

Each team in each sport had one particular guy I identified with, a guy who was my favorite. As Anthony Gargano points out in the fun book he co-wrote with Glen Macnow, *The Great Philadelphia Fan Book*, every Philly kid has a "guy."

Like Anthony, Dr. J was my guy on the Sixers and my "main man" on the whole Philly sport scene. I collected anything that had his picture on it and spent countless hours in the backyard trying to perfect the patented Dr. J finger roll (as of this writing, when I do that finger roll, I look just like Dr. J—in the fourth grade). But I had favorites on each of the other teams as well. On the Flyers, it was Rick MacLeish. MacLeish was the graceful winger who could skate circles around the competition and uncork a blistering bullet with a flick of his wrists. Eagles running back Wilbert Montgomery was my favorite Eagle. He could run around or through oncoming tacklers—whatever it took—and break off a long gain anytime.

On the Phillies, my favorite wasn't out there on the field. He was behind the mic. Harry Kalas was my "guy" with the Phils. Sure, I loved watching the Bull pound balls into the "Bull Ring" in the upper deck (that was the portion of the 500 Level at the Vet that Greg purchased for kids' groups every year). I went crazy screaming when Pete Rose slid head first into third. And it always seemed that Garry Maddox made a game-saving catch whenever I was at the park.

But Harry was my favorite—my "guy" in Philly-fan sport talk.

As a kid, there was something about Harry that appealed to me. Right off the bat, I thought it was cool having a job where all you had to do was sit and announce baseball games for a living (little did I know that years later I'd have a job that rivaled Harry's for the "All-Time Cool Job"). Harry always seemed to be "lovin' it" when he was just doing his job. You couldn't miss the excitement in his voice when he called Phillies home run shots and swapped stories with partner Whitey Ashburn. Whitey used to call Harry a "party waiting to happen."

Good call, Whitey. On the air, Whitey used to tease Harry about his life-of-the-party reputation off the air. In the spring of 1995, during a spring training game, I heard a great exchange between the two on the radio. It was the eve of the announcement about who had been selected to enter the Hall of Fame that year.

HARRY: "Whitey, I feel good about your chances tomorrow. I think this is finally going to be your year."

WHITEY: "Harry, my son called me today and he said the same thing you just said. Then he added that, if I do get selected, he's gonna catch the first flight down here because he can't wait to party with *you*!"

So yeah, Harry always looked like the guy at the party you'd want to stand around the keg with, talkin' baseball. Not surprisingly, my favorite Harry moments as a kid were the parties in the clubhouse that followed the pennant-clinching games in '76, '77, '78, and '80. Harry was there beaming, drenched in champagne and beer, his eyes moist from the sting of alcohol—all the while crying tears of joy. Those moments confirmed what every Phillies fan felt about Harry—Harry Kalas is not just an announcer. He's a fan. He's one of us. Even though he was born in Chicago, Harry is Philly, through and through.

There's another aspect of my job responsibilities that makes people like my neighbor Steve Gillin think that I have "the greatest job in the world." I get to meet people like Harry and other high-profile people. It's true. I do. And that is a dynamite aspect of my job. But I'll be honest. Many times, meeting the rich and/or famous turns out to be disappointing. They're not the people they appear to be. Too often, the rose-colored glasses we wear when we look at them get a bit fogged over and blurred when we meet them in the flesh. Harry is *not* in that category. With Harry, the guy you expect to meet is the guy who shows up.

He's always gracious to fans. He signs autographs, laughs along with people doing their Harry Kalas impersonation, and bellows his signature "Outta here" call to their delight whenever they ask. And they always ask. I've seen many fans come up to him with cell phones and ask Harry to say "hi" to their moms or dads or to record an outgoing message on their voice-answering machines right there on the spot. Harry never blinks an eye. He takes the phone and in his velvet, baritone voice "announces" into the receiver, "I'm sorry that I can't come to the phone right now, but I'M ON A LONG DRIVE, TO DEEP LEFT FIELD—I AM OUTTA HERE!!!!"

In 2000, we celebrated Harry's 30th season with the Phillies. Fans walking into the Vet that night got a great Talkin' Harry Doll. When you hit it, the doll says, "That ball's outta here!" or "Here's the pitch—struck him out," or "Phils win!" Harry's favorite player, Darren Daulton, emceed the pre-game show, giving Harry a well-deserved night off.

The Phillies did their best to keep the identity of the emcee and the other guests a secret that night. Players, family, and friends were being whisked through the corridors of the Vet, ducking into hallways and shielding their faces as they walked by. Before the game, I saw Harry, decked out in his finest white blazer, black slacks, and sparkling white shoes, pacing nervously outside the clubhouse. He didn't know who the emcee was going to be.

Out of nowhere, Dickie Noles appeared, admiring the dapper Harry.

"Hey Harry," Dickie growled, "you look great. You and Dutch [Daulton] in his tuxedo must be the two best-dressed people here tonight!" Oops. The cat was out of the bag and the mystery emcee had been revealed.

But that was OK because there were other great surprises in store for Harry that night. Harry's wife Eileen and the couple's three sons—Todd, Brad, and Kane—joined Harry on the field. So did some of Harry's favorite players—Mitch Williams (Mitchie-Poo), Glenn Wilson, John Kruk, Dick Allen, and Jim Kaat, to name a few. There was a letter from crooner and fellow piano bar singer, Bobby Rydell. And Bill Giles presented Harry and Eileen with a trip to the Caribbean Islands.

Harry gave a great speech that night and ended by singing his theme song, "High Hopes," with the fans joining in as the lyrics flashed on the scoreboard. It was one big love-in and the biggest "lounge" Harry has ever played.

I jumped on my red ATV and led Harry's convertible around the Vet. I couldn't help taking a couple of backward peeks. A teary-eyed Harry Kalas was waving to all the Philly faithful.

The Phils also brought in Harry's favorite player as a kid, Mickey Vernon. Mickey is an ex-Washington Senator and ex-Philly A who won two batting titles in Ted Williams' heyday—a feat even the great DiMaggio could equal but not top. Mickey is the pride of Marcus Hook where he grew up (the Philadelphia A's Society was instrumental in having a statue of Mickey erected there). So what did Mickey Vernon have to do with Harry Kalas? If it weren't for Mickey, Harry might not have lived the movin' on up story he has.

HARRY KALAS: "I started out as a Cubs fan but switched allegiance to the Washington Senators the day I attended my first baseball game. It rained that day. It was my first trip to Wrigley Field. During the delay, I wandered down to the first row right by the visitors' dugout. Mickey Vernon popped his head out of the dugout, saw me standing there, and invited me into the clubhouse during the rain delay. That's when my love affair with baseball started."

Harry knew early on that he was never going to make a career out of playing the game so he decided to pursue a broadcasting career. At the University of Iowa, Harry was the announcer for several different sports. Then on graduation day, he received a letter from Uncle Sam (the kind of letter the good Uncle no longer sends) welcoming him to the army where he trained as a heavy weapons infantryman. He was stationed in Hawaii and got his first big break (I think *getting sent to Hawaii in the first place* was Harry's first break) when his master sergeant called him in and told him they were looking for a broadcast specialist who could interview the troops and do short profiles on them for army radio. Shortly thereafter, he was hired by KGU radio and he found himself broadcasting Hawaii Islander games (in the new Pacific Coast League) as well as University of Hawaii games.

What was broadcasting like back then? Jimmy Fallon on *Saturday Night Live* spoofs a nasal-voiced morning record jock who works solo in the studio but fakes that he's surrounded by a boothful of zany sidekicks. Well . . . listen to Harry.

HARRY: "I never went on the team's road trips. The Islanders played teams in Tacoma and Spokane in the continental States a few time zones away. We needed to broadcast the games at a decent hour in Hawaii, so we had a guy call us long distance from the continental U.S. with the play-by-play. I broadcast entire games by reading those transcriptions. I used to hit a hollow box with a pencil every time there was a base hit. The engineer in the studio would crank up the crowd noise so loud, you'd think the game was being played in Yankee Stadium. "Of course, the transcription I was reading didn't include balls and strikes so I had to improvise each at-bat. It was Hawaii and the beautiful weather and nightlife were always beckoning so an awful lot of guys swung at first pitches when I broadcast (I wonder how many guys never got to the major leagues because their scouting report said, "shows no patience at the plate"?)! They played some *awfully* fast games!"

Harry has moved way on up from those days of fabricating the action in Hawaii. He moved on up (?) to Houston (let's see . . . Houston or Hawaii . . . you be the judge) and became part of the Astros' first broadcast team in 1965. In Houston, Harry befriended one of the Astros' young PR guys named Bill Giles. Giles, of course, went to Philly. After Bill settled into the Quaker City in '70, he enlisted Kalas to help him launch a new chapter in Phillies baseball history at brand-new Veterans Stadium. Harry joined By Saam and Richie Ashburn in the booth in 1971 and was the man on the field emceeing the pre-game festivities on the first Opening Day ever at the Vet.

HARRY: "I was excited about the move because I knew from traveling to Philly what a great sports town this was. I remember the first day at the Vet was really cold. The first ball was delivered by helicopter, and I never thought that "Irish" Mike [Ryan] was going to catch it because of the wind. Bill Giles always managed to come up with crazy ideas like that."

Little did Harry Kalas know that day that the Phillies would be handing out a talking doll in his likeness thirty years later. And he could never have predicted that 31 years later the Baseball Hall of Fame would be calling him. In January of 2002, Harry won the Ford C. Frick Award, given yearly to a broadcaster who has made major contributions to the game of baseball.

A week after the announcement about Harry's winning the Award, the Hall of Fame called *me* and said they also wanted to add the Phillie Phanatic costume to their permanent display in the Museum. They wanted to *honor the Phanatic* in the flesh—er, fur—on Induction Weekend.

Harry and I going to Cooperstown on the same weekend? Pinch me, I must be dreaming.

It was an unforgettable few days. A nonstop sea of red flowed down Main

Street in Cooperstown all weekend. I'd like to say they were all there for the Phanatic and Harry but some guy named Ozzie Smith (the lone inductee that year) was being honored and the St. Louis fans dressed in Cardinal red came out in droves for their hero too.

On Saturday, July 27, the Phanatic's display was officially unveiled in the Hall of Fame Museum. Talk about your out-of-body (costume?) experience! There was *a* Phanatic standing straight up, arms out and eyes frozen in that familiar wide-eyed stare. And then there was a second Phanatic, *the* Phanatic—that would be me—in the same costume, looking like I just stumbled across my twin brother (I don't know which role I would have played in *Twins*—Danny DeVito's or the Governator's). David Montgomery, Hall of Fame president Dale Petrosky, and HOF chairman Jane Forbes Clark joined me at the display where flashbulbs popped as they cut the red ribbon around the new display. Two hours later, at the Clark Sports Center, Hall of Famers Mike Schmidt, Bob Feller, Jim Palmer, and others participated in a Q and A session in front of a packed auditorium.

I was backstage, awaiting the official ceremony. Right before the ceremony was to begin, the door leading to the backstage area opened and in walked Harry. He had insisted that his weekend itinerary include attending the Phanatic's big moment.

I got goosebumps seeing Harry in the front row applauding as Dale Petrosky presided over the festivities. It was typical Harry—thinking of others even though he himself was being pulled in a hundred different directions that weekend.

Bill Giles hosted a kickin' tent party that night for the entire Phillies family that had made the trip. We partied on the banks of Lake Otsego. The highlight of the evening was when Harry, looking dapper in a white sports coat and matching white shoes, emerged from the darkness into the tent as the band broke into his favorite song, "High Hopes." Harry took the mic and belted out the lyrics while everyone at the party chimed in—a diverse group singing in diverse keys. The local wildlife acted strange for weeks afterward, I'm told. Didn't matter, it was fun. And it was classic Harry.

The next day, Phillie fans swarmed in from everywhere for the induction ceremonies. Forty-seven Hall of Famers graced the stage to witness Ozzie Smith's induction. Ted Williams had passed away on July 5, and a beautiful video was shown highlighting the Splendid Splinter's illustrious career. Williams' contemporary, St. Louis legend Stan Musial, lightened the mood with a rousing version of "Take Me Out to the Ballgame" on the harmonica.

When it was Harry's turn to receive his award, the Phillies fans in the crowd stood and cheered and chanted Harry's name over and over. Harry's speech covered all the bases. He thanked the Phillies for their support, the fans for their passion and of course, Whitey for his friendship.

HARRY: "I was nervous about making my speech, leading up to that weekend. To be honored by the Hall of Fame is a little overwhelming. But when I was standing on that stage, I knew 'His Whiteness' was looking down on me and I got through it OK.

"I can't put into words what that weekend meant to me. To see all those great Hall of Famers on that stage at one time and to look out at all those fans was very humbling. One of my lasting memories is the camaraderie among all the ex-ballplayers. I wound up golfing with Mr. October, Reggie Jackson, in an outing that they put together for all the Hall of Famers. I've never been much of a golfer and as a matter of fact I pretty much gave it up, but I never enjoyed a round of golf more."

Reggie Jackson drove a lot of golf balls out of the area code that day, according to Harry. But Reggie isn't hitting baseballs any longer. What a loss for the game. Just as it's going to be a loss for the Philly fans when Harry finally broadcasts to the Philly phaithful that he's "outta here." Until then, Harry's gonna keep on movin' up at Citizens Bank Park, living for the day he says, "The Philadelphia Phillies . . . Champions of the World!"

The Phillie Phanatic clowns around with Harry Kalas before a Phillies games at the Vet. Two weeks later, the Phanatic joined Harry for his big Hall of Fame weekend in Cooperstown.

(Photo: Chip Fox, The *Philadelphia Inquirer*)

HARRY THE K'S INDUCTION DAY POEM

Harry wrote this poem about the Philadelphia fans and read it in his acceptance speech on Induction Day in Cooperstown on July 27, 2002.

This is to the Philadelphia fan—
To laud your passion as best I can
Your loyalty is unsurpassed
Be the Fightin's in first or last.
We come to the park each day
Looking forward to another fray
Because we know you'll be there
We know you really care.
You give opposing pitchers fits
Because as one loyalist shouts, "Everybody hits."
To be sure, in Philly there might be some boos
Because you passionate fans, like the manager, hate to lose.
Your reaction to the action on the field that you impart
Spurs us as broadcasters to call the game with enthusiasm and heart.
We feel your passion through and through
Philadelphia fans, I love you.

STADIUM STUFF
TOGETHER FOREVER

Harry Kalas shared the Phillies broadcast booth with his friend, Richie Ashburn, for twenty-seven years at Veterans Stadium. Harry made sure that the plaque that hung outside of the broadcast booth, dedicating the booth in honor of Richie, made it over to the new broadcast booth at Citizens Bank Park. Harry and Whitey will forever be linked at the new ballpark on Ashburn Alley. A huge bronze statue of Whitey rounding second stands in the shadow of Harry the K's restaurant in left field.

WHITEY AND HARRY

Words and music written and copyrighted by Chuck Brodsky

Moonlight on the mountains,
North Carolina two-lane,
Trying to find a ballgame
No matter how bad the reception
Whitey, man, I miss you,
When I listen to the Phillies.
And there's Harry going on without you,
Harry . . . good old Harry.

Radio under my pillow,
Kept me up on school nights.
The ballgames from the west coast
Wouldn't start until eleven.
Whitey, man, I miss you,
When I listen to the Phillies.
And there's Harry going on without you,
For the first time since I was seven.

We wore red, the thousands of us,
Who'd come to say goodbye & pay their last respects.
This tough town really loved you.
I saw grown men who wept.

Bats & spikes & flowers,
Made a shrine around your casket.
And I signed in in the guestbook,
As the line filed past it
Whitey, man, I miss you,
When I listen to the Phillies.
And there's Harry going on without you,
Harry . . . good old Harry.

SCOTT GRAHAM MOVES UP TO THE WORLD SERIES

Harry Kalas has loved a lot of Phillies teams. Of course, the 1980 Championship team holds a special place in his heart. But Harry will be the first to tell you that his favorite Phillie team of all was our town's ultimate movin' on up team—the team that went from worst to first, the '93 Phillies. With Harry's personal theme song, "High Hopes" providing the soundtrack to that season, the '93 gang of "gypsies, tramps and thieves" rollicked and *macho-ed* their way to the World Series.

Harry's colleague, Scott Graham, is another guy who enjoyed that incredible ride. Scott was born a Yankees fan and grew up in North Jersey. Fortunately, salvation was at hand. Scott attended the University of Pennsylvania, and moved on up to a full-fledged Phillies fan. In 1991, Scott took a job with the Phillies as the host of the Phillies radio pre- and post-game show, *Talkin' Baseball.* Two seasons later, he found himself smack-dab in the middle of the most exciting baseball season he had ever experienced.

SCOTT GRAHAM: "I've never seen a looser bunch than the '93 Phils. They started out that way in spring training. I kept thinking that this team finished in last place the year before and now they're out there pulling pranks on one another and holding daily wrestling matches on the field at Jack Russell Stadium. I thought, 'Are they taking this thing seriously enough?'

"I've never seen a team have so much fun. They were the loudest team I've ever seen. This wasn't the only team that ever clowned around. But other teams do all that in private. The '93 guys did it out in plain view. They didn't care what anyone thought. They were going to have fun, no matter what."

The guys on the team weren't the only ones clowning around that year. Even at the World Series, the whole Phillie contingent stayed loose.

SCOTT GRAHAM: "Oh I was having fun all right, but I was a little nervous too. It was my first World Series and I wanted to get everything right. Well that didn't happen. During the pre-game show just before game one in Toronto, I'm on the air and I'm getting a signal from my producer, John Weber, from the field. He was poking his head out of the visitors' dugout and motioning into the dugout that he had lined up a guest for me to interview. My soundman was sitting next to me talking to John over the headset and scribbling something down on a piece of paper. He handed me the paper, with the name 'Duke Raggiola' written on it. I was still talking live on the air and I was staring at the paper thinking, 'Who the heck is Duke Raggiola?' Well I looked back down at the field and

John was waving frantically and pointing up to me, indicating we were ready for the interview. Not knowing who Duke Raggiola was and not having any time to find out, I opened with an innocent-enough question: 'We're here with Duke Raggiola. So Duke, what the heck are you doing here?' The voice on the other line said, 'Scott, it's Joe Garagiola.'"

Weber had been yelling into his headset: "Do Garagiola! Do Garagiola!"

SCOTT GRAHAM: "Needless to say, whenever Joe Garagiola is at a game, Harry Kalas always points out to me that my buddy 'Duke' is in attendance."

CHAPTER 16

THOME

Let's go back to the year 1930. A radio interview crackles through staticky speakers and sounds something like this.

INTERVIEWER: "Lou, you've got to be included among the greatest players who ever played this sport. People mention you in the same breath as Wagner, Lajoie, Cobb, and Speaker. Do you think you're up there with those lads?"

LOU GEHRIG: "Well, I don't think about things like that. My job is to play for the New York Yankees, and I try to do that to the best of my ability every day."

INTERVIEWER: "But Lou, your statistics have earned you a place with these illustrious gentlemen. Do you think you can supplant them in the record book?"

LOU GEHRIG: "I just try to sock the ball the best I can and hope I'm blessed with good luck. I'll keep doing that till I can't any more. Then I'd be honored and humbled if people remember me."

Now, move on up to the year 2004.

INTERVIEWER: "People are mentioning you in the same breath as Ruth, Mays, Aaron, Williams, Robinson, McGwire, and the all-time great sluggers. Do you feel you belong in that group?"

TOO MANY BALLPLAYERS: "I've put up the numbers. I think they say it all. Besides, I play in a tougher era."

INTERVIEWER: "Is your goal to beat those numbers on the all-time lists? And will you do it as a member of the (fill in the team)?"

TOO MANY BALLPLAYERS: "Who wouldn't want to beat those numbers? Big numbers mean big money for me. And if I don't do it as a (fill in the club), I'll do it wherever they pay the big bucks."

Let's stay in the year 2004.

INTERVIEWER: "Jim, people mention you now with the greatest sluggers like Ruth, Mays, Aaron, Williams, Robinson, and McGwire. How do you feel about those comparisons?"

JIM THOME: "Well, I don't really think of things like that. I'm flattered but I'm focused on winning and helping the Philies every way I can."

INTERVIEWER: "But wouldn't you like to move on up on that all-time list of sluggers?"

JIM THOME: "Well, winning a baseball game every night is the most important thing to me. I don't think about the personal achievements."

We overuse some words so much they become meaningless. Take "*gamer*" for example. At the end of a day, who isn't a gamer? Or "*hard-nosed*." From what we read in the papers, it appears that baseball has more hard-nosed guys than Geppetto's workshop. Or "*throwback*." John Kruk called his '93 Phillies pennant-winning team throwbacks. He said their old teams threw them back into the pond because they were considered lightweights (meaning they weren't good ballplayers—none of John's employers, past or present, could ever consider the Krukker a lightweight).

Throwback generally refers to a ballplayer who plays hard and works hard every day *for the sake of his team*. That definition and that word—throwback—give a starting point for what Jim Thome is about. Sure he's a gamer and sure he's hard-nosed. But though he has one of the sport's most recognizable names, he plays for his team, not for personal goals.

In a sport era awash with tiresome torrents of bravado, Jim Thome is a throwback to soft-spoken, hard-working heroes who weren't pampered, set apart, and lionized from eighth grade on. Jim Thome is grounded. Self-promotion is not his pastime.

The three interviews above suggest the modesty at the heart of Thome's throwback nature, the characteristic that distinguishes—and elevates—Jim Thome. Modesty made him an instant hero in Philly—a local deification that took less than a full baseball season. Of course, his quick start (4 of his first 5 games as a Phillie were multi-hit games) and National League-leading 47 homers (second best single-season output in the history of his adopted 120-year-old franchise) didn't hurt.

Thome bonded with Philadelphia fans with his aw-shucks, everyman mien. Thome is the anti-Leon—Leon being the self-absorbed, self-promoting star of the Bud Light beer commercials that make us laugh, but should also give us pause. When you talk to Jim

Thome, he's visibly more at ease discoursing about the team than himself. Thome wears his working-class upbringing and values on his bulging shirtsleeve.

The rest of the Phillies were a bit in awe when Thome's ticket to Philly was officially punched. The Phillies' 2003 preseason TV publicity spots featured lots of different Phillies bowing in front of his locker, paying homage to him like a god. Thome's down-to-earth demeanor immediately alleviated any clubhouse fears that a megastar was now in their midst. Thome was just a regular guy. "Yeah," as Randy Wolf observed in one of the Phillies' TV spots, "a regular guy with arms like tree trunks."

THE REAL WORLD

Jim Thome loves Philly 'cause it's *real.* Strangely, Philly has always been considered *too real* for the reality TV show, *The Real World*. In its 10 PM Tuesday MTV time slot, *Real World* has been the top-rated cable show for 12 to 34-year-olds for seven years. *The Real World* has been drawing four million viewers every season since its inception.

The show's premise is to follow the lives and adventures of a bunch of strangers living together in a big *hip* city. Hip was the stumbling point. The show had chosen New York, Los Angeles, Paris, and other similar centers of swank. The show's principals never considered Philly hip enough until the co-creator of the show, Jon Murray, got a taste of Philadelphia himself. Evidently he liked what he tasted. Murray was here when MTV was honored at PrideFest America in Philly in 2002. The vitality and beauty of Philadelphia impressed Murray. The fact that the metropolitan area is home to 250,000 college students should have tipped off any outsider that, despite deep Old World roots, Philadelphia is a complex, interesting metropolis with a heart that pumps fully oxygenated blood through a diverse set of arteries. Philly is not just about cheesesteaks, even though Philly cheesesteaks happen to be damn good.

Actually, Philadelphia has long been in the camera's eye. Way back in TV's pioneering days, *Bandstand* bopped out live from Philly. Over the years, television series and movies with a Philadelphia theme or tie-in have popped up here and there. But never before like they have now. Philly has moved on up in TV-land status, boasting three recent or current television series portraying life in the Quaker City.

American Dreams takes a look at Philadelphia during the seventies. Another show, *Cold Case*, has wowed critics with its tales of unsolved cases and the guilty brought to belated justice. Before it was cancelled recently, *Hack* portrayed a deposed policeman who drove a cab and fought crime with virtue as his only satisfaction.

They all focus mostly on blue-collar Philadelphia. With the addition of *Real World*, the City of Brotherly Love can be portrayed as a place with great nightlife, restaurants, and a cool city vibe. Oh yeah, and a baseball team and a football team that play in cool stadiums and basketball and hockey teams that play in dyno digs. And Big Five teams that play some of the country's best hoops in one of roundball's hallowed shrines, the Palestra. In reality, the real world has been alive and well in Philly for a long time. Maybe Hollywood can learn a little about keeping it real while they're in town. *Nah, never happen!*

Jim Thome was born in Peoria, Illinois in 1970. He was an all-state basketball player at Limestone High School. Thome's hometown loves its native son. He already has a street named in his honor. Thome has given back to his community, donating a scoreboard to his old high school.

He played basketball and baseball at Illinois Central College where he was honorable mention All American. Jim didn't remain at Illinois Central long. Cleveland drafted him in the third round of the June 1989 draft. He played his first minor league game as an eighteen-year-old in '89 with the Gulf Coast Indians, then blasted right through the minors. At Burlington in 1990, he hit a blistering .373 before being transferred to Kinston where he "cooled off" to .308. His efforts earned him the Lou Boudreau Award, presented annually to the minor league player of the year in the Cleveland system. He was only two weeks beyond his 21st birthday when Cleveland first called him up to the big show in '91. He shuttled back and forth between the majors and minors in '92 because of injuries. In 1993, however, at AAA Charlotte, he led the International League with a .332 average and 102 RBI and ranked third in HR with 25. Again he was the recipient of the Lou Boudreau Award. At the end of the '93 season, Cleveland brought him up to stay.

Thome made the transition to the big leagues look easy. His first three years he played third base. Paul Sorrento was the first sacker for the Tribe at the time. In Thome's first full season with the Indians, he led all AL third basemen with 20 HR. He followed with a sparkling sophomore season when he batted a career-high .314. We think of Thome as a slugger. However, he left Cleveland with a lofty lifetime .287 batting average. In five of eight seasons as a starter, he topped .290.

It was the long ball, however, that thundered him into prominence. He banged out 38 homers and won the Silver Slugger Award for third basemen in 1996. His HR total never again dipped below 30 as he launched a one-man assault on the Cleveland franchise record book. He added the Thome name to a number of AL records as well. Here are some of Thome's achievements.

• in 1996, he became only the second Indian in history to score 100+ runs, hit 30+ homers, walk 100+ times, and drive in 100+ runs (Al Rosen did it first in 1950)

• in 1996, he set a Cleveland record with 123 walks

• in 1997, he became the first left-handed hitter since Carl Yastrzemski in 1970 to hit 40+ HR and drive in and score 100+ runs while drawing 100+ walks

• in 1997, he became the first Indian to draw 100+ walks in consecutive seasons

• in the 1998 post-season, his 6 HR tied Lenny Dykstra and three others for most HR in a post-season

• in the 1998 post-season, his 4 HR in the ALCS against the Yankees set a new ALCS record

• in 1999, he became the only Indian ever to hit 30 HR in 4 consecutive seasons

• in 1999, his 511-foot blast off Don Wengert was the longest ball hit in Jacobs Field history

• in 1999, he became the first player in ML history to hit 2 grand slams in the post-season

• in 1999, he moved into third place on the all-time list for post-season HR with 16 (he subsequently tacked on one more)

• in 2001, his 47 HR placed him second on Cleveland's all-time list for home runs in a season behind Albert Belle who hit 50 in 1995

• in 2001, he became Cleveland's all-time HR leader, eclipsing Albert Belle's 242 (when Thome left Cleveland he had hit 334 and stretched that differential significantly)

• in 2002, he hit 52 HR, second best in the majors, breaking Belle's franchise record of 50 and becoming only the 21st player in ML history to top the 50-HR mark

• in 2002, he extended his club-record streak of 30+ homer seasons to 7, making him only the 15th major leaguer ever to do so

• in 2002, he led the AL in HR ratio (1 HR/ 9.2 AB) and RBI ratio (1 RBI/ 4.2 AB)

• in 2002, he homered in a franchise-record 7 straight games—the third longest streak in ML history

• his 8 career Division Series HR are tied for most in MLB DS history

• in 2003, he tied for ML lead in HR with 47

• in 2003, he became only the second player in history to record back-to-back 40+ HR seasons in two different leagues (Junior Griffey is the other)

• in 2003, he hit Veterans Stadium's final HR

Sorry to go on and on, but that's a dynamite résumé to take to any job interview. The Phillies were aware of what Thome had accomplished. They had great expectations for him. But how about Big Jim? Did Thome have any reservations or angst about coming to Philly in front of their big bad fans?

JIM THOME: "I'm excited to be in Philly. I've felt that way since I made my decision. I knew if I left Cleveland, I had to find a place where I'd be comfortable. And just as important, a place where my family would be comfortable. What a fine choice Philly was—a great place to raise a family. I'm happy my little girl Lila Grace [who was born on 12/15/02] is going to learn baseball in Citizens Bank Park.

"You don't know what to expect when you switch to a different league. I didn't want to be overwhelmed by NL pitching. They had such great names, like Kevin Brown, Randy Johnson, Greg Maddux, etc. You never should let yourself feel comfortable in baseball. The game of baseball is about making adjustments. And I can't overemphasize the role your teammates play in succeeding. You will fail without good teammates. In fact, sometimes the toughest adjustment of all is adjusting to your teammates. But that was easy here. We have great chemistry on this club and good leadership. Leadership doesn't have to come from the oldest guy. It comes from a lot of different guys. It just means no one has to police the team and everybody is on the same page. And I don't mean just the starters. Bench guys are as important as starters for a team's chemistry. Tomas [Perez], J-Mike [Jason Michaels] and the rest all helped me adjust to the NL. Those reserves watch the game carefully and study the pitchers. I learn a lot from them. I trust them and we have a great relationship. Every team doesn't have a group like we have. These guys have made themselves a key part of the team's success. They have their own identity and pride. They call themselves the 'Bench Dogs.' I think Tomas Perez gave them that name."

The Phillie Phanatic gives Jim Thome his first Philly soft pretzel during taping of Comcast SportsNet's "Meet the Phillies" program at the King of Prussia Mall.

(Photo: Chip Fox, The *Philadelphia Inquirer*)

PHANATIC PHILE

WHO LET THE DOGS OUT?

On July 17, 2003, Marlon Byrd slugged a two-out, three-run home run in the 11th inning to cap a thrilling comeback win against the Montreal Expos. With one swing of the bat, Byrd did much more than ignite a celebration in the stands with a walk-off home run. Marlon unleashed the dogs. That's right, hip-hoppers. You finally got your answer to *Who let the dogs out?* It was Marlon Byrd.

Marlon let the Bench Dogs out.

The Bench Dogs are the Phillies' flaky group of backup players. They named themselves "Bench Dogs." The Bench Dogs led the charge out onto the field that night to "greet" Marlon. When the young center-fielder touched home plate, the "beat-down" began. Back-up catcher Todd Pratt grabbed Marlon's jersey and throttled the startled Byrd. Jason Michaels, the reserve outfielder, charged through the pile of players like a fullback plowing through the line of scrimmage. Utility man Tomas Perez got to Byrd and pummeled him with a flurry of left-right combinations to the body. When poor Marlon emerged from the pile, he looked like a haggard boxer from a Stallone movie. The buttons on his jersey had popped off in the melee and he staggered back to the dugout looking a little dazed and confused.

What was *that* about, all of Philadelphia wondered. Why did the hero of the moment have to endure such a "beat-down"?

"It's a way for us bench players to get our frustrations out for not playing every day," joked Bench Dog extraordinaire Tomas Perez "When we backup guys get to the park, we start saying to one another, 'Who's gonna get the beat-down today?'"

Strange talk for a tight-knit team—tight-knit, but not wrapped too tight.

"One thing you can't be as a Bench Dog is 'normal,' that's for sure," adds Todd Pratt.

So what is a Bench Dog?

Pitcher Randy Wolf has his own thoughts: "To be a Bench Dog, you need a mind that's easily amused."

"You have to look pretty and be single. The Bench Dogs always get the girls," barked the very single Jason Michaels.

Jim Thome believes there is more to being a Bench Dog than looking good and starting shaving-cream-pie fights.

"I talk to those guys all the time," said Big Jim. "They give me advice about what I might be doing wrong, and how a pitcher is working batters—all those things."

True Jim, but those guys are more than a little crazy. Take the case of prototypical Bench Dog Tomas Perez. Tomas is a versatile player. When called upon, he can play every position on the diamond. His clutch hitting and all-around play have earned him the nickname "Secret Weapon," courtesy of announcer Harry Kalas.

But it's Tomas' penchant for shaving-cream pies that makes him a huge fan favorite. At one time or another, a Perez pie-to-the-face has victimized just about every Phillie during a post-game TV interview. At one point in the 2003 season, the pies were flying with such regularity that pitcher Randy Wolf showed up for his interview wearing goggles, like a pitcher turned stunt pilot.

TOMAS PEREZ: "The conditions have to be right if I'm going to pie somebody. It's got to be the right guy and we have to be on a hot streak. But I know the fans love it so I do it for the fans as much as anything."

What goes 'round comes 'round. Two days after Marlon got the beat-down, it came 'round for Tomas. As soon as Tomas' RBI hit off Hector Almonte had landed safely in left field in the bottom of the 11th inning, sealing another dramatic come-from-behind win for the Fightins, everyone in the park knew Perez was dead meat. First came the beat-down at home plate. The players swarmed the smiling Venezuelan at first base, igniting a brawl that rivaled most WWF cage matches.

I had run out onto the field as the Phanatic, dancing for joy after the big win and watching the players high-five their way back to the Phillies dugout. A moment later, Tomas Perez reappeared out of the dugout and took a seat in front of the TV cameras for his post-game interview.

Stadium Operations Director Mike DiMuzio darted over and blurted to me, "Tom, you've *got* to go get a plate full of shaving cream and pie Tomas as the Phanatic while he's doing the interview." Mike has seen his share of pie-ings at the Vet. From super flake Jay Johnstone in the seventies to the pie-happy '93 bunch, Mike has seen the best of them and he ranks Tomas right there at the top of the wacko list.

Without hesitating, I bolted up to the Phillies clubhouse to load up on shaving cream. When I got there, at least ten players were already lined up at the door leading to the dugout, pies in hand. Jim Thome was the first man at the door

PHANATIC PHILE

and when he got the signal from a Phillies operative on the field (we'll call him Deep Pie to protect him from Perez retribution, unless he refuses to buy me a drink the next time I see him in a bar—then *I* will be the one who lets the dogs out), Thome yelled, "It's time! Let's go!" The players all ran through the doorway, down the tunnel and onto the field where Tomas Perez sat awaiting the inevitable execution by pie. Twisters have struck with less fury. Tomas was deluged with towels and plates filled with shaving cream. The white stuff covered his head and body like icing on a wedding cake. Actually, it was the icing on the cake as far as the Phils were concerned.

The crowd, which hung around waiting to see the payback, cheered wildly. Tomas looked relieved. Tom Petty was right. The waiting is the hardest part.

The only guy who looked like he wasn't having any fun at all was the TV technician in charge of mic-ing Tomas for the interview. Once again, he needed to request a replacement pair of headphones from the Comcast storeroom. And once again, he had the same explanation for his storekeeper. Just another Dog Day at the Vet.

What does Thome feel about his new team's prospects now that he's played with the group for a year?

JIM THOME: "Of course, ultimately our goal is to win a championship and as Larry Bowa says, 'play 'til Halloween. We have the components for a strong team but we didn't come together in 2004. This game, though, it's just a feeling that you get, a winning feeling when you really have the magic. We couldn't get that feeling going in 2004. The game is tricky. You can lose the feeling fast. When things are going well, you want to stay in that zone. You want to go to the park, do well, then go home and do it all over again the next day. The game goes by quickly when you're doing well. When you're not doing well, just being out on the field is like an eternity. That's the feeling you *don't* want. We battled that feeling all year. And when it does go bad like that the fun part of this game is overcoming those bad times. I still think we can do that here."

Thome's Phillies team saw the heights and the depths in Thome's first year in Philly. Lost in the September swoon that did the Phillies in was the fabulous September 2003 that Thome had personally. Though the Marlins blew the Phils out in a late-season rush, Thome did a yeoman's job trying to carry his sinking mates. He socked 10 HR and drove in 30 in earning NL Player of the Month honors. He was the first Phillie so honored since Lenny Dykstra in May 1994.

JIM THOME: "The Marlins just got hot in 2003. But it was great being part of the final year at the Vet. Again we had great chemistry. I watched how Pat Burrell struggled. He's a promising player and we all supported him all year. Check the back of any baseball card. You'll see that practically every player has one or two off-years. Pat's a good kid. I'm convinced he'll bounce back after the past two seasons. If the rest of us play our role, we'll get there.

"The fans in Philly are so awesome! I never expected them to react like they did to Pat's struggles. They could tell he was trying and if they left him alone, he'd come around. You can feel that Philly tradition in the stands—how deep people here love their teams and how much they wear that love on their sleeves.

"The fans overwhelmed me personally. They showed me a lot of respect. They didn't know me as a person or a player when I got here and they took me under their wing. I thank them for helping make my transition easy. And to be selected for the Final Innings ceremony to greet Mike Schmidt! When he raised my arm, that was one of my greatest moments of my life. Think about it! The best third baseman ever was closing down the Vet, one of the game's famous stadiums. When I was a kid growing up, Mike Schmidt was one of my biggest heroes—a power hitter. I wanted to be just like him. Remember, I started my career as a third baseman. That was one of my most vivid recollections as a kid—Mike Schmidt jumping into Tug's arms. Anyway, it was humbling for me—all the tradition here. Look at all the guys that paid their dues here—Larry Bowa, Dallas Green, Vuke, Daulton, Dykstra, and on and on. But for me to be picked to go out there and greet Schmidty was an incredible honor and I'll always treasure that moment."

So Jim Thome, the Paul Bunyan throwback guy, is a baseball softie, touched by tradition and sentiment?

JIM THOME: "I was raised in a baseball tradition. I grew up in Peoria, which was about two hours from Wrigley Field. I used to think, even as a kid, there's so much tradition at that park! My early memories were of Bill Buckner and Dave Kingman and guys like that. My dad encouraged me to play baseball, instilled the love of the game in me. My whole family was into it. My aunt was into softball, my dad played fast-pitch softball, and my grandfather played in what was called the Three-I League. They barnstormed all around the country in the Bob Feller days. So the baseball background is definitely there in the Thome clan. We all played. I played hoops too, but I knew I just didn't have it there. I was gonna be a baseball guy.

"When I got to the minor leagues, I played on good teams. Charlie Manuel helped me at every level along the way. I enjoyed the minors. I was only a young kid. But the minors are the backbone of your baseball career. You don't realize it when it's going on, but the camaraderie, the bus trips, the quick meals at the Wendy's and the McDonald's—you learn to live the life or you don't. Our lifestyle today as major leaguers, particularly at Citizens Bank Park, is so different from all that, so it makes me appreciate what I have all the more."

And what does Thome think of his new digs at Citizens Bank Park?

JIM THOME: "I love the new park. First of all I have no regrets with my decision to come to Philly. Cleveland had a great organization and so does Philly, but I could tell that the Phillies are going to make something good happen, even if we do take our lumps along the way. They convinced me and I haven't changed my opinion.

"As for the new park, it's exciting. I've got the same sense, the same feeling we had in Cleveland about moving into a new home and feeling proud. I see the same thing across the way with the Eagles. It's an exciting time in Philly, a once-in-a-lifetime time. It's great to be here and watch the excitement grow all around the city."

PHANATIC PHILE

OPERATION THOME

When the speculation first became public that the Phils might be putting on the full-court press to lure slugger Jim Thome out of Cleveland, there was a constant buzz around the Phillies offices. The ticket office had flashbacks to 1979, when a guy named Pete Rose arrived in Philadelphia and helped boost the club's all-time attendance record to 2,775,011 (a record that was shattered to pieces in the Enchanted Season of 1993). The advertising folks were salivating over the prospects of buttressing the middle of the line-up—to say nothing of the team's ad campaign—with a player of Paul Bunyan-like proportions. Certainly the baseball people in the organization—the guys who actually have to worry about the *action on the field*—dreamed of what it would be like to pencil Jim Thome's name into the "four" spot (or three or five spot) on the line-up card every night. The video department rushed around gathering Thome footage from the Indians, just in case a press conference was announced. As for the Phanatic, I had work to do too. I needed to examine the video footage so that, during the pre-game show, I could mimic his batting stance. Did he wriggle his butt like Schmidty? Flap his arm like Joe Morgan? Raise his bat to the sky like Bobby Tolan? For a mascot that spends his life parodying the idiosyncrasies of ballplayers, these were burning questions.

On the fourth floor of the Vet, the troops were being gathered to plan Operation Thome.

RUBEN AMARO, ASSISTANT GENERAL MANAGER: "Eddie [Wade] rallied the baseball administration people together and laid out the facts and the plan to go after Thome. I was Jim's teammate when I was with Cleveland. I knew what kind of guy he is. Obviously, he's a helluva ballplayer but he is also a one-in-a-million person. No, make that one-in-a-zillion. He was the perfect guy to wrap up everything we were looking for. We had the new ballpark coming along, and we knew he'd be the centerpiece. He's a fan-friendly guy who handles the adulation like no one I've ever seen. And as a past Roberto Clemente Award winner, Jim is the kind of guy who likes to give back to the community.

"There were other big-name free agents out there, but no one was a better fit for our club than Jim Thome."

Still, there was doubt that Jim Thome would leave Cleveland. And if he were going to leave, we all thought there'd be plenty of other teams busting down his door.

ED WADE, PHILS GENERAL MANAGER: "We were very fortunate that we had the financial resources from the potential revenue from the new ballpark. We knew where other clubs were financially as well. There were other clubs out there that weren't in as strong a position to make a run for him. That left Cleveland and us. Charlie Manuel [Thome's confidant in Cleveland and who has now moved on up to be the new manager of the Phillies] talked to Jim and told him that he'd have a better chance of winning in Philadelphia. He liked the fact that we had a promising nucleus."

The minute Jim Thome's plane landed in Philadelphia the battle plan was put into action. Jim and his wife Andrea were put up in the toney Ritz Carlton in downtown Philadelphia. The next day, they visited the Vet and Bill Giles took them on a personal, guided tour of Philadelphia and the surrounding suburbs in a white stretch limousine. But the biggest sales pitch came after the tour at the Preview Center.

The Preview Center was the site formerly occupied by Maggio's cheese factory on Seventh Street, just east of the Vet and the new ballpark construction area. The Phillies bought the property two years before the first pitch was thrown at Citizens Bank Park and converted it into a state-of-the-art facility for the sole purpose of showing off the plans for Citizens Bank Park to potential sponsors and season ticket holders. When Bill Giles and his guests arrived, the wall off the main lobby opened, *à la Get Smart*, and the Thomes, along with Jim's agent Pat Rooney and some of the Phillies brass, entered the room. The whole ensemble watched a five-minute video production courtesy of "Video" Dan Stephenson.

VIDEO DAN STEPHENSON: "Ed Wade came down to the video room all excited one day. He told me we were trying to convince Jim Thome to be a Phillie. Ed wanted a video to pump Thome up on the team and the city—a video that showcased the city and showed what a beautiful place it is to live. He wanted me to show what a blue-collar sports town it is too.

"I put it together. Harry Kalas did the narration. When you have a Hall of Fame broadcaster welcoming you to town, you've got to be impressed. For background music, I used the Hooters [they're the great Philly—Ambler—rock band that opened "Live Aid" for the whole world in the eighties], along with Springsteen's "Streets of Philadelphia" and of course, Elton John's "Philadelphia Freedom." We made two versions of the tape depending on whether Jim came alone or with his wife. One version opened with Harry welcoming Jim to Philadelphia. In the other, Harry welcomed Jim and his wife Andrea. We carried out the whole operation with military precision. Ed had everything timed down to the minute."

ED WADE: "We sort of looked at it the way a college coach recruits a young athlete. We wanted to sell Jim on the city, show him the plans for the new ballpark, and show off our organization. That was our pitch. You can't do that over the phone or in e-mails.

"We treated Jim to a Flyers game and asked the Flyers to show Jim Thome up on their Arenavision board. We knew what would happen next. The crowd went wild and gave him a standing ovation. So Jim got a taste of the enthusiasm of Philly fans, but not like he did when he left the Preview Center before the hockey game."

Ed is referring to the greeting Thome got when he got back in his limo. That leg of the Thome Magical Mystery Tour wound up on every front page and every TV newscast that night. Members of the Electrical Workers Local 98 stood nearby, cheering him and wearing caps that read "Philadelphia Wants Jim Thome."

RUBEN AMARO: "Believe it or not, that part was *not scripted.* We were all blown away. It was awesome. When we got in the limo and started to pull away, Jim was saying, 'We've got to stop! We've got to stop!' I asked him if he was sure, and Jim said, 'Oh yeah, dude!'"

Jim got out and shook hands with several of them. The big guy felt in his element among this throng.

JOHN DOUGHERTY, Business Manager, IBEW Local Union 98: "All of us workers knew he was coming to town and we figured that we'd try to help the Phillies out. We made up signs and caps saying that we wanted him in Philadelphia. He jumped out of that limo and started shaking hands and talking with everybody there. I think he was impressed that we knew who he was and who his dad worked for and that we were so pumped up about his visit. You could tell that he was a working-class guy, although we joked with him that after he signed his next contract, he'd be in the *upper*-middle-class category.

"Our Union wound up sponsoring the Thome T-shirts that they gave away at the Vet in 2003 and we sponsored Jim Thome Bat Day in 2004. He's done a number of charity appearances with us and he's a real gentleman in every sense of the word. For every home run that he hits, that's how many good deeds he has done in the community—and then some."

JIM THOME: "Seeing those workers out there that morning was huge in convincing me I should come to Philly. That whole trip was impressive. The Phillies were upfront and honest with me and laid everything out on the table."

On Thanksgiving Day, Ed Wade sent a three-page e-mail to Jim and his wife, restating the Phillies' position and their desire to bring Jim into the Phillies fold.

RUBEN AMARO: "Ed made it personal. He's such a forthright, compassionate guy. He connected with Jim at a human level, and I'm sure Jim would tell you that was a deciding factor for him."

The word came on December 2, 2002. Jim Thome was signing with the Philadelphia Phillies.

ED WADE: "Right up until the last minute, I had no idea how everything was going to turn out. When [Thome's agent] Pat Rooney called and said Jim was coming to Philly, I didn't hoot and holler and jump all around like I thought I would. I just called Ruben and David [Montgomery] and told them that Jim Thome was now a Philadelphia Phillie. I think I was relieved more than anything else."

Ed left the hooting and hollering and jumping around to everyone else in the Phillies front office. And to those amazing, wacky, sometimes exasperating but always earnest people who played such a pivotal role in putting the big guy in pinstripes—the Philadelphia fans.

Movin' on Up

We may be fighting a losing battle
But having a lot of fun
Trying to win

—Peter, Paul, & Mary

What a pad! What a place! What a home! Citizens Bank Park is all we ever dreamed of. It's all we could ever possibly want . . . for now. No, we're not trying to throw a damper on things. We're just wrapping up a recurrent theme of the book. Yes, this is where our book's peripatetic and eclectic—and hopefully fun—walk through the then-and-now of the Philadelphia Phillies and Philly heritage culminates. At Citizens Bank Park, the greatest place in the world, at least for today. That's not cheeky or disrespectful or cynical. It's history and like tacos and refried black beans, history does repeat. Think back. Those thousands of Philadelphians who stormed Shibe Park on April 12, 1909 couldn't possibly have envisioned its magnificence morphing into monstrosity in a half-century or so. But it did, at least in the eyes of the sons and daughters and grandchildren of the very same crowd. Time passes, and time passages have a way of making those transformations happen. Time after time.

Who knows what the future holds for Citizens Bank Park? Maybe we've reached the pinnacle and it doesn't get better than this. Or maybe in twenty years, the latest craze will be force-field seats or holograms that put you in the middle of the action or sky transports around the park. At that point, the Phillies "new" home will become a "decrepit, out-of-date eyesore." For now, though, we should simply enjoy the novelty, intrigue, and outright fun of a Philly institution-to-be where new generations of families learn to love baseball and create happy memories. On the jaggedy graph of Phillies history, unquestionably we're on a stretch that's movin' on up.

The most energizing aspect of movin' on up to Citizens Bank Park is the *who* that's movin' on up. It's us. That's what this book celebrates. Philadelphia is the place we love to complain about among ourselves but bristle at when an outsider dares criticize us. Philadelphia is hopelessly entangled with our teams. Loyalty and love of the city—even begrudging love—is encoded in Philly natives. Does that happen anywhere else? Yep. But more importantly, does it happen everywhere else? Nope. Not on your life. In Hotel California, you can check out any time you like, but you can never leave. Hotel Philadelphia is the opposite. You can leave any time you like, but you never really check out. Whether you're Rocky, Bill Cosby, Kevin Bacon, Kevin Eubanks, Mike Tollin, or Smarty Jones, you might hit the big time and leave Philly. But you never leave Philadelphia behind.

Admittedly, none of our hometown teams boasts an impressive track record for winning. Sometimes (or many times) our hometown teams don't seem to be one *with* us. But we get the feeling they are one *of* us, not an isolated enterprise as detached from the community as some of those nameless, invisible enterprises hidden away in industrial parks. With all their foibles and blemishes, the Phils love the Quaker City. The Phillies organization teems with *Philadelphians*. They're here to stay. They're here to live and raise their families. They're not pyramiding job-hoppers. They're not that contemporary (or contemptible) breed of corporate carpetbaggers who touch down and take off with no emotional investment in an organization in a community. The Phils employ people who want to be part of our local heritage.

As for the bond between the Philadelphia community and its teams—is there an official film about Philadelphia or the Philadelphia region that *does not* feature the stadiums, the teams, the Phanatic, or Tug McGraw's leap on October 21, 1980? From the turn of the twentieth century when Phillies players in uniform rode trolleys to Recreation Park (which was expressly situated alongside the trolley tracks for convenient access) right up to the present day, the Philadelphia Phillies have been intertwined with the city they nicknamed themselves after. Yes, much as we kidded about it in the book, the nickname our hometown team invented burrowed the team deeper into the town's soul. It stamps the team as Philadelphia's exclusive property. No team outside the shadow of Billy Penn's hat will ever call itself the "Phillies," even if, God forbid, the franchise moved on out. The once-beloved Philadelphia Athletics remain the "Athletics" in Oakland, as they had been in Kansas City. Pro sport teams that relocate practically always retain their original nickname. The result sacrifices incongruity for continuity—incongruities like the Los Angeles *Lakers* (what LA lake could they be referring to? The Salton Sea?) or the Utah *Jazz* (sure, jazz and Utah go together like rap and proper grammar). Those nicknames made sense when they were the Minneapolis Lakers and the New Orleans Jazz. But the LA *Phillies*, the Utah *Phillies*? Can't imagine that. There could only ever be the Philadelphia Phillies.

So we're moving on up all these years. The past two seasons have disappointed. Life is full of disappointment—as twenty-nine other teams along with Philly each year can attest. Like Rocky, Philly fans bounce back, get up, put on the gloves each round, and answer the bell, bruised and battered. And still think they can win. That gives Philadelphia its craggy character—scrappy, feisty, yet full of resolve for each new round. Fact is—good, bad, ugly, and pathetic—we've gathered a trunkload of memories over the past (almost) century and a quarter. We may be fighting a losing battle, but having a lot of fun trying to win.

A NEW BALLPARK FOR PHILLY

To be more accurate, it should be two new ballparks for Philly. There was a lot of complaining about the Vet in its final years. Both the Phillies and the Eagles wanted to move on out of the Vet. But securing the finances, finding locations for the stadiums, and other details bogged matters down.

What were the sticking points as the Phillies and Eagles haggled and hassled for new homes? Without going into all the details, money was the root of all upheaval. But on February 9, 1999, Pennsylvania, under Governor Ridge, passed a bill that released $320 million for new stadiums in Pittsburgh and Philadelphia. That set the local wheels in motion. The Phillies, the Eagles, and the City of Philadelphia started talking in earnest about new stadiums.

When John Street succeeded Ed Rendell as mayor in 2000, he endorsed a location for the Phils' new park at 12th and Vine near Chinatown, but that decision quickly fell through. Then on an historic day, November 13, 2000, Mayor Street announced that both new facilities for the Phillies and the Eagles would be located at the South Philly sports complex. He vowed that the "sports complex will be unmatched in the country." Street's decree situated the Phillies and the Eagles in the same place they had been for the past three decades—in South Philadelphia. Things moved quickly from then on. Four days later, the city, the Phillies, and the Eagles agreed on terms to build two new sports facilities. By December 21, the city could give the Eagles and Phils an early Christmas present. City Council approved a $1 billion stadium deal for the Phils and Eagles at the sports complex.

A month or so later, on January 30, 2001, the city purchased the stadium sites—two pieces of privately owned land: the Acme warehouse property and the T-Warehouse site. Within two days, City Council approved lease agreements for both the Phillies and the Eagles.

The Phils laid out an aggressive work schedule. They had a ballpark to build. They retained EwingCole and HOK Sport+Venue+Event to design the park. On June 28, 2001, the Phillies officially unveiled the architectural design plan for a new 43,000-seat, natural grass and dirt field ballpark.

Stadium work began in earnest on July 23 when utilities relocated pipes, wires, and cables in the construction area. Construction plans called for the field to be sunk 23 feet below the street level, so a full-scale excavation kicked off on January 15, 2002 and was completed by May 27. By that time, 594,000 tons of dirt had been removed. Unfortunately, the Phils had not yet landed on the idea of selling dirt from the Vet like they did at the Final Pieces night. Too bad. At $20 a pound they would have netted a cool $23,760,000,000, enough to get the city out of debt and maybe pay in advance for those force-field seats with the change. Confused? Don't be confused. Be amused. Read "Final Pieces."

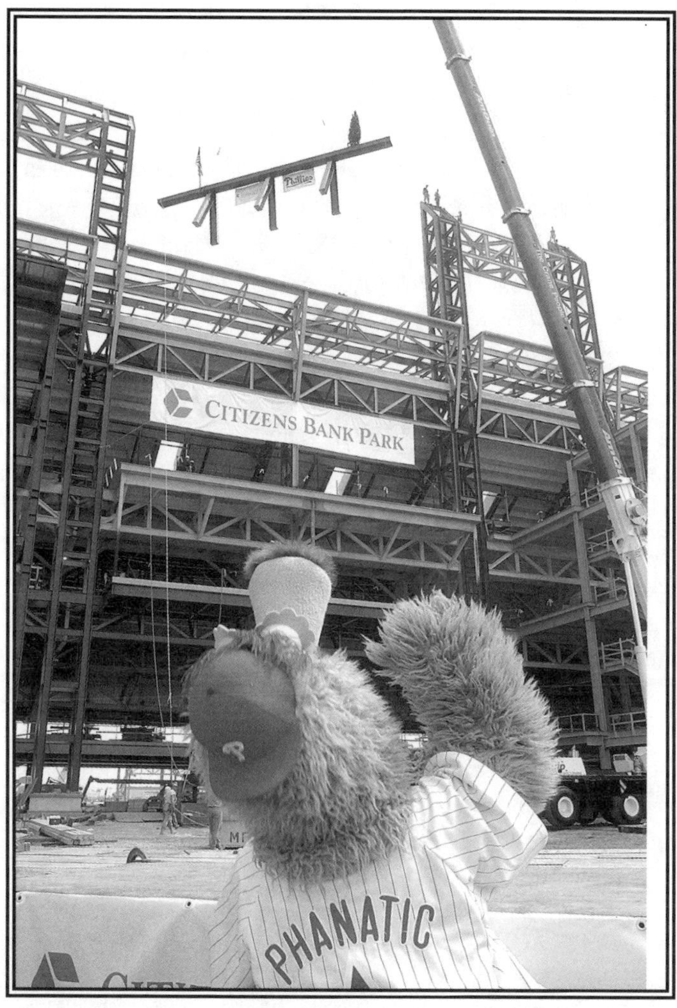

On August 12, 2003, during the ballpark's Topping Out Ceremony, the Phanatic watches a steel beam being put on top of a light tower. (Photo: Peter Tobia, The *Philadelphia Inquirer*)

PHANATIC PHILE

FINAL PIECES

Being just a young Phanatic-in-waiting back in the fall of 1970, I missed all the shenanigans the final night at Connie Mack Stadium. I've heard all the theories for the riotous behavior: it was just a sign of the times, or it was just a city blowing off steam in the days of Viet Nam, the civil rights movement, and free love. But things sure seemed a lot calmer in the year 2003 when it came time to close down the Vet. But then, things aren't always what they seem to be.

MIKE DIMUZIO, STADIUM OPERATIONS DIRECTOR: "That last season at the Vet, people really started to get nostalgic about the old place. We started noticing that little things were disappearing—things like section markers, signs on the concourse, seats, and the 'Watch out for foul ball' postings were taken as well as the little numbers attached to the backs of the seats. Why anyone would want a little label with a number on it is beyond me. It could have come from anywhere. One guy stole a toilet bowl seat [Imodium isn't sold—I guess he thought that was his only option]. He got caught when he showed it to a cop on the corner of Broad and Pattison [apparently proud of his booty, so to speak]. Overall, not a lot was stolen—nothing compared to Connie Mack's last game."

The Phils came up with a much more civil approach to dispose of stadium seats in an effort to avoid the same kind of free-for-all that overtook Connie Mack Stadium on its final night. The Phils solicited the help of popular ex-first baseman John Kruk, who starred in a commercial publicizing the sale of Veterans Stadium seats. The spot showed the Krukker walking through the aisles at the Vet, passing the blue seats while waxing poetic about the historical significance of leaving the Vet. After all the uncharacteristic platitudes, Kruk crashed back into character. Reaching under one of the seats, he wiped his index finger along the underside of the seat, raised his finger to his mouth, and licked it, muttering gleefully, "Mmmm, mustard," while mugging for the camera. The campaign worked. Over 22,000 pairs of seats were sold. The Phils charged nothing extra for those with mustard.

If the ESPN gig doesn't work out for the Krukker, he's a natural for *The Joey Isuzu Story*, if Mike Tollin or anyone else ever wants to make it—and you have *my* word on it.

But there was a helluva lot of other souvenirs, memorabilia, artwork, lockers, fixtures, lights, Astroturf, urinals, turnstiles, banners, signs, scoreboards, Liberty Bell, junk—well, you get the idea. The Phils organization wondered what to do with it all.

So on a rainy February 6th Friday morning, the Phillies hosted the "Final Pieces Auction" at the Wachovia Center, the Vet's neighbor across the street. It was a one-time happening to sell off as much Vet memorabilia as possible for a good cause. The event was a smashing success—well actually there *was* no smashing this time around. We learned our lesson from the Connie Mack closing.

The Phils raised over $700,000, and all the proceeds went to Phillies Charities Inc. From the moment we opened the doors at 10:00 AM, the fans snatched up everything in sight. They waited in long lines on the concourse to buy four-inch cutouts of the wall and turf, which were neatly packaged in wooden boxes with the Vet logo on the top. The dirt was poured into jars shaped like glass soda-pop bottles marked with the Vet logo as well as the spot where the dirt originated (first base, home plate, Lenny Dykstra's uniform, etc.). The dirt was *not* dirt cheap. Each bottle sold for $20. Over 6,000 swatches of turf, 2,500 bottles of dirt and 2,500 chunks of outfield fence were bought by the 8,000-plus in attendance.

Fans dug furiously into boxes, scavenging up old signage that hung in the stadium. Season-ticket holders scoured the place for signs sporting *their* old section number. The auction-goers snatched up posters, old scorecards, and past giveaway items.

Starting at 12:00 noon, the auction got underway and the big money started to roll in. For seven hours, auctioneers took turns putting treasured Vet artifacts up for bid. Hundreds gathered in the arena's seating area and viewed pictures of items that were flashed on big projection screens. As each item was sold, Phillies staffers accounted for the sale on computers on the side of the stage. We auctioned off players' lockers, artwork, championship banners and signage from the doomed old Vet. The original blueprints of the stadium went up for bid, as did Harry Kalas' broadcaster's chair and ex-owner Ruly Carpenter's desk. The red door—dings, dents, and all—that led from the tunnel in the Phillies dugout to the clubhouse was sold, as well as the only bat rack *ever used* in the Phillies dugout. That piece went off for the staggering sum of $5,500. The item that netted the most was Richie Ashburn's retired #1 banner that had hung in the Vet. Whitey's memento added a cool $10,100 to the coffers. Adjacent lockers once occupied by Pete Rose and Tony Perez were the next highest money netter at $6,400. Mike Schmidt's retired #20 banner added $6,100 to the tills. Schmidty's locker sold for $5,900. I even pitched in an old game-worn (and gamey-smelling) Phillie Phanatic jersey and shoes, Lysol not included. I think bidding started at $5. A delirious Phillie Phanatic fan ended up buying it for $2.99. Thanks, Mom.

It was a wonderful day and night. The Phillies family and their fans raised a lot of money for charity. True to form, the Phillies faithful came out in droves on a miserable rainy day, demonstrating again why Philly has the most passionate sports fans in the country. Some came from miles away to snatch a piece of history and they walked out with everything but the kitchen sink. And I *do* mean everything. Because while some snatched, one guy snitched. That's right. Not everything that left the Wachovia Center that night was for sale.

HEADLESS IN PHILLY

I don't know if I ever bought into my mom's favorite expression when I was a kid, namely that I would forget my head if it weren't attached to my shoulders. I'm not the sharpest knife in the drawer but I'd like to believe that I'd never forget a necessary detail like a head—maybe an eye or an ear since they come in pairs—but not a whole head. On the night of February 6, 2004, Mother Burgoyne's theory came back to haunt me. Yes, that was the fateful night of the "Final Pieces Auction."

I had been in costume all day long (I'd say I was *working* all day, but you readers with *real* jobs would scoff). At about 6:30 PM, I walked into a room I had used as a dressing room all day just off the main concourse. I took the costume off for a little breather and strolled out to the concourse. Forty-five minutes later, I walked back into the room to suit up, or costume up, one last time. I squeezed into the red spandex Phanatic legs, stepped into the big, green body, tied my shoes then reached for my head. Mother Burgoyne preserve us! It was gone (the Phanatic's head, not mine, although at that point, I figured David Montgomery was going to decapitate me anyway). My assistant Christine came into the room to help me finish suiting up. She looked at me like Ichabod Crane looked at the Headless Horseman. That headless look rocked for the Headless Horseman's shtick. But headless horseplay

YIKES! The Phillie Phanatic's head is stolen from the "Final Pieces Auction" on February 6, 2004. (Photo: Courtesy of The *Daily News*)

doesn't cut it for Phanatic shtick. I mean, I'm a handsome guy (my wife tells me that all the time, especially around her birthday and Christmas), but I'm not as irresistible as the Phanatic. Who is?

Anyway, my own mug was as green as the Phanatic's fur. Christine and I called Security but nobody knew nothing. (Yo! Remember, we *were* in South Philly. I had visions of the head winding up in Bill Giles' bed that night.) It was official. The Phanatic was headless in Philly. My mom's prophecy had come true.

Not wanting to be a killjoy the same night we had raised so much money for charity, the Phils and I decided to keep the crime quiet for a couple of days. Yeah right—like that'll work. We live in Philly, not Pleasantville. By Monday morning, the *Philadelphia Daily News* was running with the story like J-Roll rounding second on a triple. They ran a photo of the Phanatic dancing on the Phillies dugout with his head digitally removed. It was as disturbing as the final scene in *Braveheart*, well, almost. That morning, my good buds Angelo Cataldi and the Morning Crew on WIP radio were buzzing my house trying to get the scoop: "Where's the head? Who could have done it? Is this just a cheap publicity stunt?"

In the middle of his off-air interrogation, host Angelo Cataldi said to me, "Tom, we've got a guy on the other line right now claiming that he's got the head. Then Angelo jumped over to live: 'Hello, sir, are you there?'"

"Yeah, I'm here and I've got the Phillie Phanatic's head," the caller bragged. "Tell the Phanatic and the Phillies that I'm not giving it back until the Phillies make it to the World Series."

By day's end, *everyone* had the story. Every local TV station dispatched reporters to the Phillies' new offices at Citizens Bank Park, and radio stations jumped in with both feet.

"The Phillie Phanatic's head is missing in one of the most bizarre mysteries we've ever seen," sports talk-guy-turned-DJ Mike Missanelli screeched on WMMR. "Call in now with your best caper story and we'll give the best one a free t-shirt." Rhea Hughes, WIP's reigning sports babe, called me to ask for the back-up Phanatic head so they could parade it around the city on the top of a flatbed truck. They wanted to ask people on the street if they had seen a head resembling the one in the truck. Rhea quickly realized that the Phillies wouldn't be interested in having the head of the Phanatic on display like John the Baptist's after Salome danced. So, after that idea was shot down, Rhea thought that she and the gang at WIP could maybe make a papier-maché head and drive around town with it.

The *Daily News* offered a $1,000 reward in a front-page headline, "Bring Us the Head of the Phanatic." Another local radio station, 96.5 WLDW, offered a $5,000 reward and conducted a candlelight vigil in its parking lot. A couple hundred loyal listeners as well as some area mascots came out to support their decapitated comrade in what was billed as a "prayer service."

Radio shock jock Howard Stern announced on his nationally syndicated radio program that one of his sponsors, Gary Barbera Dodge, was offering a $5000 reward for the Phanatic's head. Hard to believe that the King of All Media would interrupt his steady flow of strippers and midgets in a hunt for head. On second thought, I guess it isn't.

USA Today ran a photo of the Phanatic with the headline: "The Phanatic Would Hang His Head If He Had It." They called the perpetrator a knucklehead. I did a live interview via satellite with ESPN from a small video link office in Center City Philadelphia. You know it's a big story when you get interviewed with a fake skyline of Philly in the background while a caffeine-jagged host screams at you through a plug in your ear. ESPN later ran a four-minute segment detailing the specifics of the crime and putting out a list of suspects, including Tommy Lasorda and Joe Carter (we ruled Tommy out because the Phanatic's head is several sizes too small for him). Even CNN covered the story.

Of course, no national media frenzy worth its salt would be complete without Internet buzz. A Google search the day after the story went public produced 193 hits on newspapers covering the caper.

One die-hard fan started an online crusade on eBay. Fans could go on eBay and offer a reward for the whereabouts of the missing head. Fans flooded the site with e-mails like:

"The Phillie Phanatic is the most prized symbol of my Philadelphia soul. I bleed Pinstripe Red and hope whoever stole the Phanatic's head returns it A.S.A.P. Don't let the Phanatic's Jinx jinx the Fightin' Phils."

My e-mail box lit up for days from fans and friends expressing their concern. One friend seeking divine intervention e-mailed me the prayer to St. Anthony, patron saint of items lost or stolen. I thanked him for the tip. Up until then, I had been praying to a different saint, who was probably up there thinking, "Why you bothering me? That's not my job, man."

I knew the story had really hit the big time when it appeared on the "Weekend Update" segment of *Saturday Night Live*. Peering earnestly into the camera, *faux* news co-anchor Jimmy Fallon announced that in Philadelphia the world-famous Phillie

Phanatic's head was stolen during a charity event. He deadpanned that the Philadelphia police were on the case tracking several leads. At that point, a doctored picture of a man in a business suit wearing the Phanatic's head popped up on the TV monitor behind him.

"The police believe THIS man may be a suspect," Fallon announced.

Our man Jimmy was actually right. The police *were* on the case and getting more and more peeved that the theft on their turf had become a national joke. Three of Philly's finest visited our new offices at Citizens Bank Park to get my statement and re-enact the events of the night back at the Wachovia Center. I felt like Columbo as we walked through the crime scene, checking doorways and exits that the burglar may have used. The cops were all business, acting very cop-like. They asked for the list of fans who registered for the auction, hoping the perpetrator might be on the list. They gathered video from Comcast SportsNet who taped the "Meet the Phillies" segment that evening, hoping the camera might reveal some clues. They checked the surveillance tapes at the Wachovia Center. I tagged along with them through the whole process, feeling more and more like Clouseau rather than Columbo.

The security staff was eager to assist. They had already pulled the tape from that night and handed each of us a black-and-white still photo of a lone man in the hallway just behind the break room I had been using.

"That's the guy who stole your head," one of the security guys said, proud that he had solved the mystery.

We all huddled around a bank of security monitors in the control room and studied the tapes. First, we watched the tape that was shot from the ticket windows. A heavy-set man entered the ticket office, walked into the lobby and up to the ticket window. Instead of buying a ticket, he slipped behind a door that was clearly marked "Authorized Personnel Only."

"We got this sucker for burglary now," one cop mumbled. "By going through that door, the guy jumped the charge up from theft to burglary."

The next shot was taken by a camera in the hallway just outside the break room. At 6:55 PM, the perpetrator walked towards the camera and disappeared from the field of view. For three minutes, the hallway was empty. Suddenly the guy reappeared, this time walking away from the camera. We could pick out the Phanatic's head, partially concealed by the guy's jacket.

Our group of crime stoppers walked out of the office with the smoking gun—the video tapes—in our hands. The cops were ready to set the dragnet in motion. They were ready to enlist the help of every media outlet and post the picture on every Crime Fighters news segment in town—a manhunt—well, mascot hunt—worthy of Dr. Richard Kimble.

But it never happened 'cause the thief did something unexpected. He placed a call to WYSP, the Philly radio affiliate that broadcasts Howard Stern. The DJ at the time was ex-Philly rocker Tommy Conwell who was skeptical. The station had received hundreds of crank calls since putting up the $5000 reward. Conwell told the guy to bring in the head. A little while later, the culprit walked through the radio station's lobby at 5th and Market carrying the head of the Phanatic. Stationed in the lobby was an ex-cop who called his pals at the precinct. Within minutes, the detectives working the case barged into the studio and placed the head-napper under arrest.

Back at the police station, the man struggled to keep his story straight. At first, he claimed that his kids found the head while they were sledding. A neat little story, but an obvious snow job considering there was no white stuff on the ground from Philly clear up to the Poconos. Then he admitted he had been at the auction. He said he saw two kids running through the parking lot carrying the Phanatic's head. Being an upstanding citizen, he confronted the kids. They dropped the head and ran. Apparently he picked it up and ran.

Finally, the guy came clean. He pleaded temporary insanity. He admitted that when he stumbled across the Phanatic's noggin in the room at the Wachovia Center, he somehow lost his own head.

While the interrogation was in process, the Phils and I tried to decide what our next steps should be. What should we say at the press conference? Someone suggested that the Philly cops present me with the Phanatic's head. *I don't think so*. For years, we've been careful *not* to show the Phanatic costume unattached or unanimated, and *not* to show me half in and half out of costume. The media refers to Tom Burgoyne as the "best friend" of the Phillie Phanatic. We work hard to keep that shtick going. It worked for Clark Kent. Clark made sure to wear those big-framed glasses. He never went out in public without them. Otherwise, someone might have said, "Say Clark, did anyone ever tell you you're a dead ringer for Superman?" No one has ever told Tom Burgoyne he's a dead ringer for the Phillie Phanatic.

We settled on a scenario where the cops would pull up to the press conference at the Phillies Preview Center, walk past the crowded mass of cameras and microphones and enter the building with the head concealed in a plastic trash bag. Within a couple minutes, the Phanatic would appear, head firmly attached to the rest of his body.

You know what they say about the best-laid plans. Right before the press conference was about to take place, my cell phone rang. It was Detective Stephen Caputo from the interrogation room.

"Tom, the guy just confessed."

"He killed Hoffa? He took the Lindbergh baby?" I asked.

"No, bigger than that. He admits he took the Phanatic's head. He's writing down his confession even as we speak. We've got about an hour's worth of paperwork to clean up here so we can't be there for the press conference."

We held the press conference anyway, without the cops. The show must go on. Tommy Conwell and other WYSP representatives talked about how proud they were that they were the ones who helped the Phanatic get his head back. I stepped up to the microphones, stared into the TV cameras and thanked the Philly police force for their efforts, and the fans for their support.

"Now the Phanatic can get back to the serious business of making a fool of himself," I declared triumphantly.

"Can we see the head?" one reporter called out.

"It's been a long ordeal for the Phanatic. He's resting." That's the best I could counter with. I was bound and determined to keep the press from getting a picture of a bodiless Phanatic.

After the press conference, I slipped away to pick up the head. I did *not* want to draw the attention of the press. But when I arrived at the station, there were TV trucks and camera crews everywhere. The police had scheduled a press conference of their own to announce that the suspect had confessed.

I double-parked my Phanatic van a block away from the police station. I sneaked past the crowd and into the police station where I filled out a couple of forms and recovered the head. The detectives led me down a back staircase and out to the street. With the head in a bag slung over my shoulder, I pulled the brim of my Phillies cap down over my eyes and walked briskly past the herd of reporters. I thought I had slipped by undetected until I heard someone shout, "That's him! Hey Tom, wait up! Is that the head you have there? Let's see it!"

I pretended not to hear and quickened my pace back to the van. I opened up the side door of the van, tossed in the head, and hopped into the driver's seat. Within seconds, the cameramen and reporters had surrounded the van, angling for a shot of the green, furry head. I rolled down the window, gave the thumbs up sign and a "Go Phillies" chant, and rolled slowly through the throng. The cameramen jogged alongside the van but gave up when I turned the corner. I saw open field, and sped away toward daylight like Brian Westbrook.

PHANATIC PHILE

I was relieved that, once again, I succeeded in preventing a picture of the Phanatic's decapitated head from hitting the front page. I kept thinking of that episode on *Happy Days* when budding reporter Richie Cunningham snapped an unauthorized photo of Howdy Doody's friend, Clarabelle the Clown. Clarabelle had no makeup on (heck, *no* woman will let you take a photo of her with no makeup on). Stricken with guilt, Richie opted not to print the picture in his high school newspaper, so Clarabelle could keep her image intact for the kiddies. Richie could never have worked for the *National Enquirer*.

It just so happened that I had an appearance that night at Dave and Buster's in Center City. Dave and Buster's is a huge entertainment and restaurant complex on Columbus Boulevard, along the Delaware River. They were celebrating their tenth anniversary in Philadelphia. When I jumped out of the van in full costume, every TV station in the city had crews there, covering the Phanatic's return. I waddled into the party and was greeted immediately by the Mummers who commemorated the occasion by playing "Happy Days Are Here Again." I strutted and hugged any woman I could get my hands on (so what else is new?). The cameras followed my every move as I entered the main party room to cheers and applause (so what else is new?). A Ben Franklin look-alike high-fived me. Harry Kalas announced in his best Harry voice, "The Phillie Phanatic has got his head back!" Harry held the Phanatic's hand up high and flashbulbs exploded.

So, see Mom, I didn't lose my noodle after all! I gotta admit, though, the guy who stole it had a lot in common with noodles. He was in hot water, lacked taste, and apparently needed the dough.

On the morning of September 27, 2002, the Phils hosted a Construction Workers Outing for over 1,300 construction workers and their families. The group stayed over for a 1:15 PM game at Veterans Stadium. On May 31 the following season, more than 2,000 construction workers and their families celebrated the progress of the new ballpark at the 2nd Annual Ballpark Construction Workers Picnic.

The Phils had been building the park for almost two years before they named it. Lots of suitors vied for the honors. Naming the ballpark became a hot topic in Philly. The suspense ended on June 17, 2003. That's the day Citizens Bank entered into a 25-year naming rights partnership with the Phillies. On the same day, the Home Run Spectacular—a

50-foot-high Liberty Bell that dings after each Phillie dinger—was revealed.

On October 29, 2003, a little more than one month after the final Vet game the Phillies, Aramark, and World Wide Concessions announced that they had formed a joint venture for the food, beverage, and retail services at Citizens Bank Park. Former Phil Garry Maddox is president of one of those parties, World Wide Concessions. In a related story, the Phillies announced that McFadden's and Zanzibar Blue had also partnered on a restaurant and sports bar within the Citizens Bank Park site. Located at the southwest corner of the ballpark adjacent to the third-base gate on Pattison Avenue, McFadden's Restaurant & Saloon would remain open year-round.

PHILLIES PHOODIES

Alison Barshak is one of Philly's biggest names when it comes to food. In the seventies and eighties, Alison worked in numerous big-name restaurants around the city—the Commissary, the Center Park Grille, and Apropos, to name a few. Alison grew up in the Philly area and she's a big Phillies fan (although her father hails from Baltimore, so she nobly overcame some mixed signals).

Alison tells a story about the night her parents invited "the young guy next door" to dinner at their Main Line home. He was new to the area and didn't know anyone. They "thought he might be a baseball player."

ALISON BARSHAK: "He turned out to be Larry Christensen, so I got to know Larry. One evening a short while later, I was at a party and had to park my car in the driveway next door. Later that night, a phone call came in from the Maddox residence next door. Garry was coming back home from a game and couldn't get in the driveway. I was working at the Center Park Grille at the time, and Larry Christensen walked in not long after that party. Garry Maddox was with him. Larry introduced us and we became friends. Garry stopped in frequently. He always ordered the same thing: a Caesar salad, a medium burger, and chocolate bread pudding."

At the time, Alison was becoming a name in the Philadelphia restaurant community. When Neil Stein made plans to open the Striped Bass, which was trumpeted to be one of the city's finest restaurants, he offered Alison the job as chef. That was big, bold news in those days—a woman getting such a high-profile power position. Alison struggled with the decision.

ALISON BARSHAK: "I talked to Garry quite a bit about whether I should accept the offer. Garry was real supportive and encouraging. He told me to go for it. Of course I did accept, but I lost a friend for awhile! Garry never came into the

Striped Bass to see me. I used to see Darren Daulton a lot and Bobby Clark and lots of other athletes, but not Garry. He didn't eat fish. Most of the other athletes ordered tuna because it tasted like a steak. Eventually Garry came in and tried it. He liked it and became a regular there too."

Alison has since left the Striped Bass. Currently, she's wowing customers at her Alison at Blue Bell restaurant, an awesome BYOB on Route 73 just below Route 202.

Garry Maddox helped Alison move on up to celebrity chef status. Alison in turn helped Garry move on up as a gourmet. Of course, Garry is no stranger to dining—fine dining as well as the stick-to-your-ribs variety. For the past several years, Garry has been the main man in the "Garry Maddox Celebrity Rib Burn-Off Contest" at the ballpark. At Citizens Bank Park, the food concessions are run jointly by Aramark and World Wide Concessions and the Phillies. And the president of World Wide Concessions is Garry Maddox. That's right. In the world of ballpark eats, the guy that Alison turned on to tuna moved on up to the new ballparks top tuna.

On November 7, 2003, the Phils mowed the grass at Citizens Bank Park for the first time. On November 12, the club made the official announcement that the field was ready for major-league action. On February 7, 2004, the lights were turned on for the first time, and one week later, the mammoth "Phillies" sign was perched atop the first base gate. On March 5, the Liberty Bell took its esteemed place in Ashburn Alley.

Then on March 21, the old Vet was imploded.

Goodbye, old friend—the Vet is imploded on March 21, 2004.
(Photo: Rosemary Rhan)

THE BIG BANG

March 21, 2004. That day I may have experienced the most surreal moment I've ever lived through, and that's saying something. When you make a living as a mascot, life is filled with surreal moments.

But this moment had a different flavor. This was the day the Vet would come tumbling down. On one hand, it was a time for everyone in the Phillies family to gather at the break of dawn across the street from our longtime home-away-from-home to laugh and cry a little and savor the good times we shared. On the other hand, it was kind of like waiting around to witness a public execution.

That morning, directly across from the Vet, the Phillies staked claim to a stretch of asphalt on Packer Avenue where Phillies employees, invited neighborhood guests, politicians, and the media set up camp. Crowds started milling around at 4:00 AM and by 5:00 AM, Packer Avenue was crammed with TV trucks, satellite dishes, and more than 200 media people covering the event. Fans wandered about taking photos of the doomed stadium one last time. The Mummers showed up to serenade the old girl. The Scots have their bagpipers at funerals. Philadelphians have their Mummers.

A hospitality tent was set up, providing hot coffee and fresh pastries for the bleary-eyed. The three to six inches of snow that had been forecasted the night before never materialized and the tent and stage were set up without nature interfering. A handful of dignitaries were seated in chairs in front of the stage as long-time Vet PA man Dan Baker fired off Veterans Stadium trivia. David Montgomery briefly thanked everyone for coming and finished off his remarks by turning toward the Vet and tipping his red Phillies cap.

Mayor Street spoke next and in the middle of his speech a roar went up from behind the crowd. The Philadelphia Police Department had blocked all traffic on the Schuylkill Expressway and hundreds of cheering spectators streamed across the highway from the nearby neighborhood to get a better view.

There had been lots of speculation about who would be chosen to push the button to demolish the Vet. My ideas didn't go over too well. I thought Burt Hooten should do it. Hooten had imploded on the mound at the Vet some 26 years earlier during Game Three of the NLCS, so Burt had the experience to get the job done. I thought Tommy Lasorda was a good candidate too. Tommy blew up so many times at the Phanatic's antics, I'm surprised he didn't blow the Vet up himself years earlier. For that matter, Dallas Green and Larry Bowa had some classic explosions there too. Benny the Bomb was another candidate of mine.

Benny performed at the Vet many times by crawling into a small box and blowing himself up into the air to the delight of the fans. Not the best thing for the ears, particularly when the matter between the ears is in question. Actually, I did telephone Benny and invite him, but he kept repeating, "What?" He wasn't even on a cell phone.

The Phils actually did entertain some serious thoughts about the Phanatic doing it, but there was a disconnect to that scheme. The Phanatic loved the Vet. Why would he risk losing his free rent and force himself to go apartment- or house-mooching? Still the Phanatic had a classified ad ready just in case:

Wanted: free room and board with well-stocked refrigerator and pantry for lovable, occasionally (usually) obnoxious, unkempt green mascot with body odor that could knock a buzzard off a garbage heap.

No, the Phanatic couldn't pop the charge to take the Vet down. Still, he had to play *some* role in the implosion. I dug out an old prop that I had used years before. It was a big, red "TNT" detonator that looked like it belonged in Wile E. Coyote's closet. We finally decided that Greg "The Bull" Luzinski, who was known for his mammoth Bull blasts, should do the honors. We dressed the big plunger up and printed the words "Final Bull Blast" on the side. When it came time for the big countdown, I jumped off the stage and grabbed the big detonator. Stumbling back onto the stage, I purposely tripped onto the plunger and looked back at the big stadium, making sure my pratfall hadn't set off the explosion. Hey, it was the last day of the Vet and I had to throw a little Three Stooges into the ceremony.

Following my attempt at slapstick humor, the Mayor started the countdown.

"7…6…5…4…3…2…1… Fire! Fire!"

The Bull pressed down on the plunger and a series of loud popping sounds ensued. From our vantage point, you could see the explosions being set off through the exit tunnels that ringed the stadium. Mixed in with the sounds of the explosives was the thunder of each segment collapsing sequentially like dominos. Seconds later, the dominos rolled around our way. The crowd "oohed" and "ahhed" as the concrete facility crumbled in front of our eyes. In a moment of defiance, the tall tower housing the Penthouse Suites elevator stood firm before finally giving way and tumbling to the ground. After the last of the 103 columns had collapsed in a cloud of dust, most of the crowd let out a cheer. Others stared in silent disbelief.

It took 3,000 pounds of explosives 62 seconds to wipe away a building that took three years to build and housed 33 years of memories.

Then something funny and bizarre and appropriate happened. The wind shifted as if by the hand of the baseball gods. The massive cloud from the implosion blew eastward, dusting the new park with its memories.

As fans wandered around taking pictures and toasting the fallen Vet, I stood next to the fake detonator and posed with a long line of Phillies fans snapping the remains of the day.

After the last picture had been taken, I peeled off my costume and joined my three brothers in a toast. We had all been together sitting in the 700 Level on Opening Day, 1971 for the Vet's overture. Now, 33 years later, we were together again for the Vet's swan song. We drove a couple blocks north to the Melrose Diner, another South Philly institution. Over chipped beef and scrapple (see, despite our jokes, I *do* eat scrapple), we shared our favorite moments of the Vet. More and more people came into the diner. With all the sentimentality and tears for the Vet, it was more Melrose Place than Melrose Diner. The implosion was now history, as were the scrapple and chipped beef. The Vet was down. It was going to take a long time for its dust to settle.

NOW THAT'S WHAT WE CALL A BALLPARK

So our town and our people and our baseball team moved on up together into a brand-new ballpark. Citizens Bank Park is a showcase of the then and now. It's a reflection of a unique city's pride. Let's take a look at the Phillies new ballpark.

THE STRUCTURE

Citizens Bank Park looks like it belongs in Philadelphia. The red brick exterior evokes a Quaker City feel—substantial, stable, reserved, and dignified rather than splashy or faddish. We loved the Vet but, admittedly, it was a period piece. It didn't fit the look of the new millennium. We don't get too swimmy-eyed when we think of the old Gino's franchises that used to be scattered around city and 'burbs. Nor are we sentimental about that fifties-era Linton's look for our current eateries. No, if we've learned anything from local history, it's this: what abides in Philly is the classic. Philly has moved on up as a tourist destination because of heritage and happenings—the then and now. Our old architecture is nonpareil at least on this continent. Our colonial-era rehabbed areas can't be matched. We feature the real-deal places of this nation's heritage: Independence Hall, Carpenter's Hall, Betsy Ross House, Elfreth's Alley, the Hard Rock Café. Well, OK, that last one's out of line, but not out of place. It fits nicely in Philly. All our stately and august remnants of the past mix in nicely with beautiful additions like the Constitution Center, which is impressive and dignified with great contemporary architectural riffs that jazz up the Philly melody. That's exactly what Citizens Bank Park does. It's stately, dignified, and inviting like a great old Center City ballpark from the days of yore, yet it mixes in modern fun and funk with nary a sour note.

Citizens Bank Park with its *million* or so bricks, 52,000 yards of concrete, 1.15 million square feet of building, and 100,000 square feet of 100% Kentucky bluegrass from the Tuckahoe Turf Farm in Hammonton, New Jersey is here to stay. The Phillies strived to insinuate hominess into their home and they succeeded.

The cavernous Vet seemed to swallow us all up. There are enough world and local events to make us feel insignificant. We don't need to feel that way at our ballpark. Citizens Bank Park welcomes its guests, makes fans feel like a participant in a happening rather than an insignificant spectator. Spectators, no matter where they go, never lose sight of the game—which qualifies them as true spectators. Furthermore, the park-encircling concourse opens to the outside world. It's airy and liberating, with no feeling of confinement. The increasingly beautiful Philly skyline looms over the left field fence if you fancy getting lost between the moon and Quaker City.

Perhaps most important of all, the park is ideal for the thing that has always made baseball special—bonding among family and friends. There are numerous places to talk and eat together. Parents can bring their infants along. Every one of the 62 restrooms is equipped with baby-changing tables. The park is universally designed for access to those with disabilities.

And the place is beautiful. Thousands of flowers and newly planted trees embellish the surrounding landscape. Over 800 trees will be planted on the north side of Pattison Avenue alone, including on the former site of the Vet. The largest LED video display board in the National League—39′5″ x 69′7″ (2,775 square feet)—amplifies the ambiance. In fact, scoreboards seem ubiquitous, as do shops and galleries. Ubiquitous but not tacky.

NOSTALGIA AND HERITAGE

The seventies and eighties brought the Phillies respect. The town's baseball heritage back in the fifties and sixties resided almost exclusively with the old Athletics. Philadelphia baseball meant Connie Mack, Jimmie Foxx, Al Simmons, Lefty Grove, Mickey Cochrane, and other A's. The Phillies' image was that of weak sister, and the exploits of some pretty great Phillie players were diminished if not entirely dismissed. Philly kids in the fifties heard little about Phillies heroes like Chuck Klein who had played a scant two decades before. Klein, who achieved baseball's most glorious and rarified of accomplishments, the Triple Crown, was overlooked for the Hall of Fame till 1980. Richie Ashburn, eclipsed by

New York's center field contemporaries, Willie, Mickey, and the Duke, was likewise passed over for years by the Hall of Fame. Whitey finally made it in 1995. Even the great Robin Roberts, who started five of six consecutive All-Star Games to ring in the fifties, was rejected for three consecutive years till 1976. Appropriately, he was selected the year the Phils moved on up to the top of their division with 101 wins, most wins ever for a Phillies' team.

Whether the success of the seventies-era Phils had any influence on selection committees is moot, but unquestionably the Phils *did* move on up in terms of image and respect during the Vet years. They boasted some of the finest ballplayers in the game and some memorable NL squads. Open up *Total Baseball*, baseball's "Bible," and you'll see Mike Schmidt listed as the twelfth greatest baseball player ever. Yes, the Phillies' Mike Schmidt is rated ahead of icons like Mickey Mantle, Lou Gehrig, Frank Robinson—well, figure it out. Schmidt, by *Total Baseball's* reckoning, outranks all but eleven others who ever crossed the diamond.

The Phillies at Citizens Bank Park extol Phillies tradition. Serious sport art abounds at the stadium. Art used to mean the Rocky sculpture outside the Spectrum. Ed Rendell told us that, in his view, the unique charm of Philadelphia is its dichotomy: "Philadelphia is among the most cultured of American cities. The arts are so ubiquitous here, yet it's a blue-collar city as well." That dichotomy plays in two-part harmony at Citizens Bank Park. Four 10-foot-high statues of Richie Ashburn, Steve Carlton, Mike Schmidt, and Robin Roberts were commissioned from Glenside sculptor Zenos Frudakis. Original artwork by Dick Perez is on display in the Cooperstown Gallery in the Hall of Fame Club.

Dick Perez is an intriguing figure himself. Perez got his start in baseball art when he formed the Steele-Perez Galleries with the now-deceased Frank Steele. Steele had been casually looking for an artist who could evoke the feel of innocence and nobility captured by turn-of-the-century portraits. Steele and Perez happened to meet at a party, where fate steered Perez's talents toward a lucrative, rewarding career. Perez created the portraits and Steele had the contacts. Together they developed and marketed a Donruss Diamond King baseball card series that proved a springboard for Perez's style. Perez wound up becoming the official artist of baseball Hall of Fame.

STADIUM STUFF

OPENING DAY LINEUPS AT CITIZENS BANK PARK

APRIL 12, 2004

Philadelphia Phillies		Cincinnati Reds	
1B	Jim Thome	1B	Sean Casey
2B	Placido Polanco	2B	D'Angelo Jimenez
3B	David Bell	3B	Ryan Freel
SS	Jimmy Rollins	SS	Barry Larkin
RF	Bobby Abreu	RF	Austin Kearns
CF	Marlon Byrd	CF	Ken Griffey Jr.
LF	Pat Burrell	LF	Adam Dunn
C	Mike Lieberthal	C	Jason LaRue
P	Randy Wolf	P	Paul Wilson

Perez was born in Harlem where he spent his young life. When his family moved to Wayne in 1958, he switched allegiance from the Yankees to the Phillies. Now a longtime Philly native, the Phillies and Perez were a natural pairing. In 2003, the Phils commissioned Perez to paint 32 oil paintings that now grace Citizens Bank Park's Cooperstown Gallery.

Philadelphia artist Dane Tilghman colors the Diamond Club with his original artwork. Max Mason's works hang in Harry the K's restaurant at the new ballpark. Mason, who studied painting at the University of Pennsylvania, was featured in the May 2004 edition of *American Artist.*

Perez, Tilghman, and Mason are all local artists who love baseball. Zenos Frudakis, creator of the Ashburn, Carlton, Roberts, and Schmidt sculptures, has become a local. He grew up in Gary, Indiana, the son of a Greek immigrant. Zenos studied at the Pennsylvania Academy of the Fine Arts and the University of Pennsylvania. His works can be seen all over the world. Check out his 8-foot-high sculpture titled "Freedom" in the GlaxoSmithKline building in Philly next time you're in Center City.

The stadium showcases Philly's heritage on the diamond too. Ashburn Alley houses Memory Lane, located in center field, directly in front of the Richie Ashburn statue.

Memory Lane is an illustrated history of Philadelphia baseball that covers the Phillies, A's, and Negro League teams from the city. Bronze plaques in Memory Lane honor the players enshrined in the Phillies Wall of Fame that was instituted in 1978 at the Vet. Our one lament is that the Phils didn't opt to keep the tradition of honoring Philadelphia A's along with Phillies each year. Black granite medallions depicting every Phillies All-Star since the initial midsummer classic in 1933 are displayed throughout Ashburn Alley. There's plenty of room to add new names.

FOOD AND FUN

Times change. We can romanticize all we want about the beguiling purity of baseball. The classic baseball contest is characterized by intriguing mind games, subtle strategies, etc. But the fact remains, professional baseball is entertainment and has to compete with every other form of entertainment. If the Phils and Major League Baseball botch or reject that tenet, Ashburn Alley will have tumbleweeds blowing down it. Youngsters today demand fast-paced fun. The slinky doesn't give this generation the same rush it gave previous generations. Maybe if it fired laser beams as it slinked down the steps it would. For good or bad, kids today demand their thrills in quantum bursts. That dynamic shortens attention spans. I've witnessed it firsthand. At my house, I have to break down every simple task into a simple sequence, or the task will be flubbed. For instance, to spare myself the aggravation of whining, "Why is the air conditioner running when every window in the house is wide open?" I've learned to sequence the task. First I tell the kids, "Close all the windows," and when I see that task is satisfactorily completed, several minutes later I say, "Turn the air conditioner on." Now, the childless among you might be thinking that the second order *should be* unnecessary since at some point the kids in a closed-up house in July would be perspiring like a batter facing a blindfolded Billy Wagner. But as long as the remote control is working, all 120 channels are available, and Tastykakes, snacks, and Cokes are within easy reach, modern kids would sit out a heat wave in an equatorial greenhouse with no fan before mustering enough ambition to get up from the couch and turn the air conditioner on.

Kids nowadays need constant stimulation. That's the only way they'll foster a love of the game. They've first got to love the event—call it a spectacle—of going to Citizens Bank Park. Part of that event happens to include a baseball game. As time goes by, hopefully the game will become bigger and more interesting to them. Meanwhile they can head out to Ashburn Alley and play interactive games like Run the Bases, Ballpark Pinball, and Pitch 'em and Tip 'em. The kids get play money (the kind they think their parents have) for participating. They can then trade in the Citizens Bank Dollars for cool baseball souvenirs. The tykes can do all kinds of Phanatic-related stuff at locations all around the park. And of course, the kids can just enjoy the real Phanatic's antics as well. Let's face it. Amusement parks have disappeared and given way to theme parks. Citizens Bank Park is a baseball theme park. These times demand it.

And no spectacle is complete without good grub. Besides authentic Philly steak sandwiches and Schmitters, fans can eat good and plenty and plenty sloppy on outdoor picnic tables at Bull's BBQ, which serves barbecued pork, ribs, and chicken. Harry the K's restaurant is billed as baseball's only bi-level restaurant built into a scoreboard. The High and Inside Pub is just what the name indicates. Located inside and high on the terrace level, it's a place to chat with friends and still catch all the action.

PHANATIC PHILE

Showtime!

The day everyone had waited for had finally arrived.

Opening Day, 2004.

On my way to the new ballpark that morning, I thought about the five and a half months that had elapsed since the last regular season pitch was thrown. It was the busiest off-season in Phillies history. We had said good-bye to the Vet, opened new ballparks in South Philly and Clearwater, made some key free-agent acquisitions and said farewell to Tug and the Pope. We were poised to begin a new leg in our team's journey through time. But those five and a half months that led us to Opening Day were as bittersweet as they were exciting.

For the members of the Phillies phamily, the emotional Final Innings Weekend at the Vet and the tearful post-game tribute jump-started an exciting odyssey. Many in the organization congregated in the Executive Dining Room on the fourth floor after the final game, toasting the Vet into the night.

We packed our belongings the next three months and got everything ready for the move. Think about it. If you've ever moved, you know the drill. You find all kinds of things that you didn't realize were lurking in the backs of closets and under beds—and that's just in a house. Imagine what it was like to vacate Veterans Stadium. Every day somebody discovered something new. Every old photo that was unearthed or every tacky promotions giveaway that popped up launched a new round of stories about the good old days.

January 8, 2004 was the last day the Vet was open for business. Once again, hugs were the order of the day. There were lots of misty eyes. Everyone packed up his or her belongings in huge boxes that were hauled over to Citizens Bank Park. David Montgomery called one final "town meeting" in the Vet's Executive Dining Room. As the sound of demolitions shook the room, David thanked everyone for all their hard work and loyalty. He shared his personal list of favorite moments at the stadium. He also talked about all of the intra-office romances that led to marriages during the days at the Vet. And no, there's no truth to the rumor that any of those romances were consummated in the 700 Level. David also passed around pictures he had dug up of the original Phillies sales staff at the Vet. David Montgomery, a bit younger, was pictured in the photos. So were many others who still work for the organization. Of course, age wasn't the only tip-off that the photos were snapped in the seventies. I wondered aloud if the Phils had a dress code in those days that made sideburns and plaid pants mandatory. It is hard to believe that people dressed like that of their own free will.

After the meeting, we all went outside into the sub-freezing temperatures for one last group photo. We all huddled together in front of the Vet, close to the Connie Mack statue on Broad and Pattison. I made sure that I stood next to Maje McDonnell for the final photo. Standing next to Maje, my hand on his shoulder, in front of the Vet with the Connie Mack statue close by, I could feel the generations of Phillies baseball history reverberate. And, it wasn't the shock from the demolition crew.

Priceless.

When the picture had been taken, I jumped into costume and skittered about the offices, "assisting" people with their packing and generally just getting in the way, but then you already knew that. I grabbed a suitcase and a box of junk and crashed through the front doors of the Phillies office entrance where the local TV news stations filmed me loading up the moving trucks and goosing the movers who I'm sure were "thrilled" to have the Phanatic helping out.

Four days later, the Phillies offices opened up a block away at the new ballpark. The Phanatic was there too, helping people with their boxes and offering bagels and donuts to the early arrivals. Mike Stiles, our VP of Operations and Administration, stood in the freshly painted lobby and handed out gray "Front Office Opening Day" tee-shirts.

After I had gotten out of costume, Maje pulled up to the front entrance on Pattison Avenue.

"Hey Maje," I called out. "If you're looking for Baker Bowl, you might be a little lost!"

"I used to watch the Phillies at Baker Bowl," Maje yelled back. "This is my fourth Phillies ballpark!"

We had made it into our new offices according to schedule, but it was going to be a race to the finish line to get the ballpark itself ready for the upcoming season. The Phillies had scheduled two exhibition games called the "On-Deck" Series for the first weekend in April. With construction crews scurrying about working on all aspects of the new park in the days leading up to the first game, there were times I thought that we might have been premature in blowing up the Vet. The night before that first exhibition game, in a cold, driving rainstorm, brick was still being laid and concrete poured at the entrances on the east side of the ballpark. Electricians were still hard at work lighting various parts of the park, including the main entrance on Pattison Avenue. Cleaning crews were busy getting the suites ready for the game the next day, vacuuming rugs and scrubbing down counters. Mounds of trash built up on every level of the park, waiting to be collected. At 10:00 PM, the front office staff was invited down to the Diamond Club to order food and give the waitstaff a little practice with the new, high-tech ordering system that recognizes a bar code on the game day ticket.

Amazingly enough, we were open for business on time the first day. The first fan walked through the turnstiles at the third base gate at 11:00 AM. The Phanatic wasn't going to miss out on all the fun as the first fans entered their new playpen. I hopped on my quad and sped out to the third base plaza. Thousands of fans had been lining up prior to the grand opening. People took pictures as they walked through new-fangled turnstiles. Some carried signs. Others looked around at the new surroundings, taking it all in. I was busy high-fiving fans and dishing out Phanatic smooches to the mob that surrounded me.

"Yo, Phanatic, nice place you got here," one fan called out.

"Glad to see you got your head back, Phanatic," another fan yelled.

You gotta love the Philly fans—Philadelphia really is the place that loves you back.

The pre-game festivities focused on the people who were responsible for the new baseball palace. David Montgomery said a few words as did Stephen Steinour, president of Citizens Bank. Mayor Street thanked everyone for their hard work and talked about what a special addition the new ballpark was to the city's landscape. However, in true Philadelphia tradition, the Mayor was booed—the first in a long line who would be accorded that Philly tradition.

The boos quickly changed into cheers, however, as Jim Thome walked out of the dugout and took the microphone. With the Cleveland Indians, his former team, looking on from the visitors' dugout, Jim thanked the men and women responsible for building the new place.

The crowd roared. Philadelphia *definitely* loves Jim Thome back.

The players emerged from the dugout and formed two lines that stretched from the dugout to the dirt path between home plate and first base. A handful of the construction workers were then introduced individually and ran through the gauntlet of players to take one of the nine positions on the field. When the starting players were introduced, they ran out to their positions to greet the workers and sign their hard hats. It was a living diorama of Governor Rendell's Philly dichotomy. As a cultural center, Philly was christening another architectural gem, but at the same time, we weren't about to let the guys who did the brick-and-mortar work go unrecognized.

In keeping with the tribute to the workers, the Phanatic did his fifth-inning dance with a bunch of the female hard hats who entered the field on the back of a John Deere Gator truck. Together, we danced to the theme song for the movie *Flashdance* ("What a Feeling"), shaking our groove thing down to the ground. These Philly working girls made Jennifer Beals look like a reject from *American Bandstand* (of course, if you're reading this, Jen, you can dance with the Phanatic anytime—your dugout or mine). Not to be outdone, the men on the crew joined the Phanatic on the Phillies dugout in the 7th inning for their version of "YMCA." I say "their" version because if you picture a bunch of guys in hard hats and tool belts and a very questionable sense of rhythm spelling out Y-M-C-A with their rather huge bodies, you know it's not a pretty sight.

It's no surprise that a Jim Thome blast provided the first official goose bumps at the new ballpark. He whacked a first inning home run into the second deck in right field, officially christening section 205. The Phils dropped the first game 6-5 and lost the second game of the mini-series 3-1 in a game that started two hours and twenty-seven minutes late because of rain. The temperature dipped to 36 degrees that second game but felt a lot colder because of the arctic-like winds that blew through the concourse.

Despite the weather on Sunday, the weekend was a smashing success. Fans left the new ballpark raving about the tremendous sight-lines, the abundance of amenities, and the overall atmosphere. The fans felt they had moved on up.

A week later, I was nearing the new ballpark in the pre-dawn hours on Opening Day. Again as I approached Citizens Bank Park, my mind raced. What about the Phanatic? Will the green, furry guy that Philly fans have come to know and love remain as much a part of the game-day experience at Citizens Bank Park as he was at the Vet? Will he play the same role in the new millennium as the old? Will the new place feel like home?

Traveling east on the Schuylkill Expressway towards the last exit before the Walt Whitman Bridge, I turned right and stared out at the new ballpark. The light towers lit the South Philly sky. To my surprise, there was a gigantic sign hanging under the new left field scoreboard. It was a close-up of the Phillie Phanatic, peering out to the northwest over the parking lot, the expressway, and the rubble that was once Veterans Stadium. The sign was hung the night before. I had no idea it was going up so it gave me a big boost when I saw it. I found out later it was 45 feet high by 33 feet long. The Phanatic poster was the first thing many fans would see when they approached the new ballpark. It may not match the grandeur of the huge light towers that Larry Shenk and David Montgomery remember from their youth at Connie Mack—the images that stuck with them all these years. But I hope that in some way, the Phanatic sign fires the imagination and fuels the love of baseball for some youngsters in the next generation of Phillies fans.

That morning, I walked around inside the new park. Another Opening Day—but this year was the most special Opening Day ever, at least for me. I can't speak for Maje and some of the others who have witnessed so much more history. Everywhere it was hustle and bustle. The food concession stands were being readied, souvenir shops were getting stocked, and cleaners were wiping down the seats. My little stroll allayed any fears about the Phanatic's place in the new order of things. The Phanatic's stamp is all over the new park. There's a Phanatic Phun Zone (yes, the "ph" problem moved on up to Citizens Bank Park) located on the Main Concourse. The Phun Zone is a huge jungle-gym playground, complete with tunnels, slides, and ladders, geared toward toddlers who have less chance of sitting through nine innings of baseball than Greg Luzinski has of becoming a vegan. There's also a Phanatic Phood Stand and Phanatic Kid's Corner that sells food geared toward younger fans. The Phanatic Attic is a giant retail area located on the second level of the Majestic Clubhouse Store. Fans can pose next to an eight-foot-high fiberglass Phanatic or climb on top of the ATV that he used in the last season at the Vet. The coolest thing of all is the Make-Your-Own-Phanatic stand, located down the third base line on the Main Concourse. It's a place where kids can stuff their own Phanatic doll (you even place a small red heart into the doll before you sew it up) and then choose from a variety of costumes to dress him in, like the beach bum outfit or tuxedo that he sometimes wears (after all these years, *finally a handsome* alternative to the Ken doll). Anyway, this stand is the only one of its kind in sports. Judging by its success in the early part of the season, other teams might be itching to build similar stands at their parks.

Once again, the weather was threatening but the gates opened on time. The Philadelphia Boys Choir performed and a giant American flag was unfurled in the outfield. Despite the nasty weather, the Navy Leap Frog parachute team did their thing, swooping into Citizens Bank Park as the crowd roared. There was one hitch. One member was supposed to dress as the Phanatic. If you recall, that's the way we kicked off the 1993 season. Unfortunately, the Phanatic costume he had practiced in didn't get shipped back to Philadelphia in time. I was bummed—so much for my John Wayne entrance.

So how *would* the Phanatic make his first official entrance into Citizens Bank Park? As it turns out, months before the opener, David Montgomery had the idea to bus the players out to 10th and Packer Avenue just before the game and parade them into the stadium. Remember how the players marched into center field to christen Shibe Park? But who would lead the Citizens Bank Park parade? Who would be the Phillies' Professor Harold Hill? Yes, the Phillie Phanatic. Not a bad plan "B" if I do say so myself.

What a sight it was. Traffic was stopped on 10th Street as the players assembled. The Budweiser Clydesdale horses were called in for the occasion to lead the team up 10th Street to the entrance gate on Ashburn Alley. That's where the Phanatic met them. Ashburn Alley was packed with wall-to-wall fans. Security guards made a passageway through the crowd so the team could get through. The fans were cheering like crazy, high-fiving the players and the Phanatic as we passed through.

I led manager Larry Bowa and the rest of the guys down a makeshift staircase that was temporarily installed for the grand pre-game entrance. The staircase was located in center field. It started at the top of Ashburn Alley and descended to the field itself. I couldn't ask for a finer entrance.

However, I've got to admit that for the Phanatic it *has* gotten better. Every night he wanders into the crowd, only to be swarmed by exuberant fans who are enjoying themselves in one of Major League Baseball's premier parks. Kids dance between innings to the songs played over the PA system, mugging for the cameras, trying to get their faces on the video screen. Dads grab their kids and chase after the Phanatic, because as they tell me, "That's what I did when I was a kid." For older generations, the sight of the lush, green grass and the light towers that stretch to the skies eases them back to happier times. In the stands, I can almost *feel* generations connecting, families bonding, and friends enjoying each other's company over cheesesteaks, hot dogs, and Schmitters.

PHANATIC PHILE

It's really true. If you build it, they will come. And they do come, a packed house of happy fans every night. In *Field of Dreams*, John Kinsella looked out over that ball field his son built in the midst of the cornfield. He told his son Ray, "Yeah, there's a heaven. It's the place where dreams come true." Looking out over the people having fun at Citizens Bank Park, the Phillie Phanatic would have to echo Ray Kinsella's reply, "Then maybe this is heaven."

On January 8, 2004, Phillies employees gather for one last time in front of the Vet. Four days later, Citizens Bank Park opened for business.
(Photo: Courtesy of the Phillies)

We're gonna cheer and boo
And raise a hullabaloo
At the ballgame today
At the ballgame, the wonderful ballgame
Today

So we've moved on up to Citizens Bank Park, another great place for baseball—not the last place, not the ultimate place, but another place. Times change and time marches on as we've seen throughout the book. But Citizens Bank Park in its time is another terrific place to cheer and boo and raise a hullabaloo—things that nobody does better than Philly fans. As for the team . . . yeah, 2004 didn't have the storybook ending we'd all hoped for. Philly don't play fairy tales or even phairy tales. So, how about the future? Is the future of our Phils bright? As always, who knows? No one. Who cares? Everyone. That's Philly. Philly always has a muddled, intriguing future with passionate people debating it because our teams are as important as breathing to Philly fans—maybe not as important as eating, but just as important as breathing.

Think back to spring 1979. The Phils' future was so bright they had to wear shades. The hometowners had nabbed Pete Rose, *the prize*. By the fans' reckoning—as well as the reckoning of most baseball experts—Charley Hustle was the lost chord in the Phils' great symphony that they could never manage to score in the seventies. They didn't score it in 1979 either. In fact, Philadelphia slipped from first to fourth (out of six teams) that season.

By October of 1979, the Phillie future looked frustratingly muddled once more. Then marvelously "it" all came together. In 1980, the Phils gave the city its greatest sports rush ever.

In frustrating contrast, think back to 1964. All looked rosy. A scant twelve games remained. The Phils were ahead of the field by 6-1/2 games. The future was so rosy, so certain, that the Phils printed up World Series tickets. By the time the presses finished churning, those tickers were as worthless as continentals. (Times change. Nowadays Phillies '64 Series tickets fetch plenty—so do continentals.)

Yes Forrest, our Phils are like a box of chocolates. We never know what we're gonna get. But the Phils know what they'll get—devoted, hopeful fans—Philly fans who dive into that box of chocolates year after year even though we know deep down it's probably full of nougats (that's my least favorite). We can't resist.

Somehow teams like the Phils and Cubs and Red Sox (well, the pre-2004 Sox) mirror real life for their fans. The loyal locals watch their heroes fall short more often than not.

Nonetheless, more than any other city, they bond with their teams—imperfections and all—in a manner that defies good sense but results in a helluva lot of fun.

In Philly, we've had a helluva lot of fun. We've had a helluva lot of derailments and disappointments too along our historic 121-year move on up. But we've had magic moments as well—moments when all the world seemed right, moments when anticipation and hope and reality smacked headlong into each other in an unforgettable cosmic collision.

Players come and go. Teams and seasons drift into oblivion. The fans, the city, remain. Ultimately Philly's movin' on up story is about soul and spirit and resiliency—the soul, spirit and resiliency of Philly and its people. That includes Philly expatriates like my son in California. He's a bona fide Californian now, dude. But he'd sooner give up sushi than bleed Dodger blue.

Here in Philly, hope abides along with heritage, history, and happiness. Those four h's never die in this intriguing city. They just change residence every few decades. Despite the team's lackluster 2004 season, next spring and every spring thereafter, Philly's 4-H Club will be alive and well. All four have moved on up to One Citizens Bank Way.

STADIUM STUFF

CITIZENS BANK PARK FIRSTS

(all from 4/12/04)

Pitch	Phillies LHP, Randy Wolf, 1:32 PM
Batter	Reds 2B, D'Angelo Jimenez
Hit	D'Angelo Jimenez (double, 1st inning)
Single	Reds 3B, Ryan Freel, CIN (2nd)
Single by a Phillie	Randy Wolf (3rd)
Double by a Phillie	Phillies 1B, Jim Thome (1st)
Triple	Reds RF, Austin Kearns (9th)
Home run	Phillies RF, Bobby Abreu (1st)
Walk	Reds C, Jason LaRue (2nd)
Walk by a Phillie	Phillies CF, Marlon Byrd (3rd)
Sacrifice bunt	Reds RHP, Paul Wilson (2nd)
Stolen base	Marlon Byrd (3rd)

Run	D'Angelo Jimenez (1st)
Run by a Phillie	Bobby Abreu (1st)
RBI	Bobby Abreu (1st)
Strikeout	Reds CF, Ken Griffey Jr. by Wolf (1st)
Wild pitch	Wolf (1st)
Win	Wilson
Loss	Wolf
Save	Reds RHP, Danny Graves
	Other Firsts
Grand slam	Braves CF, Andruw Jones, 5/27/04
Cycle	David Bell, 6/28/04 vs. Montreal
Win by a Phillie	LHP, Rheal Cormier, 4/15/04 vs. Cincinnati
Save by a Phillie	LHP, Billy Wagner, 4/15/04 vs. Cincinnati
Triple by a Phillie	SS, Jimmy Rollins, 4/18/04 vs. Montreal
Inside-the-park home run	Rollins, 6/20/04 vs. Kansas City
Error	Thome, 4/20/04 vs. Florida
Postponement	4/14/04, Phillies vs. Reds, due to rain
Night game	4/16/04, Phillies 4, Expos 2
Four-hit game	Thome, 4/16/04 vs. Montreal
Game without a homer	4/20/04, Marlins 3, Phillies 1 (6th home game of regular season)
Multi-homer game	4/21/04—Marlins 8, Phillies 7, 12 innings
Extra-inning game	4/21/04—Marlins 8, Phillies 7, 12 innings
Triple play	8/19/04—Todd Pratt vs. Houston Astros (Ensberg to Kent to Lamb)

I THINK WE'RE GONNA LIKE IT HERE

Words and music by Skip Denenberg

This is the ode to Citizens Bank Park that Skip Denenberg composed. Its a song for every sesaon.

I might be feeling optimistic but I've got a good reason,
"Ya gotta believe" that this might be the season,

There's something special about this year,
That's got me hoping for a souvenir
And we've got a new home, I think we're gonna like it here

Can't wait to meet the new faces and our old friends too,
And watch them light up the sky like only they can do,
And make some memories with our kids,
Just the way our daddies did
And we've got a new home, I think we're gonna like it here

(Like it here)
Yeah we're in for a treat and there ain't a bad seat in the house,
(Like it here)
Got a view of the city that everyone's talking about,
(Like it here)
And it's just the beginning of many more innings to shout,
(Like it here)
We'll miss our friends who've gone
(Like it here)
But they'd want us to carry on
(Like it here)

I think we're gonna like it here

I might be feeling optimistic but I've got a good reason,
"Ya gotta believe" that this might be the season,
It happens this time every year,
I'll be fighting for a souvenir
And we've got a new home, I think we're gonna like it here
Yeah we've got a new home, I think we're gonna like it here
Welcome to your new home, I think we're gonna like it here

Havin' a Ball, Skip Denenberg's complete CD of Phillies songs can be ordered at 1-877-GO-PHILS or www.phillies.com